Finding My Voice

RUSSELL WATSON

Finding My Voice MY STORY

EBURY
PRESS

1 3 5 7 9 10 8 6 4 2

Published in 2008 by Ebury Press, an imprint of Ebury Publishing
A Random House Group Company

The Random House Group Limited Reg. No. 954009

Addresses for companies within the Random House Group can be found at
www.randomhouse.co.uk

A CIP catalogue record for this book is available from the British Library

The Random House Group Limited supports The Forest Stewardship Council
(FSC), the leading international forest certification organisation. All our titles
that are printed on Greenpeace approved FSC certified paper carry the FSC
logo. Our paper procurement policy can be found at
www.rbooks.co.uk/environment

Mixed Sources
Product group from well-managed
forests and other controlled sources
www.fsc.org   Cert no. TT-COC-2139
© 1996 Forest Stewardship Council
FSC

Printed and bound in Great Britain by Clays Ltd, St Ives PLC

ISBN 9780091922917

To buy books by your favourite authors and register for offers visit
www.rbooks.co.uk

I'd like to dedicate this book to everyone who has helped support me through my illness; especially my two loving daughters Rebecca and Hannah.
Lots of love Russell x

October 2007

'Russell, can you hear us, mate?'

Not really, no.

'Russell, hang in there, pal.'

I'll do my best. Can't promise anything.

'Stay with us, pal.'

I manage to raise my head.

'Not too heavy for you, am I?' I ask.

Typical. I'm drifting in and out of consciousness, I can barely see – my vision's all but gone. Been getting worse since early this morning after a night of near-continuous vomiting, when it began to feel like I was viewing the world through neon-coloured mesh, when I started to think this wasn't just food poisoning, this was something much, much worse. And all I'm really worried about is whether I'm too heavy for the paramedics. Like what are they going to do? It's not as if they're about to pop down the ambulance chair and go, 'Well, yeah, as it happens, you are a bit hard on the old back, Russell, you wouldn't mind walking the rest of the way to the ambulance, would you?'

'Believe me, mate, we've carried them out a lot heavier than you,' laughs the paramedic.

My eyes flicker. Lights flash and distort. I drift. In my head I'm back at the City of Manchester Stadium, July 2002, the opening of the Commonwealth Games. I'm singing for the Queen, for an audience of billions. The song: 'Where My Heart Will Take Me'.

It's been a long road, getting from there to here.

'Stay with us, mate.'

It's been a long time, well, my time is finally near...

And I'm drifting...

'STAY WITH US.'

There's a slap on the back of my hand, a hard, continuous slap. My eyes flicker open.

'Do you know where you are, Russell?'

'Yeah,' I manage. Or maybe I don't. Maybe I just nod my head.

'Do you know your date of birth, mate?'

Yes, it's November...

But I'm drifting out of consciousness and the next voice I hear is Gary's. He's asking the paramedics if I'm going to be okay and the paramedic's telling him that it's serious, that I'm in a bad state. Got to get my temperature down because I'm at 38.9 degrees and if I get to 40 something bad happens – something called pyrexia. Causes convulsions.

I hear the ambulance doors shut. Through brightly coloured wire mesh I see paramedics reaching for me, undoing my clothes, hear the word 'temperature' mentioned and I think, I'm dead.

And now I'm on my back, somewhere else, and there's a flash. Then another flash, and another. And I become aware of lights flicking past overhead. It seems so familiar. From the movies, I guess. And I hear doors banging and I think, I'm dead. Lying there half-cooked, thinking, That's it, I'm dead.

'He's haemorrhaging,' I hear. 'Get him into theatre. Get him into theatre *now*.'

Is there a worse word in the English language than haemorrhage? Maybe cancer?

'Come on. Into theatre. *Now.*'

I lose consciousness. Blissfully.

I find out later that the tumour was literally in danger of imploding, taking my brain with it. I discover that the tumour had swelled so much the resulting pressure on my optic nerve was in danger of causing permanent blindness. I live by the matter of an hour or so. That's all it is.

They take the swelling down with anti-inflammatory medication but I remain on the critical list. Mr Leggat comes to see me.

'I know you've been looking at surgeons to deal with this,' he says to me, 'but you're at severe risk, you need an emergency operation and I'm one of the top surgeons at this kind of procedure. I want you to let me do it. I can do it for you. I can get it out.'

I take some convincing.

'I need to see my children first,' I tell him. 'No operation until I've seen them.'

All I can think about is the kids. Rebecca and Hannah. The most important people in my life. These experiences change you. Maybe once upon a time I might have put my career before my children, but not now. Not ever again. I live for my singing. But I'd die for my kids.

Which might happen, says the look on Mr Leggat's face as he stands.

'You'd better get them over here, then,' he says.

Helen brings them. They come to my room and I watch the colour drain from their faces when they see me, their dad, in bed, modelling the new line in near-death chic.

Someone closes a door, so we can have a little privacy.

December 2007

Here's something that might come as a bit of a surprise. Chris Tarrant. He swears like a trooper. Honest. I've never known anyone swear so much. We're standing waiting for the Queen at Buckingham Palace and he's like, 'When's the fucking Queen going to fucking appear then?' Chris Tarrant? Torrent, more like. Nice guy though.

Still, I can talk.

This morning a courier arrived to pick up a camera. We'd been using this camera to film some material on the making of the new album, *Outside In*, which we finished in mid-October. It's now mid-December, and in the meantime I've completed the album, moved house and almost died.

We can't, believe it or not, locate this camera at just a moment's notice. If you want to send a courier for it, camera-people, here's a tip: a bit of warning might be nice.

Which is what I told Gary, who was dealing with the courier, and who was probably grateful that it was him dealing with the courier and not me, and that I was remaining in the kitchen, pacing it, narky. Because I'm not a morning person at the moment, not since the operation. Mornings aren't good. And nobody wants me storming out to give a courier a gobful. You'd hear a bit of Chris Tarrant language then. So I stalked, riding out the bad mood, knowing that a good one will be along again in a minute and I'll be myself again, back to the old Russell.

I have lunch. Victoria brings me some more pills and I take them. How many am I on now? It's like every time I reach to take a sip of Coke there's a new cluster of pills, placed there by Gary or Victoria, ready for me to take. The cortisol is the most important one. The tumour was a pituitary adenoma – that's its proper name, although I just call it 'this bloody thing', or something worse – and it affects the pituitary gland, which is what they call the master gland. It gets you up in the morning, it deals with growth hormones, endorphins, that kind of thing. It basically controls and regulates the flow of your hormones so if it gets damaged you're in trouble; your body underproduces the hormones you need, so you need to take them in pill form. Which is what I do. Testosterone, growth hormone, stress hormone. All of them come in pill form, and when those pills wear off I have to take more. It's why I'm so down one minute, same old Russ the next.

Mornings I stalk and grouch. Afternoons are better. I have a laugh with Gary and Victoria, a few games of pool or table football. I'm not really supposed to work out, but I do. A room of the house is my gym, and there I've got a bike, cross-trainer, punch-bag, weights. Running is absolutely, strictly forbidden, so I've put the running machine in the garage. I use the rest of the gear instead. Got to get strong. Got to be strong for what lies ahead.

I go out for the odd drive. Not really supposed to, but come on: I'd go mad otherwise, cooped up all day.

I do anyway. Go mad, that is. You do, don't you? I watch the odd DVD, play on the Xbox or PlayStation. Management call and tell me the album's doing well, at number 12 in the charts. Outselling the Spice Girls they tell me. Which is good going considering the only promotion I've done for it is...

Actually, I haven't done any promotion for it. Not unless you consider news footage of me being wheeled out of hospital with a bandaged face as promotion. I suppose it is in a way. But even so, it's not exactly Parky, is it? Maybe the old me would have been worried about that. Thinking, Now I've got to do this show, or that show, or be on this radio station or get in that newspaper. Not any more. All I care about are my kids. All I care about is being strong. About wanting to be well. Taking pills, working out, getting a bit stronger every day.

They're saints to put up with me, Gary and Victoria, they really are.

Especially when things are likely to get worse.

This tumour's my second. The first one was apparently taken out during an operation in London in September 2006. I say 'apparently'. We'll come to that. Either way, this time I found myself being carted away by paramedics and had Mr Leggat fixing me with a look and telling me, 'Let me do this. I know I can do it.'

So they went in. Last time they went in through the nose, this time through the top lip. And when the doctors had finished, most of the tumour was gone.

Most of it. Not all.

There's still a bit left. It's small enough to deal with using radio-therapy. Which is good, I suppose. Except, I have to have the radiotherapy. Five weeks of it, to be exact. For five days a week, starting on January 2.

I had my hair cut yesterday. Cut short. So that when it all falls out it won't be such a shock. Somebody asked me if I was worried about it. About the hair falling out, I mean. But come on, least of my problems, my bloody hair. That'll grow back they say, and most of my mates have lost their hair anyway. So no, it's not the hair that worries me. It's the sickness, the fatigue, the mood swings, the other side effects. The five days a week of spending an hour a day inside some kind of radiation accelerator. I'm claustrophobic for a start, and that worries me far more than losing a bit of hair. For hair loss I can go skinhead for a few months, wear a hat. It's not like I can hide the claustrophobia.

So I've got that to look forward to. I have a laugh with Gary and Victoria, but all the time I've got it lurking in the back of my head, hanging around in there: *radiotherapy.*

I say, 'Why, thank you very much, Johnson,' in my best Jeeves impression when Gary brings me a sandwich. And in the back of my mind is my hot date with radiotherapy.

Victoria brings me yet more pills and I say, 'I hem most obliged, Victoriah,' in the same pampered-posh-bloke voice. And there lurking in my mind is the second of January. The radiotherapy.

So I work out, to get strong, because I really believe that if I'm strong, both mentally and physically, then I'll beat this. I really do.

And I go to the hospital, once a week at least – I get fitted for my radiotherapy mask next week, to protect my face while they're zapping my brain. It's all go, you know. And I watch the odd DVD, play on the PlayStation, get on Gary and Victoria's nerves, think about the future.

Sometimes, to stop myself thinking about the future, I think about the past instead.

Most days in 1975

'Are you going to make it go faster?'

This is me, a little Mancunian voice in the garage of a house in Irlam, Manchester, where I'd stand looking down at my father, who would be tinkering with the car. When he wasn't at work, at the Irlam steelworks, that's where he'd be: in the garage, underneath the car.

He'd look up from where he knelt or lay, oily rag in one hand, spanner or something in the other, streak of grease across his cheek. Manchester warpaint.

'Russell, it's a *Hillman Imp*. It goes as fast as it goes.'

'Yeah.' I would bounce on my toes. 'But are you going to make it go faster?'

He'd sigh, shake his head, as though to say, That boy. That bloody lad. Then get back to work, doing whatever it was he was doing to the Hillman Imp in the garage of our house on Sunningdale Drive.

Sunningdale Drive, Irlam, Manchester. That's where I grew up. Before that we lived on an estate in a village called Flixton. We lived in Flixton when I came into the world in 1966. On November 24, 1966, to be precise. Born at Davyhulme Park Hospital (the Trafford General these days) to father Tim and mum Nola. Little sister Hayley came along later, and that was it for us. We weren't a big family. Neither were we a particularly remarkable lot. And if I had to describe my childhood in one word, it would be this: uncomplicated. Uncomplicated and mainly idyllic. Which is four words, I know, but which pretty much sums up my entire childhood anyway. Oh, it gets harder. Don't you worry about that.

So, my memories of the Flixton house are hazy at best. I do remember one thing, maybe my earliest recollection. I recall being put on the front of my dad's Royal Enfield 260 and taken for a ride, just a few faltering, *phut-phut-phut* yards down the street. Not far, but enough for it to make an impression, obviously. What else? Well, I remember a bay window and there being loads of kids around. Then, I was – what? – two, three, four, when we moved house. Moved to Sunningdale Drive in Irlam, Manchester, just across the Manchester Ship Canal.

It was a step up for us. Dad had got a job at the steelworks. He worked on the cranes, this at a time when almost the whole of

Irlam was employed by the works: thousands and thousands of workers, miles and miles of steelworks. Literally as far as the eye could see, almost a town-within-a-town. Go there now, of course, and it's the Northbank industrial estate. Because in 1979, after a near-century of steel manufacture for first the Partington Steel and Iron Company, then the Lancashire Steel Corporation, and next British Steel, the Irlam works shut down for good. Dad went to work for a firm in Warrington after that, making wire.

Our house was a bungalow, one of many bungalows on the estate. Like a lot of them we'd had a dormer installed and this is the bedroom I shared with Hayley. It had yellow patterned lino on the floor and a wonky dividing line drawn down the middle of the room to separate my bit from hers. We used crayon.

There was a little garden out the back, a small drive out the front and then of course the garage, scene of these father–son talks.

'Are you gonna make it go faster?'

'Russell, it's a… oh, never mind.'

I would run, escaping my father's exasperated look, into the street, joining my mates there. Or, more likely, getting them to join me. Because Sunningdale Drive was a cul-de-sac, so we used to take it over and I was always the ringleader, dragging the other lads out to play. Woe betide you if you wanted to stay in and watch *The Hair Bear Bunch*, *Bagpuss* or *The Banana Splits*.

'Is Michael coming out to play, Mrs Bird?'

He was one of those I used to hang around with. Michael Bird. We called him Birdy. No idea why.

Doyley. He was another. Johnno. Still another. Their mums had to get used to Russell Watson ringing on the doorbell just after tea, regular as clockwork.

'Russell Watson's at the door,' she'd call over her shoulder. I could smell cooking from inside the house. Mashed potato and boiled veg. 'He wants to know if you're coming out.'

'Nah, I'm watching telly tonight,' was often the reply, shouted from within the house.

'Come on, Birdy!' I'd lean into the doorway, calling to Birdy, or Doyley, Curzy, Johnno… Whoever it was who just wanted a quiet evening in. 'Come on, we need the numbers, it's four against five.'

Sigh. A sigh you could hear from the front room to the door.

'All right, I'll be out in five minutes.'

What a pushy little sod, eh? Never took no for an answer.

Like I say, the back gardens of the houses on Sunningdale Drive were tiny. They were just about big enough to lark around in, and if you were playing by yourself, maybe enough for a little kickaround. But no good for anything more organised. Instead, we took games out onto the street. It's become a cliché now, the whole 'jumpers for goalposts' joke. But that really was us. Two cardigans at one end. Two cardigans at the other. The street was long enough for a decent game of football and I'd done enough work rounding up the players, so there were usually about ten of us playing.

We'd play all day, if we could. If there was no school. Until the sun went down most days. Mums in the kitchens, Dads at work. And if it was the weekend then Mums in the kitchen and Dads in the front room dozing off in front of *World of Sport*, or in the garage working on Hillman Imps. Doing Dad stuff.

Later, I'd be called in.

'Russell, it's time for bed.'

'Aw, Mum!'

'Russell, will you come inside!'

'A bit longer!'

'Come on, it's getting dark!'

And reluctantly, I'd take myself indoors. Reluctantly, always reluctantly. The next day, out again.

And that house in Irlam was where I lived until I got married and left home. My mother still lives there. She and my dad were

Chapter One

together for forty years then split up, the daft sods. He lives in Atherton these days, him and his new lady. Mum is still in the family home, still at the bungalow on Sunningdale Drive, where the neighbours are virtually the same now as they were then. Most of the kids have moved on, of course, but not the parents. Most of those same Mums and Dads – who I used to pester night after night – are still there. The Burns family, who lived next door to us. Still there now. As are the Woods, who used to live at the end. And so are the Birds. So, yes, apart from my mum, out of about ten or eleven houses on the street I'd say five or six of them still have the original owners in them. The people who lived there when I did. It's hardly changed; I drive around it now and it's still so recognisably the place where I grew up, where I discovered football and music, where I never really wondered what I wanted to do with my life because why would I? It was all here on Sunningdale Drive.

We didn't see much of Dad, to be honest. He worked hard. Everybody did. And for him that meant a lot of night shifts. He'd get in as we were getting up, and he'd be knackered, absolutely dead on his feet. His was a life of back-breakingly hard 12-hour night shifts and if he got weekends, he'd do weekends as well. Then he started doing these 'mid-shifts', they were called, all kinds of strange hours.

That was what you did back then. You worked to support your family, and though I didn't see much of my dad growing up, we never went without. Ever. It sounds like an old cliché, but there was always food on the table, a telly in the corner of the room and family holidays courtesy of the prized Hillman Imp in the garage. I remember it being a massive event when we got that car. Dad had bought it new, the old L reg, and I recall him driving it back from the garage. We all stood outside on the drive as though we were about to greet royalty. Then, gliding into view, the sun reflecting off the windshield, the paintwork gleaming, this shiny red car enters Sunningdale Drive, Dad at the wheel. We let out a collective 'Wow', and I remember just looking at this car in awe, the newness of it. It was sparkling on the outside; its interior pristine and fragrant with that new-car smell that transports you whenever and wherever it fills your nostrils. They even do 'new-car smell' air fresheners these days. That's how powerful the scent is. People want to revisit their own Hillman Imp moment.

It was the cheapest little car on the road at the time, but we were all so proud of it, Dad especially. When he wasn't underneath it, tinkering with it ('Are you gonna make it go faster?'), he'd be out there cleaning it, polishing it. No joke, he'd clean the wheels with a toothbrush. I bet there aren't many who do that any more.

And looking back, some of my fondest childhood memories are linked to that car. We used to go to North Wales a lot. Mum and Dad straight-backed in the front seat. At the rear, me and Hayley. No seatbelts in those days, of course. We'd be sitting there with all our toys out, a right little playroom spread across the back seat: Action Men, dolls and teddy bears. Just playing in the back of the car until we got to wherever we went.

We used the car for day trips and for longer holidays, too. I've made up for it since, of course, but I didn't leave the United Kingdom until I was in my early twenties. Ibiza just wasn't an option for our family; instead we'd have a chalet or a cottage in Llandudno, somewhere like that. Somewhere me and my sister would inevitably find a stream and spend hours playing in it.

The day trips, the Llandudno holidays. I remember them more as feelings than anything else. What sticks in my mind is the excitement of the planning, the fun of the journey and feeling tired on the return; that warm, snuggled-up feeling of falling asleep in the back of the car and dimly registering strong arms gently picking you up and taking you into a warm house and then to bed. The next thing you knew, you were waking up in your own bedroom the next morning, when it was Monday, and life got back to normal: Mum in the kitchen, Dad at work.

Being kids, Hayley and I didn't really spare much of a thought for our poor old dad, out on the cranes, earning a crust to keep the roof over his family's head on the night shift. Nope, we just thought: Great, we can play up Mum a bit more, go to bed a bit later than usual, watch a bit more telly. All that kind of stuff.

They were both pretty even-tempered, truth be told. Of the two, Mum was the one you could wrap around your little finger. Dad, he was calm as well, but with him we had that 'wait till your father gets home' relationship. Dad was Dad. He had this other life and he brought little bits of it home with him: the smell of the factory, the weariness that settled across his face when he dropped into a chair at the end of the day. He had the steelworks, the other place. It made him an enigma.

Mum. Well, she was just Mum, wasn't she?

She was massively protective. Over-protective, you might say, although as far as I was concerned she was just stopping me having fun. Because up until 12 or 13, as old as that, I wasn't allowed out of the street – not beyond the boundaries of Sunningdale Drive.

'Are you coming out on your bike, Russell?'

That would be Johnno, Birdy, Curzy, Paul Bennett or one of the others. *Their* mums used to let them out of the road. *Their* mums used to let them go cycling round some of the other streets on the estate. But not mine.

Looking back now, perhaps that's why I became the ringleader, the game rounder-upper. I wanted to keep the lads on Sunningdale Drive for games of football. Mum was protective, so in return I had to learn to be outgoing, unafraid of knocking on people's doors and, yes, pushy. Now, I'm good with pre-show nerves, I don't get intimidated easily and I get on with most people I meet. Maybe that's where it all started. Perhaps I've got my mum to thank for being able to get up there, do my thing.

Even so, at the time...

'Oh, but Birdy's mum—'

'I don't care what Birdy's mother lets him do. The answer's no, Russell.'

The radiogram playing in the background. Mario Lanza most

likely. It sat on the side in the kitchen and would be going all day long, providing the soundtrack to my regular appeals for freedom.

The answer was always no. So in my continuing push to make my road the social centre for the Irlam Under-10s set, we had the famous Sunningdale Drive Super Striker tournaments. Organiser, yours truly.

And if you're thinking, 'Super Striker?', then the chances are you didn't grow up a lad in the mid-1970s, because it was *the* toy. It was a football game. A bit like Subbuteo, but not. In the box you got a plastic moulded pitch instead of the cloth you used to get with Subbuteo, so it was a bit easier to set up. Plus you had a rebound wall, which meant you weren't forever fetching the ball off the floor, although it did used to crack at the edges. Also in the box you got two teams of players. But instead of flicking the players like you did with Subbuteo, you tapped down their little plastic heads to make them kick the ball. There were ten of them, so it was a five-a-side game. As far as I can recall they came in red and blue colours; I don't think they came in actual club colours, although I could be wrong. What I do remember is that I used to paint them. They needed painting for the Super Striker tournaments.

Watland Town was the venue. And Watland Town's stadium was either in my bedroom, just over the crayon dividing line, or in the garage. At first I let the other lads use my players, which had been customised, so each had a name and number, meticulously painted on. But soon the other kids were doing the same thing. They'd get their own team together, customise their own players. Believe me, it was a serious business, especially when there was a tournament date fixed – again, organised by me.

I'd draw a programme, write up fixture lists, then we'd have draws for various different cups. Sometimes we'd play away, we'd go to somebody else's house. But mainly the tournaments were held at the theatre of dreams – Watland Town. In my bedroom we'd set up the pitch and lie surrounding the field of play with our elbows on the floor, feet in the air, laces of our plimsolls dangling.

In the garage, Dad used to let me put up a wallpaper table, so sometimes we used to stand around that, cheering on our respective teams, ten or more lads in the garage, crammed in there, the Hillman Imp on the drive outside.

I used to make little cups, too. No joke. And whoever won the cup got to keep it for week. Before the next tournament at Watland Town.

I did the same thing with Subbuteo, too, organising tournaments and stuff, although it's the Super Striker matches that really stick in my head. And I think if I'm honest – and I'll probably get hate mail from hardcore Subbuteo heads for saying this – I preferred Super Striker. When I think of Subbuteo I think of it taking hours to set up; of it having lots of players that always needed gluing because they were always breaking.

But when I think of Super Striker I think of fun. I think of a bedroom full of my mates, carefully painted teams and homemade cups for the winners. Afternoons in the dormer at Sunningdale Drive.

Still, there's only so much you can do. You can't organise Super Striker tournaments for ever, and at 12 or 13 I was *desperate* to leave the cul de sac, and Mum, if you're reading this, I'm sorry to say but I did sneak off on the odd occasion. Because when you're 13 and all your mates are off on their bikes, and you're not allowed – *banned by your mum* – well, it's embarrassing, isn't it? What self-respecting lad wouldn't risk it? Wouldn't risk a bollocking to explore their surroundings?

So, yes, sorry, Mum, but I did. Only a couple of times, mind. Other than the odd thing like that, though, I was pretty obedient as a kid. We both were, Hayley and I. All the more surprising when you think that we were never smacked, either of us. There was never any physical punishment, just bollockings. Mainly these would be from Dad. No doubt the last thing he wanted to do after a 12-hour shift was give me or Hayley a bollocking, but that was the way it worked in the Watson house.

The dreaded words: 'Right, Russell Watson, you wait till your father gets home.'

Then what felt like – and probably was – hours. Twisting like a worm on a hook. In agonies of anticipation. Okay, so there were never beatings, no smacks. But Dad was scary. He so much as raised an eyebrow and you were browning your trousers.

Sometimes she'd let me off. Either forget or contrive to forget. I recall feeling, at times like that, as though it was a little secret I was sharing with my mum.

Other times, though...

'And how has Russell been today?' Dad would ask.

'He's been very naughty today.'

And the eyebrows would lift.

Uh-oh...

Other kids used to get the smacked behinds. Not us. Things were different back then and smacking your kids wasn't frowned upon like it is now, but even so, it never happened in our house. They had other ways of keeping us in line. Like going to bed. Every kid acts up at bedtime, right? Sharing a room, Hayley and I acted up more than most.

'Right, you've gone to bed to go to sleep, now get to sleep.'

This was Dad. All you'd need was one floorboard to creak and he'd be up the stairs like gangbusters.

'It sounds like the bloody roof's caving in down there,' he'd shout. 'I told you to get to sleep.'

All parents do it, don't they? Exaggerate, I mean. I do the same these days. Memo to kids. It doesn't *really* sound like the roof's caving in. You don't *actually* sound like a herd of elephants.

If it continued, our apocalyptic house shaking, we'd get a final warning: 'Right, if you don't want to go to sleep, you can come downstairs.'

Of course we wanted to go downstairs. Come on. We wanted a sneak peak at *Kojak*, *Rising Damp* or the one every self-respecting kid wanted to see: *Hammer House of Horror*.

But we'd get downstairs and he'd say, 'Right, you can stand in that corner until you're tired.'

What?

We'd stand in the corner for about ten minutes, hearing, but, crucially, not seeing the TV. And it wouldn't take long.

'I'm tired now.'

'Right. Well, go on and get to sleep.'

And off we'd go, tails between legs.

And that was pretty much it. That was as harsh as the discipline ever got. I did tell you I had an uncomplicated childhood, didn't I? Because I'm sorry if you were hoping to read all about how Russell Watson suffered as a kid, but he didn't. About the worst thing to happen to the ten-year-old me was being told I couldn't leave the cul-de-sac, and even then Mum had to let me go in the end. She had to. Apart from anything else, I was mad keen on my bike – on building my bike. And what was the point of building your own bike if the only place you could ride it was up to the top of the street and down again?

Back then, we used to scan the Grattan catalogue, and if you're of a certain vintage I bet you did the same thing. Later, of course, we used to look at the (ahem) underwear section (and again, if you're a lad and you're of a certain vintage, don't try to pretend you didn't do the same). But in those days it was the toy section we pored over, for the Action Man toys, the Scalextric, the Subbuteo and the Super Striker. That and the bike section. And wow, that Grattan bike section. The holy triumvirate of the three Raleighs:

the Strika, Boxer and the one everybody wanted: the Grifter. The racing bikes. The Raleigh Chopper.

Untold hours I used to spend looking at the catalogue. So much so that the book would end up flapping open to the bike pages if you put it down, the corners dog-eared, the colour faded on the pictures of bikes I liked, worn away from hundreds of finger-points. 'That one. That one. That one.'

I never had a bike from the catalogue, though. You had to pay something like a pound a week for the rest of your life if you wanted to get a Raleigh Grifter from the catalogue. And my dad was a crane operator at the steelworks. Raleigh Grifters just weren't an option.

So I built my own bike, one that was made up of parts. All of us used to do it. We'd get an old piece of second-hand scrap and just add to it. Get some nice handlebars for it, improve the brakes, the brake shoes, stuff like that. Next, get a couple of new tyres, maybe give it some new grips, some reflectors for the wheels. Just adding to the bike, always adding to it.

So anyway, yes, you're 12, you've got this gleaming bit of pedal-powered machinery at your disposal. You want to get on your bike and ride, as Queen might say.

'Be careful, then,' said Mum, in the end, after what felt like days and weeks and even months of pestering. 'Just be careful, Russell. Please.'

Deep down, I understood. Mum's attitude towards me sprang from the fact that she had two brothers who were both born mentally handicapped: one younger, one older. So I think she saw me like a gift almost, something to treasure, and around me she tried to create this protective force field. Looking back, it was an environment that was, I think, one of the main reasons why it took me such a long time to grow up and realise what I wanted in life; why I really wasn't thinking about being an adult, or how I was going to make money or any of the things that children are supposed to do when they get to a certain age.

It was like a cocoon, made up just of Mum, Dad, Hayley, Sunningdale Drive, the garage, the kitchen, the music constantly playing and cardigans on the road. Maybe that's why writing it down it all sounds so quaint and a little bit too perfect, like something you'd expect to see on telly on a Sunday evening just after *Songs of Praise*. It sounds like that because it was created to be like that. By Mum.

For example, and you won't believe this, but I remember when we first got a video recorder, Mum used to edit bits over the violent scenes in films. And believe me, we're not talking that violent here, either. We wouldn't have been watching it if it was. The first time she did it, I forget what the film was, but I remember that suddenly in came some footage of a brass band. Right at a good bit.

'Oh, Mum.'

I think what she'd done was to change the video channel during the recording, and it just happened to be a recording of a brass band, but after that it became an in-family joke.

'Right, we'll have to put the brass bands on.'

It didn't matter too much. Violent films were never really my thing anyway. And staying on the cul-de-sac, well, I could still play football. The only thing you could have done to really hurt me at that age was take away my football, because that was my one, enduring, all-consuming, passion: football. And who was my team? Who was the club I grew up supporting, and still support to this day?

It was Everton.

I'm pulling your leg. It was Manchester United, of course.

Imagine my bedroom. Well, my half of the bedroom at least. If you're imagining it messy, then stop. It was never messy unless there was a Super Striker tournament taking place, or maybe if I had all my toy soldiers out or something. Mainly, I was as neat and tidy then as I am now, almost obsessive, actually. Back then, I used to collect plastic toy soldiers, and as with the Super Striker players I would spend hours carefully painting them. Sometimes I'd save up a bit of pocket money and buy the metal-based ones from a specialist shop. Action Man, that was another toy. It was big back then, all the kids had them.

But tidy, you understand. All these toys were kept in their right place, not strewn across the lino. Then you've got the bed, and on the wall above that, my collage of football pictures clipped out of magazines, out of *Match* and *Shoot*. Almost the whole wall covered with pictures of United players.

Why United? Probably because I was from Manchester, United were doing well at the time and I liked the kit. Most of my mates supported United, too. But I will say this: you know that old chestnut about how only true Mancunians support Manchester City? A load of rubbish. It's just that United's fame has spread universally. (Now I'm going to get hate mail from Subbuteo enthusiasts *and* Manchester City fans.) Whatever my reasons were for supporting them, they didn't include my dad. He didn't really have much interest in football. Or, if he did, he was just too busy making the butty to indulge his interest. So I never went with him. When I did go to the football, it was with a mate, Stephen Hancock, and his dad. The first time I ever went with my own father was years and years later when... well, I'll tell you about that in a bit.

So. I had the posters. What was next?

'Russell, how would you like the Manchester United kit for your birthday?'

Traditionally, little boys don't really like kissing older ladies (it's the old-lady smell, the make-up), but I gave Grandma Watson a right smacker then. I gave her another one the next day when she took me to a shop, the name of which I've since forgotten, sadly lost in the mists of time. What I haven't forgotten, though, is the kit. Shirt, shorts, shinpads, the whole deal. And something else I haven't forgotten is the way I felt, standing in the shop, new kit on, gleaming red. I looked at myself in the mirror, Grandma Watson a smiling figure behind, but somehow out of focus and pushed into the background, relegated – sorry, Grandma Watson – by how bloody great that kit looked. How I'd love to say that I looked in the mirror and knew there and then that my future was to be inextricably linked with the club that I loved, but what am I, Doris Stokes? No, I just looked in the mirror and thought: Check me out. I'm wearing a Manchester United shirt.

It was a great moment. Up there with the first time I was ever handed a school football kit, when I was chosen for the Irlam Endowed Primary School squad by Mr Walsh, the PE teacher. True, it wasn't exactly difficult to get picked for the team. It was a bit like, 'You're in, son. You're in, too. And we'll need to find a couple of others from somewhere...' But even so, I was on the team.

At first, I played on the wing. Then I ended up in goal, which is the position I was playing when Irlam Endowed entered a local schools seven-a-side trophy.

It was absolutely leathering it down that day. I'd never seen rain like it. Hard, fat rivets of it punching into the churned-up pitch of Moorfield School, the hosts of the tournament. I wiped my face, keeping the water out of my eyes, staring down the muddy water-logged field at the action in the opposition's box. St Theresa's were the enemy. A handy side, a feared side. My nerves settled, watching my team squander a chance at the other end, wincing as the ball was scrambled away from their goal-line, but encouraged to see Endowed keeping up the pressure. Come on, Endowed, come on.

Score: 3–3. The dying seconds of the semi-final. Talk about a crunch-time. One more goal and the winning side would go through to face the hosts, Moorfield, in the final. Tough game, for sure. Moorfield were the form team. But *the final*.

I was nine, maybe ten. Nothing had ever been so important. I'd never wanted anything more than what I wanted at that moment, which was to see my side put one past the opposition goalie.

Okay, there was one thing I wanted more. (I sluiced water off my face again, knocked my keeper's gloves together.) I wanted not to be the one who let in a goal at this end. I wanted to win, of course, but I sure as heck didn't want to be the one responsible for us losing, especially as I'd been playing well. The rain and mud suits a keeper. Mud makes a keeper look good, because you can dive and slide, collect a slow-moving ball in a blur of goalmouth gymnastics.

And here they came. The ball cleared from the other end, arching over the heads of the players and plopping down to the pitch and not bouncing or rolling, just dropping, more like a cannonball than a football, and sitting there.

And chasing the ball, an army of tiny mud-men, advancing towards me. Kids so covered in mud all you could see of their faces was wide, determined eyes and bared teeth. My defence was way out of position. They'd been up helping the goal effort and were now madly scrambling to get back and defend their goal. I moved off the line, brushing rain from my eyes, glancing at spectators who looked like something from a pencil drawing, smudged and separated by the rain. Walshy was there, the PE teacher. His hands were cupped to his mouth and he was shouting, bawling at the defence to get back. Support. Support.

The opposition forward reached the ball. One of my defenders tried to tackle but missed, sliding across the front of their striker and sending up a sheet of muddy water as he did so. Nothing between me and their forward now, only muddy pitch.

And then the whistle blew.

I sank to my knees. In relief, partly, but more because I knew that was what goalies are supposed to do at the final whistle of a tense semi-final. Goalies sink to their knees. Even ten-year-old ones.

But there was no time. No time for all that. Because unless you take a taxi to Mars when England play in international tournaments, you'll know exactly what happens when the score is level at the end of normal time in a semi-final. You get extra time. During which nobody scores. Then you get penalties.

Which is the way it went. I stared downfield at their keeper, who stared back, and we were like two little gladiators, and more than ever – even more than before – I didn't want to be the one responsible for Endowed leaving the contest.

We each saved our first one. I saved my second then watched heart in mouth as their keeper dived to meet his second. And dived the wrong way. Skidded uselessly into the far post as the ball rolled across his line.

All I needed to do now was save. Save this one and Endowed was in the final. I knocked my gloves together, crouched low. Their forward approached the ball and we were eyeballing each other, doing our moves, the same moves we'd seen on *Match of the Day* a thousand times. Even at ten we understood. We knew that football's all about performance, all about drama. It's no wonder it goes so well with opera.

For a moment I thought he might slip on his run-up. Slip and then slice it across the face of the goal. But no, he was more sure-footed than that. He was better than that. And the ball was bobbling, skidding across the mud, heading straight for the bottom left-hand corner.

In slow motion, I threw myself at it. My Gordon Banks moment. I dived and skidded, finger-tipping the ball away round the post. Saved the goal.

Time stood still. Their forward stood, his head in his hands, playing his part to perfection, as I bounced to my feet, threw my arms in the air and was mobbed. Absolutely mobbed.

'Oh, what a save, well done, son.'

Walshy was there, first off the touchline, grabbing me and throwing me on his shoulders, the rest of the team arriving, too, clapping me on the back, reaching to shake my hand as I sat on Walshy's shoulders, the hero of the hour.

I thought: I could get used to this.

In the final, we won 3–2, beating Moorfield in a supreme giant-killing effort that nevertheless still lives in the shadow of the semi-final in my memory. Not long after we went to a ceremony at St Theresa's where Tommy Docherty, then the Manchester United manager, presented us each with a winners' medal.

But that night – the night of the tournament – I remember getting home and saying, 'Mum, we won, we won!' Bouncing excitedly all over the kitchen. And her saying, 'Oh, really? Very good. Well done. Now get in that bath. Look at the state of you.'

'But, Mum, we won.'

'Just you get in that bath, Russell Watson.'

They don't really understand, mums don't. All she was worried about was me getting mud on the soft furnishings.

She was right to be, of course. It took three baths before I was clean. The first two I turned the water black, and in each one I sat and wallowed, thinking about making the crucial save. How good it felt.

That's what football does. It's the same with music. It brings you those moments in life that take you out of yourself. And for the nine, ten-year-old me, buying the kit, saving the goal. These events would be the high points of my childhood, the moments that shaped me.

And I haven't even mentioned Old Trafford yet.

CHAPTER FOUR

I've been to Old Trafford for some truly momentous occasions.
Some that were momentous for the club, some for me, some for us
both. But there are two that really, really stand out. The second one
is the time I went with my dad – the time I'm going to tell you
about later.

The first one, though…

'All right, Russell, do you want to come to Old Trafford with
me and me dad?'

Um, let me think about that for a… Okay. I've thought. Yes,
please!

Hanky was my best mate then, in junior school this was. He
would stay one of my best mates through most of high school, too.
As I say, my dad had little interest in football, and anyway, he
worked too many hours. Meanwhile, Hanky's dad worked for the
GPO, and didn't have to work weekends, so there was nothing
stopping him from taking me and Hanky to *Old Trafford*.

After Grandma Watson bought me my Manchester United kit,
I'd taken to wearing it around the house. In fact, I still wear sports
gear around the house, even in the studio. I remember my
recording engineer, Josh Abbey – a New Yorker – saying to me,
'You know when the temperature's dropped to below minus ten,
'cos that's the only time Russell stops wearing football shorts.'

Sorry to break this to you if you imagine me standing in the studio

togged up in the full tenor gear, but *The Voice, Encore, That's Life* –
all recorded in shorts. Comfort, that's the thing.

Anyway. The kit. I'd worn one around the house pretty much
full-time since I'd got my first one, and today was no different.
That morning I pulled on my United shirt and pair of jeans (not the
shorts, of course; I'd have looked like the bloody mascot), a United
hat and a United scarf, with badges all over; I used to collect
Manchester United badges. And in my full get-up I walked round
to Hanky's house. What am I saying? I *ran* round there, the sun on
my face; beautiful summer's day it was, the season just starting,
bringing with it those precious few games when you can stand on
the terraces in shirt-sleeves.

'All right, Hanky,' I said, out of breath at his door.

'All right, Russ.'

Hanky had already been going to the football. His dad had a
league-match ticket book, which meant Hanky was an old hand
when it came to Old Trafford. And you know what it's like when
you're a lad and you've got experience at something like that? You
act all blasé about it, like, hey, no big deal.

Me, I was a first-timer and I was a boy-shaped packet of pure
excitement, all wrapped up in United red. But I wasn't going to
show it. I was acting all blasé, too.

'Are you ready then?'

'Yeah.'

'Great.'

We piled in his dad's car, which was bigger than my dad's
Hillman Imp, a big Eastern Bloc car, a Lada or a Skoda, something
like that, drove into Manchester, excitement silently building.
Then, as Hanky's dad parked his car what felt like miles away from
the stadium, I found myself dealing with a little worm of disappointment shifting in my stomach. Like, oh, is this it? As though
I'd been expecting Mr Hancock to park right next door to the

stadium and see Lou Macari on his way into the ground. Instead, there was... well, there was no one actually.

So we walked.

And walked.

And it felt like we walked for miles. But the thing about attending a football match – the same with a concert – is that you start off alone, but gradually, as you approach the venue, you're joined by fellow supporters. This day was no different. Slowly but surely the streets began to fill with people as they appeared from side roads, both ahead of us and behind us, or were discharged from the rows and rows of terraced houses that lined our route. Imagine *living* that close to Old Trafford, I thought. Imagine how great that would be.

Even closer now and the streets were thronged with men and boys; their one common factor the red they all wore, the red of United, worn in hats and scarves and shirts. The disappointment from before was all gone. Instead, the anticipation was building. I was part of something. Part of something that was almost religious in its ability to bring people together. The buzz building and building.

Next, two things came at me. First, the ground. I'd seen Old Trafford on telly, but only the inside of it. Here it was in the flesh, rising way, way above our heads, a huge mass made of concrete and wood but still somehow alive. A stadium on matchday seems to breathe, move and make a sound all of its own as fans congregate. You can't beat it. To experience it for the first time: *wow*. My senses were at overload just taking in the place. The people, the atmosphere.

And the smell.

Again, wow. The next thing to hit me was the whiff of the hot dogs and hamburgers, the vendors with their vans and trolleys. We'd had an ice cream on the way down but still my stomach did a hungry flip. And then we were making our way to the gates. I remember feeling so small, almost treading on Mr Hancock's heels to keep up as we reached the turnstiles.

'Give it a good push, son,' said the guy at the turnstile.

Around us the sound of the gates was deafening. *Clack, clack, clack*. Fans pushing their way in. Huge metal gates they were. Or at least they seemed huge to the ten-year-old me. And I couldn't get mine to open. I pushed but it wouldn't budge. Mortifying, it was.

'Go on, son, give it a good old push, eh?'

I gave that gate a Herculean shove and at last it shifted, propelling me off the street and into the ground. Into Old Trafford.

We were in the Scoreboard Paddock, the terrace opposite where the away fans stood. And whenever I went with Hanky and his dad from then on, that's where we went: the Scoreboard Paddock. Remember, we didn't have seating then. It was terraces, an angled concrete plane onto which hundreds, maybe thousands, of fans would cram. We came to it from behind, climbing steps up to it, the smell of hot dogs now replaced by cigarette and cigar smoke. I was hearing banter around me, supporters talking about the game to come, about the side, the manager. Hearing language I rarely heard. Strong language. Grown-up blokes talking in an unguarded, grown-up-bloke way, making me feel as though I'd joined some kind of secret society. At the same time, I was thinking, I'm going to watch the footy. *I'm going to watch the footy.*

Then onto the terrace, where the sensation was incredible. The noise hit me first of all. From outside the stands it's like a hum, as though the stadium itself has something to say. Out in the ground, though, the volume slams into you: chants, songs, an indescribable noise that is simply the sound of anticipation. There's nothing like it. Nothing like the feeling of walking out on to the terrace to watch your team play.

On the other hand, maybe there is one thing like it. When your team scores.

The thing with terraces is that they're always moving. There would be surges, and these could be as scary as they were exhilarating, and they would come in waves. One moment the crowd would seem to relax, exhale, loosen, and I felt able to breathe, move and look around. The next, a surge. Behind you, ten thousand blokes all moving forward. A couple of times I felt myself pushed against a barrier and it was terrifying, genuinely terrifying.

Then, United scored, and the whole terrace rejoiced. For a second or so the crowd seemed to open out, and I whooped and screamed, watching players congratulating each other on the field and grabbing hold of Hanky at my side. He and I had dropped the whole blasé act. No place for that on the terrace. Not when you were watching your side, cheering them on one minute, fighting for breath the next.

The crowd surged forward. I caught a whiff of Bovril. That, meat and potato pies and cigar smoke. And dimly I thought: Where are all the people eating the pies and drinking the Bovril? How can blokes smoke a cigar in this? There isn't the space to scratch your knee let alone decant a thermos and shove a pie in your face.

Funny thing is, though, those crushes never stopped me. Never even gave me pause for thought. After that, I'd try to get to Old Trafford as much as possible, and once inside me and Hanky would always do our level best to get as close to the front of the terrace as we could.

I couldn't afford to go as much as I would have liked, which at that time would have been every game. But I went as much as I could. Even then, it wasn't cheap. The first thing I did when I was old enough was to get a paper round because I wanted money and I wanted to be able to do what I wanted, which was go to the football. Doing that gave me an early appreciation of the value of money that I've never really lost. From an early age I was always trying to earn a few spare bob, whether it was to help fix up my

bike, go and watch United or, later, buy musical instruments –
when the music bug bit. There was the paper round; plus, in the
school holidays, I'd go round with a bucket and sponge offering to
clean people's cars. Always looking for ways and means of making
a few quid to feed the addiction.

I was in my last year of primary school when Grandad died. It's one of those childhood events that I still wonder about. What effect did it have on me as I grew up?

Dad came to school and I was called out of class. I first saw him through the frosted window of the classroom door, recognising him in the corridor, just the shape of him there, and somehow instinctively knowing that things weren't quite right. Dads don't belong in school. Dads are in garages and in front of the TV. They don't belong in the school corridor, looking slightly pained and uncomfortable and out of place.

He took me to my peg then we got in the car to go home.

Grandad was my mum's father. He and my gran had split up when his boozing became too much. When I was very young, this was. They lived in Flixton before the split and my only real memory of him was playing the piano, plus we used to make sandcastles in the back garden, but that's it, pretty much. Just the piano and sandcastles. I was still so young when he and my gran split up – when he moved away to live with his new lady, a woman called Gerry.

We drove to Anglesey. Which is flat, I remember thinking. There, on an estate, in a prefab bungalow, was a sombre collection of people collected together to mourn my grandad. Everybody wore an expression of shock, my mum and Gerry in particular. He was so young, that was it. Only in his mid-fifties. Hayley and I hung around the fringes, keeping out of the way, eating bags of crisps and clinging to the wallpaper.

We were there for a day or so. The atmosphere was grim, and it took me a while to adjust. It was so different from Sunningdale Drive, where the music was always playing; where Hayley and I filled the house with noise, and kids played footy on the road outside. Here, it was as though the needle had stuck in the grooves between tracks, the silence bearing oppressively down upon us all.

It was the first time anybody around me had died, and I'm not sure it had hit me. I remember wondering why everybody was crying. I would glance across at mother and she seemed in shock, alternating between weeping and simply sitting, staring out of a rain-streaked window. I didn't understand. Grandad had died? But why? What had Grandad died of? People murmured and I over-heard snatches of conversation.

'... so young...'

'... at his age...'

'... the drink...'

'... the booze. It was the booze...'

I wanted to be back in Sunningdale Drive, away from the gloom.

'Russell?'

Gerry called to me. I was on the way back from the kitchen, a beaker of orange squash in my hand.

'Yes?'

I looked at Gerry, whose position in my family I didn't really understand. She addressed me, staring at me intently as she did so.

'Do you know what his last words were, your grandfather? Do you know what he said?'

I shook my head no.

'He was lying on the carpet, and he said to me, "God, I hope

Chapter Five

Russell never ends up like this, make sure Russell never ends up like this."'

Gerry held my gaze, then straightened and walked away. I took a gulp of my orange squash and went to find Hayley.

I never forgot what she said, though, even though it took me years to work out exactly what she meant: the booze had killed Grandad, and he didn't want me to go the same way; his dying wish was that I wouldn't make the same mistakes he had.

And I haven't, touch wood. I've always had a fairly sensible attitude to alcohol. I never drink during the day and although I like a glass of wine or three, I don't go crazy (not these days anyway).

We travelled back to Salford but life didn't quite return to normal. It never did. Grandad dying affected Mum in ways that wouldn't become fully apparent for literally years after his death. She grieved. She grieved for a long, long time, and I think in many ways she grieves still.

To my shame, I never really gave it too much thought. I knew something was up, and I knew it had to do with Grandad dying, but somehow it didn't involve me. You know what it's like when you're a kid – kids are self-involved little buggers at the best of times and I don't suppose I was any different. Football, bikes, TV. Repeat chorus. I simply waited for normal service to resume.

But she'd be crying a lot, especially in the weeks immediately after Grandad had died. It wasn't like I'd wander into the kitchen and catch her doing it, but at night, after Hayley and I had gone to bed, we'd lie awake in the dormer, listening to her sobbing, and the next day, I'd ask Dad, 'What's wrong with Mum?' and he'd say, 'Your mum? Don't worry about your mum, she's all right.'

But she wasn't. She'd pick up, be okay for a while, then be down again, and it could all happen very, very quickly, with a speed I've since learnt – because these days I know from experience – has a lot to do with medication. As the years passed, the periods during which Mum was depressed grew longer. They tended to coincide with the anniversary of Grandad's death, just getting progressively worse as time went on. Dad would protect her, tell us and other people that she was just poorly, the radiogram in the lounge silent.

CHAPTER SIX

December 2007

Almost Christmas. I'm forcing myself to be Christmassy, mainly for the sake of the girls, who I'll be seeing on Christmas day, the first full Christmas day ever. Well, not ever, obviously, but the first time since the divorce. The first time in six years or so.

I'm really looking forward to it, I think to myself, in an up moment.

I'm dreading it, I think, in the next moment, when my hydrocortisol levels are low, the world outside seems grey and the future black.

Maybe if I wear this red baseball cap. Maybe that'll make me feel a bit more Christmassy.

I try. It doesn't. I keep it on anyway.

So what might Santa bring me this year? I wonder. Well, I know he's going to bring a nice new course of radiotherapy. And to go with that, I've had an early Christmas present. A lovely new... Well, I was going to say 'mask', but it's not really, it's more like a medieval torture device rendered in plastic. It's like your worst nightmare and I've got to wear it for the radiotherapy sessions. The fitting was Friday, and when someone said it was for a mask, in my mind's eye I pictured – what?, oh, I don't know, Mickey Mouse? Not what I got anyway. Not something that looks like a prop from *Witchfinder General*.

So I get to the hospital, the Christie, and there I go to a room where a very pleasant nurse stands waiting to greet me. She's holding a gum-shield-type thing.

Biggest gum-shield-type thing you've ever seen.

'That's not going to fit in my mouth,' I tell her, and she looks from that to my mouth. I can see her thinking, Hang on, this is the bloke who does the classical singing. The one who never stops talking. Could talk the hind legs off a donkey. Of course it's the right...

'Oh, give over,' she says.

I open my mouth as wide as it will go and once again she looks from her gum shield to my mouth.

'Oh,' she says, 'you do have a small mouth, don't you.'

'It's the lungs that are big,' I tell her.

'Right.' But she's not interested in my lungs. She turns and fishes for a fresh gum-shield thing. I end up with the size just above small.

In goes the gum shield, which, now it's in, isn't a gum shield. You know when you go to the dentist and they take an X-ray of your teeth? It's like that. You bite on it while they fill your mouth with blue gunge. *Ugh*. It's like having a mouthful of superglue. Which you have to leave in for...

'About sixty seconds, Russell,' says the nurse. 'And whatever you do, don't move, all right?'

So I don't. It feels more like an hour, but I stay dead still. And all the time I do I'm thinking, Don't move, Russ. Don't move because you don't want anything to go wrong. Not for the sake of a tiny movement.

After the minute is up, the nurse moves across to take the mould from my mouth. It won't budge.

'Oh,' she says. 'It's not coming out.'

'Hmgrth,' I say.

I'm starting to get a bit panicky because I've got this great big bloody thing stuck in my mouth. There's so much blue gunge in there it's started going down the back of my throat.

Gary comes over. I stare up at him, eyes wide.

'Try wriggling it,' he says. 'You maybe just need to get some air in it so it'll just pop out.'

'Hmgrth,' I repeat but have a go myself, wriggling this bloody gum-shield thing, until, *clunk*, out it comes, and – oh, joy – brings a filling with it. My mouth fills with blood, but I don't get the opportunity to worry too much about it, because now we're going into the simulation room.

'The what?' I manage.

'The simulation room, haven't you been told about it?'

Oh yes, of course I had. In all this excitement I'd kind of lost track.

So I go in.

'Just lie on that table please, Mr Watson.'

I do as they say, even though I don't like the look of this. I make jokes. Always making jokes. But somewhere inside I'm not laughing. A little voice is reminding me, 'You're claustrophobic, Russ. Best leg it, eh?'

I ignore the voice and lie down. Two bolts clamp either side of my head. They ask me to put in my new mouthpiece. I'd only just got used to not having it there, but I do as I'm told and in it goes. It has a metal bracket protruding from the front. This then feeds into a frame which clamps down above my face. They bolt me into place. I can't move. I feel like cattle. Like a strait-jacketed patient in an eighteenth-century mental hospital.

I don't like this.

'Are you okay? Is everything all right? Are you comfortable?'

'Hmgrth,' I manage, trying to say no, but unable to because I've got this thing in my mouth, and what am I, Roger de bloody Courcy?

And then all of a sudden, I think: no, I can't do this. Lying there with exactly that going through my head. I can't do it. Like a little kid going: *I can't do it. Won't do it. Can't make me.*

My palms are sweating. I'm close to panicking. Inside I feel as though I'm having volts passed through me. Internal needles flicking to the red part of the dial.

And then: 'Oh come on, Russell. Come on, you soft, *soft* bastard.'

I take control. I think, This is it now. This is the first step now to getting rid of this thing once and for all. Not having to go through the pain and anguish of telling my children again that I've got to go for major surgery on a tumour. Not having to actually have the surgery.

So that's what I do. I focus on the kids; on the light at the end of the tunnel, on knowing that at the end of all this, the tumour will be gone. Gone for ever.

It spurs me on, I focus, my insides settle and the needles come out of the red. Even so, later, when I'm leaving the hospital, I catch sight of myself reflected in the exit door. I don't look much like me today. Not that bloke with the big lungs. The one so full of confidence who's performed for royalty and gave a cheeky wink to George W. Bush.

No, I don't look like that guy.

Things don't improve the following Monday when I have to go for an MRI scan. Not only does the MRI scan set off my claustrophobia, but I relate MRI scanners to bad news. You can't blame me for that. Me, I so much as look at an MRI scanner and the Grim Reaper puts out the Welcome mat.

For example, first one ever, my introduction to the exciting world of MRI scanning, was in America, the Cedars-Sinai hospital in LA, when the headaches had become so debilitatingly painful that I'd just had to seek treatment. During the recording of *That's*

Life, my fifth studio album this was, and wouldn't that have been ironic? If I'd died, I mean. A posthumously released album called *That's Life*.

The result? 'Mr Watson, you have a conjoined tumour in your head that's about the size of two golf balls.'

Fast forward through my first operation and I went for a follow-up scan, expecting to be given the all-clear. But no. Bad news. The tumour hadn't all gone. I started looking around and weighing up treatment options, until all that was rendered irrelevant when I found myself being carted down my own stairs last October. Rushed into hospital and straight into – yes – an MRI scanner.

So, no. I don't associate MRI scanners with halcyon, never-to-be-forgotten days. I associate them with death. Fittingly, they're like coffins. Hospital staff slide you in, and once in there's very little room. You, wearing a protection mask – which makes you feel even more claustrophobic – and just a small slit, like the kind of thing you might expect to see on a suit of armour. You look through your slit and out there is a mirror so you can see the medical staff in the operating room.

When I went in I told the nurse, 'I'm a bit nervous, to be honest.'

'Oh, you don't seem too bad, Mr Watson,' she replied, cheerily. 'You should see some of them we get. They take one look at the scanner and won't come in through the door. We can't even get them to come in and sit in the room, they're that scared. We have to give them drugs. So don't you worry, Mr Watson, you'll be fine.'

I've got to say this, the staff are brilliant. In the last couple of years I've gathered a better-than-average experience of hospital staff, in hospitals in Los Angeles, London and Manchester, and these are the most unflappable, down-to-earth, capable people you could ever hope to meet. One of their great skills is taking something that seems to you to be so alien and so wrong, like, 'You want me to slide in that coffin-looking thing? Give over, will you,' and making it seem so commonplace and everyday. It's the best way of relaxing you, and for a moment or so, with the comfortingly matter-of-fact medical staff settling you down, you do feel okay. As though everything's going to be all right.

So I slide into the MRI scanner. I think about the kids. As so often, I use them like a mental anchor, keeping my mind from concentrating too much on what is happening to me, because there's a noise.

It's deafening.

They give you earplugs, which must take the edge off it, but even so. It's like a huge, engulfing roaring sound.

I peer through my suit-of-armour slit, see the people in the control room, and I'm thinking, How do they look? Are they laughing? Was that a laugh I saw, or was it a grimace? Have they caught sight of something on one of the screens they have there, and whatever it is is so big, so bad, that they can't help but pull a face?

When surgeons go through the MRI pictures with me, they point at areas of my brain and I stare, trying to see what they see, trying to square this image with the one I have of my own brain, which is the picture we all have: a certain shape, a certain colour. It all looks black and grey to me, though.

And yet after every trip to the hospital I leave with what can only be described as a feeling of euphoria. I tick off another visit on my mental calendar and think, That's it, one step closer to being rid of this thing.

December 18, 2007

'You should've seen our Russell when he was little. A right little bugger he was.'

This is Crnab, my grandma, on my mother's side. She stayed in the area after splitting from my grandpa. She remarried, to a chap called Tommy Aldred, and I've got so many fond memories of going with them both on short holidays to Wales. But Tommy's no longer with us, sadly, and Crnab now lives in a little bungalow. She has care workers who go round; my mum goes a lot. Gary and I have brought her some flowers and a Christmas card, then taken her out for a drive.

Crnab likes to tell stories, especially stories that illustrate what a little handful I was growing up. She tells the story of how we were out for a walk one day, on our way to the sweet shop, when the sky suddenly seemed to go black, almost as though someone had drawn a black sheet across it.

We looked up to see a huge flock of birds, a black mass of them and I said, 'What's that, Gran?'

'That's migration, Russell.'

'No, it's not your gration,' I replied, 'it's everybody's gration.'

Then she tells the other story, the one that's legendary in our family. The one that sounds like it should come from the first reel of a 1940s Hollywood biopic. How we were driving past a really nice house one day and I pointed at it and said, 'One day, Gran, I'm going to buy that house.'

Plus, of course, the tale of how she came to be called Crnab. The game of Scrabble that was dragging on one day. So long that she decided to cut it short by laying down the word 'crnab'.

'That's not a word,' I said. 'You can't have that.'

'What do you mean, I can't have it?' Because she can be a right battleaxe, my gran; you wouldn't mess. 'What do you mean, I can't bloody have it?'

I said, 'It's not a word. I've never heard of it.'

'It *is* a word,' she insisted.

'Then what does it mean?'

'I can't remember, but I know it's a word, I've heard it before.'

'Right, c'mon then, let's get a dictionary.'

We looked it up, and sure enough, there's no 'crnab' in the dictionary, she had to admit defeat. But somehow the name stuck and since then I've always called her Crnab. When she opens her Christmas card, she sees I've written it out to Crnab and she looks at me.

'You've never forgot that, have you, Russell?' She smiles.

'No, Gran,' I laugh, 'and I never will.'

She's great value, my gran. It's a good day. For perhaps the first time I feel a bit Christmassy, but any festive thoughts are quickly chased away by the big black dog I've got sitting in my head. The tumour. The radiotherapy I need to beat it.

CHAPTER SEVEN

Crnab's right, I was a right little bugger growing up. And you know that programme, *My Name is Earl*, where the main character goes around saying sorry for the mischief he's done? Well, if there was a Russell Watson version (*My Name is Irlam?*), I'd be paying a visit to the following...

1. The people of Ferry Hill Road

That's more or less everybody who lived on Ferry Hill during the late 1970s, but especially Catapult Codger, Treaty Beattie, Australian Cow and anyone else who was in any way inconvenienced by the Grand National.

The Grand National was a race up Ferry Hill Road, which was the road between Sunningdale Drive and Eldon Road, quite a steep hill. Round there became my stomping ground right from the moment Mum relaxed her boundary rules. A bunch of lads could have a lot of laughs on Ferry Hill. And we did.

The idea of the Grand National was that you went through people's back gardens. Over fences, through shrubs and rose bushes, hurdling walls. However you got to the finish line, you had to do it over the back gardens – and all without getting caught by neighbours. There was me, Hanky, Paul Waring, Gareth Tudor, a right load of us. We'd get together at night, all dressed in black gear, camouflaged like our Action Men, and the Grand National would begin.

'On your marks, get set…'

Do you know what a load of boys trampling through back gardens sounds like? Well, imagine a brontosaurus trying to put up a tent in a garden centre. Try as we might, there wasn't all that much stealth to this game, so, of course, we'd get caught by the neighbours.

There was one we called Catapult Codger, who we used to wind up something rotten. We'd go into his garden and make noises just to get a rise out of him.

'Who's that?' we'd hear. 'Who's that? Is that you again? Is that you lot again?'

He'd go back into his kitchen and reappear with his catapult, firing stones at us, sending us diving around in the gloom at the bottom of the garden, near wetting ourselves with laughter.

'I know who you are and I'll be down to your parents.'

There was another time when Gareth Tudor was trying to get over a fence and a bloke we called Australian Cow came running out. As he escaped, Tudor's glasses fell in Australian Cow's garden and Tudor was inconsolable, squinting at us afterwards, going, 'Oh no, what am I going to do? Me glasses. Me mam's going to go mad.'

So later we had to mount an operation to get them back. Needless to say, Tudor couldn't do it, so I crawled into the garden to rescue them instead. What a hero, eh?

Then there was the time we accidentally broke Treaty Beattie's window (actually, it was Gareth Tudor again) and we all had to club together to pay for it. And somehow I managed to do that without my mum and dad noticing. We called her Treaty Beattie because she gave us sweets. One night we took all the slats out of her fence and neatly piled them up in her garden. The next night we went back and replaced them, after word had got round that some little yobbos had been at her fence. Whether it was that or the window incident, but we stopped getting sweets from her after that...

2. Gareth Tudor, and anyone passing the VG shop who thought it was raining Maltesers

First, Gareth Tudor, for pushing him into the silt that time. Me and Hanky. It was just too tempting. There was Gareth Tudor. There was a big pile of mud.

He was wearing brand-new trainers as well. Gareth Tudor's mum went mad about it. We got into trouble and I was confined to the house for a while afterwards. Grounded, they call it these days.

Then, after that, was the Dennis the Menace Fan Club incident.

What it was, at school they were giving away the old school team football kit, which had red and black stripes, like the old Manchester City kit. Me and Hanky took one or two of these kits each and hatched a plan to get a bit of cash – or 'grub money', if you were into the *Beano*, which we were. The plot we devised was worthy of Dennis himself.

With our black and red shirts, we told Gareth Tudor and another friend about the Dennis the Menace Fan Club, which would cost them a fiver each to join. In return for their fiver we gave them a shirt (free from school); a badge that we made ourselves, badly, with felt-tip pens, cardboard and glue; and a little certificate, on which we'd scrawled, 'You are now a member of the Dennis the Menace Fan Club.'

There used to be a VG on Bury Hill. With the money from the Dennis the Menace Fan Club scam, Hanky and I paid it a visit and bought Maltesers, boxes of them, like the ones you get in the cinema. Clutching our booty we climbed up on top of a storage building to eat them. After a while, we'd had our fill of Maltesers. We took to lobbing them off the roof instead, chuckling at passers-by who were gobsmacked as Maltesers hurtled out of the sky at them, like a tiny chocolate asteroid attack. Then we went home and watched *Superstars* on telly.

The next day, Gareth Tudor's mum went absolutely mad.

3. *Mum, for the puff pants incident*

I think that most mums in the 1970s must have had a crack at making their own clothes. You don't see them much any more, but they used to have these patterns that came in a bulging white envelope with a colour drawing on the front. And it was fine if your mum wanted to put herself through the agony of making and then wearing the clothes. Absolutely nothing wrong with those envelopes so long as they featured drawings of grown-ups on the front. What struck fear into the heart of every schoolchild was if the white envelope had a picture of a kid on it.

In all honesty, I'm not sure if the puff pants came from one of those patterns. If they had, then they were some kind of experiment gone wrong. Instead of making a pair of Oxford bags with pockets down the side, which were the 'in' kind of trousers at the time, Mum had created a monster, a mutant breed of trousers: the puff pants. Where Oxford bags were baggy, the puff pants were skin-tight. Where bags boasted pockets down the side, the puff pants instead had them along the hip. But worse. Much, much worse. The puff pants were bright pink. No self-respecting male would be seen dead in these trousers. But my mum had made them, and if I'd told her, 'Mum, I'd rather die than wear these trousers in public,' she would have sat down to knit me a coffin. Whether I liked it or not, I was going to wear the trousers.

'I've made them, you wear them.'

'But, Mum, look at them.'

'They look fine to me.'

I stared down at them. If streetwise and cool and acceptable-in-front-of-your-mates was at one end of the spectrum, then the puff pants lurked wretchedly at the other end.

Even so, I had to wear them, much to the amusement of my mates at school, who instantly dubbed them puff pants. (Not very PC, I know, but it was the 1970s and we were kids, what can I say?)

'Mum,' I wailed that night, 'all the lads at school have been calling me puff pants. I'm not wearing them pants again.'

'Yes you are, Russell,' she said, resolute as a breeze block.

'Aw, Mum.'

'I made them pants, they're lovely pants, I don't know what they're talking about.'

Still, they went in the wash that day, and I got to wear normal trousers for the next few days or so. My playground shame became a memory. Until, inevitably, the day came when I had to wear them again.

'Oh, Mum...'

'Those pants are absolutely gorgeous, you look lovely in them.'

No way was I going to go school like a badly dressed Barbie doll for the second time. Instead, I hid a pair of regular, non-embarrassing trousers in my satchel, and on the walk to school, I hid behind a bush and changed into them. She was none the wiser; I never wore those puff pants in public again. In fact, I think the first time she learnt the truth was years and years later, during a TV programme when the story came out.

4. My dad, my mum and the deputy head, for playing with matches

The only time I saw my dad close to giving me a wallop was when I found a box of matches. I can't have been much older than seven or eight then, and like most kids I was fascinated by matches. These ones I'd light and just watch burn. But what an idiot, I was doing it up in my bedroom, blowing out the matches then sticking them between the floorboards so they'd fall down – this in a dormer made out of wood. A full box of matches I went through. Just striking them, staring at them agog, my seven-year-old mind endlessly stimulated by the flame, then putting them out and dropping them between the floorboards.

Then, one day, there was a problem with the central heating. The kind of problem that required Dad to get the floorboards up.

Like they used to say in the *Beano*: 'Ulp.'

I was thinking, How can I get them? How can I get the matches before my dad sees them?

Answer: you don't. Your dad pulls up the floorboards and throws a wobbly.

'Where have these bloody matches come from in here?'

'I don't know, not me.'

I'm not the world's best liar.

'It is, ain't it?'

'No, it's not, no honest, it's not me.'

At the time our kid was three or something, so Hayley's hardly likely to be the culprit, is she? I got the corner treatment, made to stand in the corner until I came clean and admitted it.

'All right, I did it.'

And I got absolutely roasted for that. Roasted.

'*You could have burnt the house down.*'

I wasn't allowed out for what felt like years, but was probably only a couple of days. Still, though. I genuinely think that was the closest I ever came to a good hiding.

Then, there was the smoking incident. I was at high school by then, and what had happened was, Mum had bought me one of those nylon parka coats, the ones with the fur-lined hoods that came out from your face like a snorkel. You know the ones I mean. Just about every school kid had one in the 1970s. They were cool at the time, and what could possibly add to that? What could I do to make myself even cooler? I decided to try a cigarette. Me and Hanky, ever the partners in crime, got hold of a box of ten Embassy. Ten Embassy, a box of matches and a packet of Polo mints probably. The cigarette made me feel sick. Thankfully I never got into that particular habit. The matches, though. That was a different story. There I was up to my old tricks, lighting matches, when one blew back, hit my parka and left a hole in it, the nylon all melted around the edge, no question of it being anything else but a burn hole.

'What's that on your coat? What's that there on your coat?'

She didn't miss much.

'What? Where? Where?' I was doing that thing where you suddenly feign blindness or memory loss. Putting off the inevitable.

'That. There on your coat, it's a hole.' She peered closer at the melted nylon. 'It's a cigarette burn. Have you been smoking?'

'No, it's not a cigarette burn.'

'Well, what is it, then?'

'It's from a Bunsen burner.' This piece of thinking I would love to use as an example of the razor-sharp Watson mind at work, and not the desperate flailing of a kid trying to avoid an inevitable bollocking. Which is what it was.

'From a Bunsen burner?' She looked disbelieving. As well she might.

'Yes.'

'And what were you doing wearing your coat in class?'

I flailed again. 'Uh, the electric had broke down. The heating wasn't working so we were made to wear our coats in class.'

'Were you?'

'Yes.'

'Right, I'm ringing the school.'

'No, you don't need to—'

Too late. She did, and all the time this little problem I had with the match was getting bigger. I should have just come clean about the match in the first place. But now she would think I was trying to cover up evidence of smoking. And, worse, she was getting the school involved.

The next day, me, her and the deputy head met, and during a meeting I sat on my hands. Bent my head low and quite comprehensively folded under questioning.

No, the heating hadn't broke down. No, I hadn't burnt my coat on a Bunsen burner. And no, I hadn't had chemistry that week anyway, so I hadn't used a Bunsen burner. In the end, there in the deputy head's office, I came clean, admitting that I'd burnt the hole with a match.

Later that night my dad went off on one.

'Are you still playing with bloody matches?'

Looking back, I wish I'd just thrown away the cigarettes and the matches and eaten the Polo mints instead.

CHAPTER EIGHT

The burnt parka happened in the first year of secondary school, and it was to set the template for my school life from then on.

I never got on there; didn't like it. It was as though all of a sudden everything got a bit more serious. We weren't supposed to mess about any more. Now we had to knuckle down to work and I wasn't prepared to do that. I wasn't ready for it. I wanted to stay at junior school, messing about with my mates, playing football, working on my bike and painting toy soldiers. Instead, secondary school got tough, both academically and in the playground. Around 20 Salford junior schools streamed into our secondary, Irlam High, and the first year was a blur of playground fights as a pecking order was established. Some involving yours truly, it may or may not surprise you to know. And I got a reputation as a right little terrier, had a few good moves. Nine times out of ten I'd be protecting a mate or finishing something somebody else had started, and my style was all about psychological warfare; I used to intimidate my opponents, striding towards them, teeth bared, tearing off my blazer and shirt at the same time. After a few of those I had a reputation as a bit of a nutcase, someone you don't want to mess with, which was fine by me. When you're at school a fighting reputation is worth its weight in gold. Pretty soon you don't need to worry about fighting at all. You just coast along on that big, bad rep of yours.

Of course, it's a terrible thing to be doing, fighting. But you know what? If it hadn't been for playground scraps I might never have become such good mates with Steve Gleave, so we might not have formed the band, I might never have considered singing as a possible career option and I wouldn't be speaking to you now. Who knows? One rush of blood to the head, your whole life changes.

'Russell.' This is my mum speaking, calling me to the front door.

'Yeah?' I was in the front room watching TV. It was teatime, so something like *Blue Peter* or *Newsround*, maybe a copy of *Roy of the Rovers* on my lap. 'The Safest Hands in Soccer', that was one of my favourite stories.

'There's someone at the door. He'll be out in a minute, love. What is it we can do for you?'

'I want another fight with him,' came the reply, and in the front room I jumped, startled. It was Gleavo. I'd had a scrap with him earlier in the day. We were mates at school, but for someone reason forever lost down the back of history's sofa, there had been a disagreement and we'd ended up slugging it out. Outside the school gates, this was. There hadn't been a clear winner. We'd traded punches and that had been it; I'd left him with some marks, but he'd caught me a right crack round the side of my head and my ear was still throbbing. But now – now he'd come round to my house. And, worse, he was talking to my bloody mother.

'You what?' she said at the front door. Her tone had changed. I wanted to disappear into the comfy chair.

'I want another fight with him.'

'You want to fight him? Why?'

'He did this to me,' and I had to imagine Gleavo on the doorstep, forlornly pointing to whatever bruise I'd given him.

'*Russell.*'

Reluctantly I went to the front door.

'Did you do this to this lovely lad?'

'Yes,' I admitted, looking from her to Gleavo's wounded face.

'Get up to your room,' she roared at me, then to Gleavo, 'He's not having another fight with you. Get off home.'

And that was it. Thanks to Steve Gleave's wounded pride and battered face, I got a complete bollocking. But even so, we ended up being best mates. I can't remember exactly how a truce was bartered, but it was, and we ended up hanging about together. Later, he'd be best man at my wedding to Helen. And it was with Gleavo that I really, properly, discovered music; with him that I played my first-ever gig.

Music had always been there in my life, mainly thanks to my mum and dad. I've mentioned the radiogram before. It sat on the side in the kitchen, a huge thing, chipboard case. You pulled the top down and inside was a record player, radio and space for storing vinyl.

It ran white-hot in our house, that radiogram. Mum had it going all day long, playing classical music. In that kitchen was my first exposure to Tchaikovsky, Chopin, Wagner, Schubert, Bach, the Enigma Variations... Her father – my grandad who'd died – had been a pianist, almost concert standard, so she'd inherited a love of the piano. Liberace was a favourite. Mario Lanza another. She had a phase of playing James Last all the time. All day long. Play one side of the vinyl, a wipe of the hands on the tea towel, flick over the record to play side two. Next record.

Then Dad would get home.

'Shall we put one of mine on?'

It wasn't like he'd get back and impose his music on us. It was all very democratic and civilised, and sometimes the classical would stay on all evening – many a night I fell asleep with classical music floating up to the dormer from downstairs. But Dad was more into rock and country and western, and if it was his turn to put something on the radiogram then it would be Dire Straits, Johnny Cash, Gordon Lightfoot, John Denver. Nothing too rocky, though. He was never allowed to go mad.

Me, I liked both Mum and Dad's taste in music. To me, then, I didn't really see them as being particularly distinct from one another. It was all just music to me. And that attitude would serve me well in the end, because later I'd be mixing classical with rock and pop during my sets and people would love it – they hadn't seen it done before. Thanks to my musical background, it never even occurred to me not to do it. Why shouldn't I? It was all just good music.

Growing up, I adopted my own favourites. Madness and the Jam were two early hits in the Sunningdale Drive dormer. I had a little tape recorder. Again, if you were brought up in this era you'll know exactly the kind of tape recorder I'm talking about: rectangular, boxy thing, buttons like a piano keyboard. I'd make tapes on it, mixing my records with those belonging to my dad, so Madness would sit next to John Denver, and I'd listen to it in the dormer, occasionally singing along, mimicking the vocals. That was something I was always good at: impressions. I could mimic virtually anyone, and once again, it would be part of my early music life that I'd later exploit, gaining a name for myself on the club circuit.

School days passed in a haze of larking about and being crap at maths and geography. I played football as much as I could and my interest in music grew. I clowned around and did impressions of the teachers. I took up the piano for a while, but it didn't last too long, even though I got quite good. At fifteen or sixteen I started playing the guitar, around the same time as I left school with just one CSE grade one, in English, to show for my trouble.

And it hit me. I had to *do* something now.

I didn't want the kind of job my dad had, that much I knew. Years of seeing him arrive home from work, dirty and shattered, had made me realise that I wanted a nice comfy job in an office. So

I went for an interview. I honestly can't remember exactly what for, but it was something to do with computers; me, having barely even seen one. We'll get back to you, I was told, and they never did. So it was necessity rather than choice that sent me to the door of Worsley Technical College, where I spent the next twelve months on a YTS course. At the time it was either that or go on the dole, and I didn't fancy the dole; I needed to be able to afford my clothes and music. As it turned out, though, college was brilliant.

I suppose you might say I was a bit of a late starter. Between you and me, I was still playing with Action Men at fifteen. Worsley Tech changed all that. In short order I discovered the delights of booze and girls, dividing my time between the pub next door to college and hanging round the trainee hairdressers, for whom I was a regular and willing guinea pig.

'Russell, your hair's purple,' my mum would tell me, after yet another disastrous session as a hairdresser's model.

'Yes I know, it should have been black but it didn't quite work out.'

I went out with one of them, Tracey Steele, a beautician, and probably my first-ever serious girlfriend, my first love.

And all the time – always there in the background – was football and music. By now I could play the guitar, and Steve Gleave and I had been dabbling around putting bands together. Back at Irlam High, we'd formed the Crowd.

God, we were awful. There were four of us: me and Gleavo on guitars, his brother Rob on drums – and he was quite good on the drums, he was probably the only one out of us who could play properly – and Phil Wilkinson, who played bass. None of us could play that well. Steve was all right, but Phil was still learning while we were getting together. We didn't much care, though, about technical ability. We were just a group of kids who got together because we were mates and we were into the same music; because we wanted to play instruments and aspire to something. At that time it seemed to us that there were two ways of getting out of working in a factory: either football or music. And I wasn't very good at football. That semi-final save against St Theresa's was about as good as it ever got. Somehow, I knew. Maybe deep down I felt it. Music was going to be my way out.

We played covers mainly. The Beatles, the Jam, Small Faces, a bit of the Who. I was on backing vocals. Even so, I can't say we were exactly serious about it. We'd got the look down pat, though. We even had publicity pictures taken in the park: really cheesy, tacky pictures of us wearing 1960s gear. Mod was the thing then, of course. We had side partings and wore wraparound shades, boating jackets, drainpipe pants and pointed shoes in black and white. Boy, did we think we looked good.

But that was as professional as we got. The Crowd was never meant to be, and as a foursome we never even did a single gig. However, me and Gleavo had a bit of a rapport going, and we'd meet together and work on songs. Gleavo was (and still is) a handy songwriter. In the meantime, my mum, who used to know just about everyone in the area, had got the two of us a gig.

I say 'gig'. It was an evening at the Craig Hall Day Centre, where the average age of the punter was 75. Didn't matter to us, though. It was our first gig. Plus, we'd been promised payment. Chocolate biscuits and cups of tea.

We turned up. Both of us hardly gone sixteen, carrying our guitars, setting up in the corner where the day centre had thought-fully provided a little PA for us. It meant we had microphones, and I'm not sure if Gleavo felt the same way, but I remember feeling a thrill at that. My first gig. With microphones.

We set up, the pensioners assembled and we began our gig, Gleavo saying, slightly tentatively, 'Hello, we've come to sing for you.'

A couple of Beatles songs – 'Help' and 'Yesterday' if I remember correctly – a few Jam songs that I'm not sure went down that well and a Style Council number.

After each one, the residents gave us a polite round of applause. One bloke in particular, though, was even more appreciative. About seventy, eighty years old, he was sitting at the back, from where Gleavo and I became aware of what can only be described as a furious activity. The old chap – and there's no other way of putting this – was pleasuring himself while Gleavo and I were up there singing Jam numbers.

Barely able to contain ourselves (well, someone had to contain themselves) we watched as a care worker crossed the room as unobtrusively as possible, leaning into our biggest fan and saying something he didn't hear, either thanks to declining faculties or because he was, um, 'enjoying' the music so much.

She tried again. Still no answer.

Then, raising her voice, she said, possibly louder than she'd intended, 'That's enough now, Sid, eh? Put it away now, there's a love.'

Later, enjoying our payment of chocolate biscuits and tea, the same care worker joined us.

'Sorry about Sid,' she explained, 'he's not done that for a while. I think he must have liked you...'

Thinking back on it now, that was my first-ever review.

There's got to be something more than this, I thought, dragging myself out of bed. Time: 7 a.m. Weather report: bloody cold. There was nothing sunny about Sunningdale Drive on those mornings.

There must be something more than this. Must be.

The radiogram played but I wasn't listening, gulping down tea and breakfast on autopilot, throwing on dirty jeans and lacing up my steel-toecap boots, pulling on my coat. Work was about two miles from home and I rode there on my bike, foggy with sleep denied to me.

'All right, Minty?'

'Yeah,' I said, still bleary-eyed from bed. Tired from the mad dash to work. A bit peeved because – yet again – I was late.

In the changing rooms I pulled overalls on over my jeans, and on top of those another set of plastic overalls, like aprons, to keep the oil off me. Then down to my workstation.

'All right, Minty?' said another of my fellow workers, as I made my way down.

'Yeah, ta,' I said.

'Right, right, Russell,' said Steve, the foreman. It was the same old drill, every morning. As he spoke I looked over the factory floor, a huge pitch-sized space, the high, curved ceiling inset with searing bright fluorescent striplights, two or three of them blinking now, the tubes on their last legs. 'We need an oil change on this today,' continued Steve, indicating a machine nearby. There were row upon row of these machines lining the factory floor, darkly glistening. At them sat workers dressed the same as I was, just settling into the day; some laughing and joking with mates; some grim-faced, tired and yawning. Already the factory air was heavy with the smell of metal and oil, and somewhere a radio played 'I Want to Break Free' by Queen.

'The sump needs doing and then there's a couple of drills need grinding and...'

But I'd stopped listening, dreaming already of 11 a.m., break time. In the meantime, I decided to make the oil change last as long as possible, give me a chance to have a chat with the lads around the machine, catch up on the football results, the weekend gossip.

'How's it going, Minty?' said another, this as I took my position at the machine.

I squinted at him, saying, 'Can I ask you something, mate?'

'Yeah, fire away, Minty.'

I noticed that my fellow workers were all looking our way with interest.

'Why is it you all call me Minty?'

They dissolved into laughter. 'Because you always turn up after eight, mate, that's why.'

The name stuck.

'You should write a book, Russell Watson,' the manager, Robin, said, on his way past one day.

'Oh yeah, why's that?' I said, half knowing what was coming next.

'Because I've never heard so many excuses for somebody turning up late. You've got a different excuse every day. Your dog died. Your cat died. There was an accident.' The manager was ticking off excuses on his fingers. All of them, I'm ashamed to say, were genuine Russell Watson compositions. 'You've had a puncture on your bike. Oh, what was that the other day? That was a cracker, that was. Oh, that's right. It was raining.'

The thing was, I'd make a concerted effort to get there. Every day. But it would be like a scene out of a film: me, dashing towards the clocking-in machine, card in hand. The clock showing 8.00.

Then changing to 8.01. Just as I clocked in.

'Russell Watson, late again,' Robin would sigh. Almost every day began that way.

This was where my YTS had got me. Sabre Repetition in Irlam. We manufactured turned parts, and my job was as a trainee learning how to set lathes and run them to make nuts, bolts, washers and spares for just about anything that needed a nut, a bolt, a washer or spare. Radio transistors, washing machines, parts for cars, you name it: if it needed a turned part, Sabre Repetition could supply.

I'd got the job after leaving college. Leafing through the *Manchester Evening News*, and there it was, a position that not only called for the qualification I'd gained at Worsley Tech, but was close to where I lived.

For the interview I took a trip into Manchester and kitted myself out with a Baumler suit. About £175 it was, this suit, and I thought I looked the cat's pyjamas in it. I was already into my clothes by then. Hanging about with the guys from the Crowd, I wore suits, panels on the back and side vents, and we always prided ourselves on being clean-cut. Through college it was V-necks, Fred Perry T-shirts underneath, or a white Fred Perry with a black jacket and a pair of jeans and brogues. I needed a job just to keep the fashion victim in me satisfied.

Ted was my first manager at Sabre Repetition. He was an oldish guy, bald, a nice bloke who didn't take any crap. It took him all of five minutes to work me out. He'd be walking round, checking everyone was busy, and I'd be sitting there doing sod all and trying to get away with it. Trying to do the bare minimum to earn my £75 a week.

Because I hated it, I really did. The job just wasn't me. It took no artistic flair, it required no imagination or drive. There were lads there who were very good at the job, and it's a skill – it might not have floated my boat, but it was skilled labour all right. It just wasn't a skill I was ever interested in acquiring.

There was a clock on the wall at the end of the factory and I'd be watching it all day. All day, every day. Pretty much the only thing I ever applied myself to while working in that factory was the business of studying the second hand's journey around the clock face until the little hand pointed at eleven, the big hand pointed at twelve, and it was time for tea and biscuits.

I had to fill the hours in between breaks, though, and I tended to do that by having a chinwag with whoever would listen. With Steve gone, off to give some other poor bastard his daily duties, and Robin and Ted elsewhere, I'd have a chat with some of the lads, then go and natter with the girls who were stationed in a different part of the factory, on what we called the second op jobs.

Second op was a living hell, a waged purgatory. What it was, we would make the nuts and bolts and then they'd go to second ops, which was like a production line. Just horrible. On second ops you'd get a trolley full of nuts and bolts and what you did was you got the nut and you'd stick it in a machine which would thread it, put a little ring in it, chamfer it, polish it, clean it out with oil, then pop it out the other side. You'd get a certain amount of trays each day for each worker to do.

Second ops was mainly staffed by women. Except if I was on it. Because if Robin was really fed up with me skiving then he'd put me on second ops, which was like the Sabre Repetition equivalent of being in solitary confinement. Because not only was it the most tedious work available anywhere in the entire universe, but Robin would make sure to put me on a machine as far away from anyone else as possible.

I'd see him coming down the factory floor and I'd know – I'd know he was after my blood. It was the only reason he ever came down to my end of the factory.

'Eh up, Dave,' I said to one of the other younger lads who worked there, 'Robin's on his way over. I bet he's going to put me on second ops. Better try and look busy.'

Too late.

'Russell,' said Robin, arriving at the machine.

'Ah, yes, are you all right, Robin?'

'Yeah, mate, are you?'

'Yeah, yeah, not bad.'

'Yeah, how's it going down here?'

'Not bad, yeah, you know, working as hard as I can, mate, under the pressure, you know.'

There was a pause, then he said, 'How do you fancy a little spell on second ops?'

'No, I'm all right actually, mate.'

He said, 'No, I'm thinking of putting you on second ops for a week.'

I said, 'No, I'm all right, mate, I think I'm doing all right here.'

He said, 'Let's see how you do for the next couple of days, shall we?'

It was like a threat. So over the next couple of days I'd be thinking, I don't want to go on second ops. But he got me.

After the eleven o'clock break for tea I watched the second hand lead us into lunchtime, half past twelve to half past one. After that, it was the slow march to three fifteen. Another break. More tea and biscuits. A natter. Then to 4.30 p.m., by which time we were winding the machines down, turning them off, cleaning shavings out of the trays, changing the oil if it needed doing, then out of there for 5 p.m., at home by quarter past.

Unless I was on nights, of course. Twelve-hour nights, these were, eight till eight, absolute killers. I survived by bringing in my guitar, giving the lads lessons. At least people were a bit more laid-back on nights. I'd have the foreman and a couple of the lads sitting round while I gave them basic guitar lessons. Learn Guitar the Russell Watson Way. Singing my Beatles songs. Doing impressions. All the time just trying to get through the days and nights by having a crack, taking the mick, doing impressions of Ted and Robin, winding people up.

One lad, called Brian, was younger than me and he let the tyres down on my bike one night as a practical joke, which he thought was hilarious. I came out and it was absolutely leathering it down with rain, got on my bike, wondering why all the lads were standing round laughing.

'Oh, right, very funny, who's done my tyres?'

No honour among factory workers at 5 p.m. They gave Brian up, so a few nights later I got hold of a double ladder, got his bike out of the bike shed and put it on the factory roof.

'Watson, you bastard,' he said, when he saw it. 'Where's the ladder?'

'Dunno, mate, sorry.' I rode off home, laughing. Chalk one up to me.

The next morning I woke up for work, dragging myself out of bed. Seven a.m. Cold. Nothing sunny about Sunningdale Drive.

There must be something more than this, I thought. There must be.

I met Helen in 1987. We bought a house together in 1990. We married at St John's Church, Irlam, in 1993, when Gleavo was my best man. We split up in 2000. It wasn't what you would call an amicable parting. We fought before we split up, we fought during the divorce and then – just for good measure – we fought afterwards too. Things were said in the press.

So it's difficult for me to talk about her for that reason. I can look back at other memories and my feelings about them remain fixed in time. But it's different with a relationship, especially one that ended as badly as ours. You can't isolate moments in the past and revisit them objectively; it's tainted by what's happened in the meantime.

And with Helen and me, it's been very tainted. A lot of water went under the bridge.

We met in the Hollins Green pub, which was where me and the lads from work used to hang out. Our hunting ground. And I'd seen Helen in there. I can't remember who got talking to whom, but I do recall that I was standing by the fruit machine, just leaning against it with my hair slicked back, trying to look cool, and we got chatting, exchanged numbers. Then, another day, we met up. We kept on meeting and the relationship developed, the same as any relationship does. Next, we're going to the cinema together, then I was invited to meet her mum and dad. We became an item.

I was still at Sabre Repetition when we got together. Not long later, I went for a job at Hunts in Patricroft, a firm making crankshafts. It was the same kind of work as I'd done at Sabre, and it was further away from where I still lived on Sunningdale Drive, but the money was better: £90 a week. I togged up for the interview, dazzled the company manager, Phil Smith, who interviewed me, totally selling him on my blinding engineering skills, and was given the job...

Then I got there and did absolutely nothing. My very first day at Hunts I realised I was out of my depth. There was a machine there called the A-line, which turned out specialised crankshafts, and it had about six or seven different ports, all for different tasks. Huge thing, it was, and I didn't have a clue how to operate it. Standing there on my first day, I knew Hunts wasn't for me. It was as not-for-me as Sabre Repetition had been. Although at least at Sabre I knew how to work some of the machinery.

So how did I cope? Same way I did at Sabre. I skived, made jokes, took the mick and impersonated the foreman, a chap called Dave we nicknamed Smiler because he never did. He used to say, 'I can see you, Russell, watching me, watching you, watching me.'

That was his catchphrase. If they ever make a sitcom about life at Hunts, kids'll be saying that in the playground.

And he got a lot of opportunity to exercise his catchphrase, Smiler did. He was on to me from day one. There was a huge crankshaft machine I used to hide behind, to get out of work, but he'd catch me skulking there: 'I can see you, Russell, watching me, watching you, watching me.'

I'd say, 'All right, Dave, I'm on with it, mate, yeah?'

'Well, I'm watching you.'

I nailed his voice, of course, and took to using it on the lads. They'd be in the tearoom in the morning and I stand out of sight in the corridor, doing my best Smiler impersonation: 'Right, lads, come on, let's be having you, shop floor.'

'Piss off, Russell.'

'Come on, lads,' I'd persevere, 'none of that. Let's be having you out there.'

This went on for a while, until one morning I came in about five to eight, not quite due on the shop floor yet, and I stopped outside the tearoom, put on my best Smiler voice: 'Right, lads, come on, let's be having you, let's have you on shop floor now, lads, come on, stop messing around in there with tea, come on, let's be having you.'

And instead of the usual 'Piss off, Russell' from the lads I heard my impersonation coming back to me: 'Very funny, Russell.' Serves me right I suppose; Smiler was sitting in the tearoom.

I could do Phil Smith, too, as Rabbit would testify. If Rabbit wanted to pull a sickie, he used to get me to tell management; he asked me to do it one day because he wanted to place a bet. God knows why it was going to take him all day just to place a bet, but anyway I did what he wanted. Then, about halfway through the morning, I put on my best Phil Smith voice and phoned him at home, telling him he'd been seen at the bookies, trying not to crack up laughing as he attempted to talk his way out of it.

'Well, yeah, I am ill but the thing is, I did have to go to the bookies… Just a minute, is that Russell bloody Watson?'

It used to get me into trouble, too. One bloke, Andy, a huge Geordie lad, got wind of the fact that I'd been taking him off behind his back.

'Someone's told me you've bin tekkin the fookin' piss oot o' me,' he said one day, this huge, displeased bloke in my face. 'Yerrbin tekkin' the fookin' piss oot o' me accent.'

'No, I haven't,' I told him, face like an angel.

He said, 'That's not what ah've fookin' heard, but I'll tell yer what, if ah fookin' hear yer tekkin the piss oot o' me, ah will fookin' have yer, d'ya hear me?'

'But I've not. I can't even do your accent,' I said, butter wouldn't melt, already thinking about the fun I was going to have replaying this incident to the other lads.

My denials were getting him angry, I could see. He was worked up just confronting me. Me trying to wriggle out of it was getting him even more wound up.

'Don't you lie to me, mate, ah'm fookin' gonna have yer.'

'Andy, I've not been taking the piss—'

But I didn't get a chance to finish my sentence because he came at me, advancing on me like an angry Geordie bull at a matador convention. I was faster, though, ducking behind one of the huge machines. I couldn't operate them properly, but they made a great refuge.

'Come here, ah'll fookin' have yer,' he roared, chasing me around one machine, then another. Me almost killing myself laughing. Lucky for me, the big man was out of breath first.

'I'll get you, yer wanker,' he warned, tuning away, and I let him get a safe distance before calling him.

'Andy?'

He turned. 'Yeah?'

And in my best Geordie accent I roared, 'Fook off.'

'You're a bastard, Watson,' he shouted back, 'ah'll fookin' have yer.'

I got away with that one, though.

Just as with Sabre, the work at Hunts wasn't for me, and every morning I had the same sinking feeling as I got out of bed. They must have liked having me around, though, maybe for the entertainment. It certainly wasn't my productivity that saved me from the boot.

'We're not getting much production out of this line, Russell,' said Smiler one day. 'I'm not sure what to do with you.'

He wasn't wrong. I was on a grand total of five crankshafts a day.

I said, 'Well, you know, there's a lot of problems with it, Dave. It keeps breaking down. The belt's not working properly and it's only been here like six months, mate, you can't expect miracles overnight.'

'All right,' he said, doubtfully. 'I'm going to try one of the other lads on it for a couple of days.'

'Yeah, all right, Dave, great.'

Frowning, he moved off. 'I'll be watching you, Russell. Watching you, watching me, watching you.'

Not long after, this other lad, George, ambled across to take over on the machine.

'Listen, mate,' I said, drawing him to one side, 'do me a favour, eh? Don't go crazy on your first day, you know. It's all right to do, say, seven or eight. Just don't go mad, eh?'

At the end of the day they tallied up the crankshafts he made, comparing his score with mine from the previous day.

Russell: 5.

George: 110.

The writing was on the wall, wasn't it? No matter how I looked at it, engineering wasn't for me. I had decided not to follow in my father's footsteps, yet here I was. I needed to get out.

So when my chance eventually came, I took it.

December 20, 2007

We go to buy a Christmas tree, Gary and I. People stare.

True, people often stare, but this is slightly different. I think they're surprised to see me on my feet for one thing. Everyone's seen reports of me getting rushed into hospital and how I'm going to have radiotherapy in the New Year; the last time I was on TV I was being wheeled out of the hospital with my nose in some kind of bandaged sling. Maybe because of that, some folk reckon I should be sitting in a bath chair with a rug across my lap, coughing gently into a hanky and ringing a bell for my nurse.

Two ladies follow us around the shop. We are stalked as we try to pick out a Christmas tree and it's strangely unnerving, but at least they're not trying to point mobile phones at me, take my picture. I get other, slightly taken aback, looks. A woman passing by takes it more in her stride. 'Good to see you, Russell,' she says. 'Good luck with the treatment.'

'Cheers, love.'

It's not so bad. There was a time I was out and this group of hoodies clocked me, shouted out my name. There I am, turning around, thinking: Yes, you're down with the kids, and one of them shouts, 'Russell, yer shit!'

That cracked me up.

What wasn't so funny was the last time I went out for a drink with some mates, that was bad. Some drunk girl totters up to our table. 'Hey, mate, yer the opera singer intyer? It's me mate's birthday. Sing happy birthday for us, would yer?'

'Look, sorry, I'm just out for a drink with my mates.'

And she totters off and I watch her go, knowing that she's going to tell her friends what an uptight miserable twat Russell Watson is, and they'll tell their friends, and they'll tell their friends, and each time the story will become distorted until it goes that Russell Watson waltzed into a bar and demanded that some girls celebrating their mate's birthday were ejected.

Back home, Victoria reminds me about a hospital appointment. I need constant reminding these days. What I had – what I've got, I should say – affects the memory, so my recall for dates and appointments has diminished dramatically. Luckily, I've got a lot of people around me to help jog my memory.

'Thank you very much, Victoria,' I tell her, adopting the voice of a convalescing pensioner. 'You're so good to me, dear, you really are. Whatever would I do without you?'

She grins and leaves.

It was worse before the emergency operation. I'd be walking about the house, scratching my head, going, 'Where are my car keys. I'm sure I put them round here somewhere...'

And Gary would open the fridge.

'You know you couldn't find your keys, boss?'

'Yeah.'

'They're in the bloody fridge.'

If I lost something we'd have to look everywhere for it. In the freezer, coffee machine. I'd have to retrace my steps, trying to work out where I put them. 'Okay, and then I opened the washing machine, and... aha! The keys are in the washing machine.'

You know what, though? Something I do remember is the

registration number of my dad's Hillman Imp: XNC 486L. Weird that, isn't it?

I work out then later watch a film, a Bourne film. Time for the brass bands, I think, watching Bourne get into another violent scrap. Bourne's not quite doing it for me, though, so I switch him off and schlep to the kitchen for a tin of Diet Coke. On the way out there I pass the grand piano that sits in my hall and I plink the keys as I go past. In the kitchen I fetch the Coke and decide that maybe I'll have a couple of games of footy on the PlayStation. On the way back to the TV I pass the piano, reach out to plink the keys, then stop.

I plink a key, try my voice a little. Then another key, trying it again, voice filling the hall. I put the Diet Coke can down and do some scales, trying some of the harder notes. Then a top C, which I nail.

Feels good. I was struggling with my high-end stuff before the operation, but here I am belting it out, maybe because my voice has had a rest, and they like that, voices do, they like a rest. I'm belting out another high C, pleased to hear it, when I get a dizzy spell and have to stop. It's like a reminder, the dizzy spell. *Don't you go getting ahead of yourself, still a way to go yet. Don't forget your little rendezvous on January the second (and that's one date I haven't forgotten; funny, that).*

I leave the piano, go back to the TV, pick up the videogame controller.

It's no good, though. No amount of PlayStation helps. I pull on a baseball cap and take a drive just to get out, take my mind off the radiotherapy. I go to Sunningdale Drive where streetlights bronze the little cul-de-sac, feeling bad for the kids who live there now because there's no room to play in the street these days. Too many cars. The lights are on in my old house, Mum in there, but I don't stop, not tonight. I reverse, pull away, indicate right, find myself taking a drive that goes past my old school, then past Eldon Road and the house I shared with Helen, the bottom of the route of the Grand National, Sabre Repetition, which isn't there any more, it's a Lidl now…

I know it sounds as though I'm taking some kind of maudlin tour, revisiting my old life, but I'm not. My mum still lives in Irlam. So do Helen and the kids. This is *still* my life. When I say I never forget where I came from, you better believe it. I can't forget. People growing up, they always want to escape where they're from, head for the bright lights, but I was always too happy with my life to want to escape. Where I lived, that *was* the bright lights. I always knew there was something more for me out there, though; felt it in my gut.

And anyway, if I did want to escape, I haven't done a very good job of it, have I?

I go past where the VG shop was. Where Hanky and I pelted passers-by with Maltesers. Past where Craig Hall Day Centre used to be, not far from the old steelworks. Heading for home and trying not to think about the R word, I drive past the Railway Inn.

CHAPTER TWELVE

February 1990

'Go on, Russell, give it a go.'

We were in the Railway Inn, halfway through a mini Irlam pub crawl. A weekday night, so we weren't overdoing it and the Railway Inn was only the second stop of the night. Weird. Sometimes I wonder, what if we'd just walked past, deciding not to bother? What if I'd not fancied going out at all: 'No, love, I'll give it a miss tonight, you go, eh?'

Watched a bit of telly instead; waited for Helen to get home: 'Ah, you missed a good night, Russell. They had a talent contest down the Railway Inn.'

'Oh, right, any good?'

'Yeah, not bad, not bad. Tea?'

But I did go out, and we didn't walk past the Railway Inn or decide to go to the White Horse instead. We strolled in, right slap-bang in the middle of something they were setting up. A Piccadilly Radio talent contest. Singers wanted. There was a DJ compèring; a little stage area set up in the corner; expectant, nervy people sitting round, the DJ cajoling latecomers to join in.

'Anybody fancy having a go?' he asked us as we walked in, and we laughed at the suggestion, waving him away – 'No thanks, mate' – getting the drinks in and taking our seats.

What if I'd stuck to my guns?

Out were me, Helen, a couple of other mates and a bloke called Tony Wragg, who I knew because he lived on the same street as Helen's mum and dad: Astley Road. Somehow or other we'd got wind that we both played the guitar. 'Oh you should say hello to Tony down the road, he's always carrying a guitar around with him.' That kind of thing. Tony and I had got together to jam, meeting at Helen's mum's house and practising.

'You should get up there, Russell,' they said, as we took our seats.

'Yeah, Russell,' said Tony. 'You'd be good.'

Really? I thought. Why? It's not as if I fancied myself as a singer. True, I'd sang along to Madness in the dormer, I'd done the gig with Gleavo and, as anyone on the nightshifts at Sabre Repetition could tell you, I could hold a mean Beatles tune, but even so. Incredible to think, really: ten years later they'd be calling me The Voice. Up till then the main thing I'd used it for was taking the mick out of the blokes at work.

'Nah,' I said, looking over at the gear they were still setting up in one corner of the room; at a banner saying, 'The Piccadilly Radio Search For A Star 1990'. This, we found out, was one of the early heats. They were taking place all over.

The DJ hunkered down, busy doing something. Just behind him was the microphone stand, a lead snaking down from the mic and pooling on the carpet. A lonely microphone on an empty stage, always something about that sight that seems to tell a story. I tried to imagine myself standing behind it. No guitar for protection. No Tony Wragg or Steve Gleave or blokes from the Crowd.

'Come on, get up and give it a go, Russell.'

I laughed, shaking my head no. But a little insistent voice had started up. *They're right, you can do that. Easy. You can get up*

*there. Done it before. Let's face it, your first-ever gig you had a
member of the audience knocking one out during the set. What's
the worst that could happen here?*

'Go on,' said someone at the table, 'you do a bit of the old
singing, play the guitar and that. Why don't you give it a go?'

'Nah, I'm fine just sitting here,' I replied. But really I think I'd
already made up my mind. My little voice had decided for me.

'Go on,' cajoled my mates.

'Oh, all right then. I'll go and give it a go. Just for a laugh, mind
you.'

Someone fetched a list of songs to choose from. I scanned the
selection.

It wasn't like Tony and I were trying to form a band or
anything, but we'd had one gig a couple of weeks earlier. At the
Tiger Moth pub, this was. He'd rang up: 'All right, Russ? Got us a
gig, do you fancy doing it? Fifty quid. Twenty-five nicker each?'
'Yeah, mate, yeah, why not?' Turned up with our guitars, a bit
nervous, played the guitar, did a bit of singing, the usual Beatles,
Jam and a bit of Neil Diamond. Spot on. But it wasn't as though
my vocals were ever centre stage. And song-wise the best I could
offer was a working knowledge of music from *The Jazz Singer*, the
Neil Diamond version that came out in 1980. The big hits we'd
learnt from it were 'Hello Again', 'America' and the one I chose
from the list in front of me at the Railway Inn that night: 'Love On
The Rocks'.

There were ten or twelve other singers, all doing their bit. When
it came to my turn I pulled a face and strode up to the microphone,
sang 'Love On The Rocks'.

I got through it well enough, I thought. I'd done a pretty pass-
able impression of a bloke trying to sing a Neil Diamond song.
Yeah, not bad. And I sat down, basking in my little moment of
glory as everyone assured me it had gone okay, that people in the

audience had seemed to respond well. According to them I'd had the biggest cheer of the night.

The DJ totted up the votes cast among the audience. Sitting there waiting for the result, I wasn't sure how I felt. Actually, yes – yes I was. I wanted to win.

'We've got two people going through tonight, based on the votes,' announced the DJ, head down behind his booth. 'And the first contestant through is... '

I realised I was holding my breath and let it out as the DJ announced the name of the runner-up, who would be going through to the next round. It wasn't me. At our table we gave each looks that said, 'Ah well, gave it a go.'

'And the winner tonight and also going through to the next round is... *Russell Watson.*'

Our table erupted, someone got a celebration round in. Next day I had work and I was suffering a bit, but only a bit. I was already looking forward to the next heat.

Piccadilly had promoted the show in pubs across the whole of the North West. Four hundred singers went through the first round. There was a second set of heats at another pub and I won that, too.

And something had changed. It was me. That second heat, I wasn't smirking any more, not taking the piss or doing it for a laugh. My version of 'Love On The Rocks' had gone from strength to strength. It's a sad song in the key of A minor, a sad key, but I was giving it full pelt. I was giving it everything. What had changed was that suddenly I'd realised I really wanted this. I'd spent years in factories dreaming of something else, but never quite working out what it was. Now I knew: it was this. And I thought I could do it; I thought I could make it work. Other contestants I knew were already doing the pubs and clubs and making a living out of it. So could I.

Winning my heat brought me down to the semi-final where the four hundred original contestants had been whittled down to twenty. It took place at the Three Crowns in Stockport, and walking in there that night, it was obvious things had got a bit more serious. The place was rammed, the noise of conversation almost deafening, the air thick with smoke, hanging in the air like rolled-up hammocks. At one end of the room was a stage with a 'Piccadilly Radio Search For A Star' banner draped across. There were lights. And behind that lonely microphone on a stage, technicians from Piccadilly assembled their rig.

I don't know how to explain it. It was like I was on a stove and someone had just turned the gas up. If I'd had any doubts, if I needed that one final shove in the right direction, then this was it. It felt as though I was stumbling into my calling. You've got to remember, before then I'd never thought about my future and I'd certainly never thought about fame. These days every kid in the classroom says they want to be famous, but not back then, and certainly not me. I was never one of those Lena Zavaroni types, prancing about in their bedrooms with a hairbrush. I worked in a factory. So what I saw, walking into the Three Crowns that night, was not just a way out of the factory – although it was that – but it was what I wanted to do. I'd grown up with this formless, nagging feeling that there was something else out there for me, something outside the boundaries of Sunningdale Drive. Walking into the Three Crowns that night, I realised I'd found it.

It's funny. That feeling was so strong and so incredibly enveloping that it seems to have obliterated most of my memories of the night. I remember what I was wearing, how could I forget that? It was a Hawaiian shirt I'd bought from the underground market in Manchester and it was probably the most expensive shirt I'd ever bought. The most revolting, too. I had on a pair of black pants, plus a pair of patent-leather Pierre Cardin shoes. I don't remember preparing for the night, though. Did I rehearse? Who was even there? A similar crowd to those in the Railway Inn that night I'd first entered the contest. Most of the evening, though, most of it's a blur.

We took our seats in the audience. We were towards the back, I think. A compère called the contestants up, one after another.

'Right, lairdees and gennerman, we've got Joe Small on now. Let's have a big hand, if you will, for Joe Small. Joe Small, lairdees and gennerman!'

Joe Small stood and a spotlight picked him out as he made his way through the audience. I watched him climb up to the stage. It seemed huge to me, that stage. There was a light show, a backdrop. It was proper. It was full on. There must have been two hundred people in there. I've played Wembley Stadium since then, 76,000 people in the audience. But that night it felt like everybody in the North West was packed in that pub.

Joe Small got a decent reception, as did the next contestant, and then the one after that.

One guy, in particular, was very good. He sang 'You've Got A Friend' by Carole King and he sang it well, big applause from the crowd rather than the polite smattering that had tended to greet the other contestants. He's the winner, I thought.

And then: 'Well, lairdees and gennerman, we've got Russell Watson now, coming up to sing Neil Diamond's song, "Love On The Rocks". Russell Watson, let's have a big hand for Russell Watson.'

Tony Wragg said, 'Good luck, mate,' and then I was striding up to the stage, climbing up, taking my place and blinking through the lights at the crowd. Funny thing, you can't see everybody, just the first few rows or so, their faces looking at you, staring your way, as though saying, 'Come on, then, entertain us…' Standing there, I had a feeling of intense, exhilarating loneliness – and I fed off it to sing my number.

'Love on the rocks…'

From the reaction of the audience, it went down well. Really well. My first real, 'Wow, that went *well*' moment. I returned to my seat, everyone telling me that I'd done brilliantly, got a great cheer, biggest cheer of the night. One more singer, then they announced the five finalists.

Carole King bloke got through. Deservedly. He'd been great and his was the first name to be read out, the first of five finalists whose song would be played on Piccadilly Radio for the listening public to vote on the winner.

The second name called out was mine.

We'd all been coiled up like springs, unconsciously pushing ourselves into our seats, fists clenched, so that when my name was read out the entire table seemed to spring up. *Yes.*

And I remember thinking, Christ, I'm going to get played on the radio. I'm a factory worker from Salford and they're going to put me on the radio. I'd gone from being one of four hundred to one of twenty, and now one of five – a one-in-five chance of winning this thing, for pity's sake – plus they were going to put my song on the radio. And it's funny, because when you get well known and your records start selling – which mine do, I'm glad to say – you get radio reports and you look at these things, thinking hmm, just seventy plays on Capital this week, and you forget – it's so easy to do – how it felt that first time. In the years since, I've done the lot: I've done *Parkinson* and *Jonathan Ross*. I've made a documentary, had TV specials and a *South Bank Show* done on me. I've sung for the US president, for the Pope and Prince Charles, but there was something about that first radio play. Just knowing it was going to happen. It felt like I'd made it.

The final was on a weekday. I went round to a mate's house.

Everybody else was at work, probably listening in on their work radios. As I walked round to my mate's house, I remember thinking, I can do this, I can actually win it. People are digging what I'm doing here, they're liking it.

Carole King bloke was going to win it, though.

We'd been asked to phone in at 1 p.m., and they put us on hold, the five finalists.

'Hello, is that Russell? Are you with us, Russell?'

'Yeah, yeah, I'm here.'

'Great, mate. Hold it there, yeah? We'll put you on in a minute.'

Jeff Ward and Pete Shreeves were the two DJs. Earlier, they'd played all five songs, all of them recorded that night at the Three Crowns. 'Love On The Rocks' had come on and I'd been grinning ear to ear.

Carole King bloke was going to win it, though.

I was recording it. (I wonder what's happened to the tape? Probably in a box somewhere. Probably in Mum's garage.)

'And the runner-up is...' There was a pause during which I offered up a silent prayer to the god of pissed-off factory workers.

The name read out was the Carole King bloke.

'And the winner of this year's 1990 Piccadilly Radio Search For A Star is... Rrrrrrrussell Watson.'

I'd got my mates to ring in, of course, and all of my family. Crnab had rung about forty-five times.

Jeff and Pete were telling me, 'Well, Russell, we've had an absolutely brilliant response to "Love On The Rocks". It's been absolutely fabulous,' and there was me thinking, That's it, I've made it, I'm going to sing for the rest of my life.

Things moved quickly after that. Tony Wragg called me about an agent called Dave Oldfield who had someone from his office at the final. Then a day or so later Dave Oldfield came to see me sing, at a pub called the Plough in Cadishead.

You couldn't miss him, Dave Oldfield. He's what you might call 'proper Manchester'. An agent of the old school, he had slicked-back grey hair and gold chains, and he spoke in a deep Mancunian drawl, slow and abrasive, like sandpaper on Prozac.

'Hiya, mate, how are you doing, Dave Oldfield, nice to meet yer.' He stuck out his hand to shake, thick gold rings on almost every finger. 'I'm liking what I'm hearing, son, I'm liking what I'm hearing. I think I can get you out three nights a week.'

This was what I'd wanted to hear: that he'd take me on. And three nights a week, too.

'Really?' I said. 'What sort of bread?'

'Well, you're looking about £55 to £60 a night,' he rasped. And already that was around £50 a week more than I was getting at the factory. I almost bit his hand off.

The next day I got into work and went to see Phil Smith. I don't know what it was, maybe I just felt the planets were in alignment then. That I'd won the talent contest and an agent wanted to take me on. Maybe I thought that there might not be another chance.

'I'm leaving, Phil, handing in my notice.'

He looked at me. 'Why, what are you going to do?'

'Um, I'm going to be a singer. I've decided that's what I'm going to do.' And was there a little note of uncertainty peeking in at the end there? Nah, of course not.

'Sing what?' said Phil.

'I want to sing songs in clubs. I want a change,' I told him.

He frowned at me. 'We'll see you next week, then.'

'No you won't, pal,' I said and that was it, the proverbial oily rag had been thrown on the floor. I was going to embark on a career in music.

Shortly after, the *Manchester Evening News* rang me about winning the Piccadilly contest and I told them I'd ditched my job. In the following edition of the paper was a photo of me with a headline along the lines of, 'Piccadilly Winner Throws Down Oily Rag For Life in Showbiz'.

It meant there was no backing out now. Not unless I wanted the next headline to be, 'Piccadilly Winner Sheepishly Picks Up Oily Rag And Asks For Job Back'.

CHAPTER THIRTEEN

'Okay, I'm going to sing an Elton John number for you now. This one's called "Sacrifice".'

Dave had got me some gigs in my time, but this one – this one took the biscuit. This was worse than the Red Cow where I'd played the week before; where I'd sung them 'Dancing On The Ceiling' and the place was so full of dope smoke, most of them *were* dancing on the ceiling. Doing something on the ceiling anyway. Sometimes, if you wanted to be a bit flash you might take along a bit of dry ice. Not in the Red Cow. Smoke was already provided. I came out of there as high as a kite.

But this was worse. This was the Holly Bush. Dave had got me the booking, telling me it was 'a nice lickle pub', which was what he always said, but we hadn't been together long enough for me to work out that every pub in Manchester was, according to Dave, 'a nice lickle pub'. Sure, he'd sent me to the Red-Eyed Cow last week and he'd told me that one was a nice lickle pub, too. But that was just a misunderstanding, obviously. I mean, it wasn't like all the nice lickle pubs could be like the Red Cow, was it?

So I'd turned up at the Holly Bush with all my gear. This old pub, it was in Wythenshawe, right in the middle of an estate. I pulled up in my brown Austin Maestro (oh, the amount of times that thing broke down), got the gear out of the back, hauled it in. The way it works is that you bring your stuff in, have a word with the landlord, say hello, introduce yourself, then set it up. People don't take a blind bit of notice, you're just the turn setting up. In years to come I'd use that time wisely, but this was early on in my career and I kept my head down, got on with sorting out my gear. It was all stuff I'd bought from A1 in Manchester just a few weeks earlier, when I'd wandered in telling them I was about to start singing in the pubs, and what would I need? Speakers, stands, tape recorder, amp, reverb system, microphone, I was told. I was blowing my savings on this stuff.

A company called Ameritz specialises in doing backing tracks, so I'd bought some of those, too, building up a set of Beatles, Elvis, Lionel Richie, Elton John: faster, rockier numbers for when the joint was jumping ('Jailhouse Rock', 'La Bamba'), plus some slower ones: 'Love On The Rocks', 'Sacrifice'. I used to begin with those, just to get the measure of the place, to see how the audience reacted. Thing with working the pubs and clubs is, if an audience doesn't like something or wants something different, they tell you. A blast of an Elton John ballad when they're in the mood for 'Blue Suede Shoes' and I'd hear, 'Play something faster, mate,' sending me diving for my fast tape.

Looking around tonight, though, I wasn't sure I'd want my fast tape. This lot I wanted in a nice, calm, laid-back state of mind, because there was an atmosphere in the Holly Bush, an unmistakable crackle in the air. Looking around from behind my PA, I could sense a tension, as though something was going to kick off.

Nine o'clock rolled around and I got the nod, went up to the mic and introduced myself.

'Hello, my name's Russell Watson and I'm going to be singing for you tonight.'

I turned to my tape recorder and switched it on. Not exactly high on the wow factor, my show back then. I wasn't big on stage-craft. I mean, of course I wasn't; I'd only just started. That was where I was *learning* my stagecraft. But looking back, it was ropy in those early days. For the first two years or so, I used to operate the tapes myself, so between songs there'd be this awful silence. All you'd hear were people clearing their throats and me, fumbling with cassettes. Then it was suggested I got help, so I started taking someone along to do it for me. All of a sudden there was an almost seamless transition from one song to the next. Instantly my show became more professional.

'Okay, I'm going to sing an Elton John number for you now. This one's called "Sacrifice".'

I sang the first line of the song.

And in the next moment all the doors burst open and there were police everywhere. Through the front door, in through the fire exit. Plain-clothes and bobbies with helmets on. Storming into the place, descending on tables, pulling customers to their feet.

The place seemed to erupt, everybody shouting at once, the solid wet *thunk* of pint glasses being knocked over on tables, the landlady standing behind the bar, watching the whole scene with her hands on her hips.

I stopped singing 'Sacrifice'. I stood behind the mic, watching open-mouthed as this scene out of *Gunfight at the OK Corral* unwound before me. It was incredible. Police shouting at blokes. Blokes shouting back at police. Girlfriends shouting at police to 'Let him go, willya'. Police shouting at girlfriends to 'Shut up'. Blokes shouting at police that 'Oi, you can't talk to my missus that way'. Police shouting at blokes that 'I'll talk to her any way I like, you're under arrest, son'.

Nil points for working out that it was a drugs bust, and almost as quickly as it had started, it was over. I watched as about half the pub's clientele were led off, arms in half-nelsons, girlfriends either still mithering about police brutality or else being led off as well, for obstruction.

The backing track to 'Sacrifice' tinkled prettily on behind me.

'Eh, you? What are *you* fookin' doing?' said the landlady, coming from behind the bar and appearing in front of me.

'Sorry?'

'I said, what yer fookin' doing?'

'Well, I've just stopped because...' I said, and indicated the room, where the last of the luckless drugs lot were being frog-marched away.

'Stopped?' screeched the landlady, almost dropping her fag. 'It happens every fookin' week, just get on with it, will yer, for fuck's sake!'

'Right. Okay.'

And I started singing 'Sacrifice' again. The atmosphere had changed after the drugs bust, though, and by the end of the night I was doing my rock and roll, the Elvis numbers, and it was like something out of the *Muppets*, everybody up on the tables dancing. No idea what they were on, but it was working for them.

Playing the pubs, I'd do a few songs from 9 p.m. to 9.30, then 10 to 10.30, then 10.45 to 11.15. By closing everybody would be absolutely leathered. It could be really rammed, too. So the best thing to do was wait until the place had cleared out before packing up. By the time I'd got my equipment loaded up, it was one o'clock in the morning. I'd drive home, lug the kit out of the car and into the house, wishing I could turn in straight away but I never could. I'd been performing, and it takes me a couple of hours to wind down, so instead I'd watch a bit of telly, have a cup of tea, maybe a bite to eat. It was usually two or three o'clock in the morning at the earliest before I'd get to bed and be able to sleep.

The next day, I'd be up around midday. To make ends meet I was working for Ameritz. I'd made a friend there, Pete Tyson, just from buying my own tracks, and through him I raised a bit of cash on the side doing vocals and overdubs in their studio.

Then, if I'd been lucky enough to get a booking that night, another nice lickle pub.

'I'm going to miss you,' said my mum.

'Well, I've been around for long enough, you ought to,' I replied.

I was twenty-three. Who still lives at home when they're twenty-three? Our kid had flown the coop years before and she was younger than I was. Add to that the fact that my horizons were broadening. That year – 1990 it was – I was learning to stand on my own two feet, to take control of my life. A lot of blokes just drift, they fall into a groove and spend their lives in it, maybe telling themselves they had more to offer but they never really had the time to explore it; they had to bring in the butty. I didn't want that. It was as though my time at Sabre and Hunts were some kind of prophecy: I'd seen myself in dirty overalls, getting home at the end of the day and walking into the kitchen where my mother stood. And I'd thought: No. I can't do that for the rest of my life. I can't. I want something else.

So I was moving out. Not exactly far, but then it wasn't about distance. It was about finding my feet then standing on them.

'Oh come on,' I said, 'it's only Eldon Road.' (And it really was 'only Eldon Road', a five-minute walk if that.) 'You'll be hanging out the bunting soon as I leave.'

We took all my belongings, which, thinking about it, probably only amounted to a bed, which we dismantled and put in the back of my Talbot Sunbeam. I still wonder what happened to my other stuff. The football programmes mainly. I wonder how many other kids have had priceless football programmes consigned to the bin?

So I moved, to Eldon Road, where Helen and I lived more or less until we split up. We didn't have a deposit, so we'd got one of those 100 per cent mortgages; probably thought it was a good deal at the time. We were wrong about that, as it turned out.

And 1990 was also the year of the World Cup, of course. Italia 90. I didn't know then, but events there were to shape what I'd end up doing. Like everybody else I was moved by the Three Tenors, and of those, Pavarotti, because he, for me, was the standout voice of the three. Carreras in the 1970s was very strong and Domingo's a great musician, but technically, the best voice was Luciano's. Hearing them, and hearing 'Nessun Dorma' accompanying the England team's progress in the competition, it became clear how close football and classical music could be – the huge, inspiring passion of it. For the first time, maybe since Mario Lanza, classical music was being reclaimed by the general public. Set to the images of triumph, heartbreak and defeat in Italy, it became suddenly so relevant, its beauty and power so apparent.

It's not like I sat bolt upright in the sofa one day proclaiming, 'Yes! For I have seen the way forward. From this day on I shall dazzle the general populace with my moving renditions of classical music!' I didn't. But being brought up on classical music, thanks to Mum's radiogram, I was already comfortable with it. And there in Italy, as England crashed out of the semi-finals, with Gazza crying, Lineker making that famous sign to the bench and Pearce and Waddle mucking up their penalties, the seeds for my future were being sown.

In the meantime, though, there was another small matter to contend with closer to home. Helen was pregnant.

Another mouth to feed. More nice lickle pubs.

CHAPTER FIFTEEN

'Why's it called Fraggle Rock, Dave?'

'No idea, son. No idea.'

It was a Sunday afternoon gig. A place in Manchester, and I was told to get there before opening hours for this one, 'Because it gets packed and you can't get the gear in, so you need to get there at eleven, all right, son?'

'Sure, Dave, yeah.'

I got there about 11 a.m. and I swear there was a queue of about forty punters waiting to get in. Eleven o'clock. Queuing to get in, they were.

I was on at midday, and it was insane, the maddest, insanest place that I've ever been. I started singing and there were chairs flying all over the place, everyone was up on the tables, they were leathered by one, absolutely wasted. The whole place caved in, giving it the big one, but not aggressive, just having a good time.

Some of the rough places I played, though, you wouldn't believe.

There was one place I did in Standish. I walked in and the room was about as big as the average front room. It was hardly big enough for a game of pool – and there was a pool table in it. There was this atmosphere, too. The pool players straightened from their game as I entered, skinheads to a man. Great. I turned to the bar, taking in the place. It was one of those pubs that seem to deny entry to outside life. Some pubs are like that; they're like a world within a world. Thick with cigarette smoke, a plotting murmur always audible.

'All right?' I said to the landlord, looking around this tiny, foggy room, thinking: I must've got the wrong place, the landlord's going to direct me somewhere else. He'll say, 'You didn't think you were doing the singing here, did you, son? Oh no. There isn't the room to swing a cat, let alone put a turn on. No, you go out the door, turn to your left...'

But he didn't say that. Instead, he pointed over to a corner, saying, 'Over there.'

'Where?' I looked, thinking he must be indicating some cavernous room I hadn't yet seen.

He said, 'There, next to the pool table.'

Two skinheads saw us looking their way and scowled.

'But there isn't room; they're playing pool,' I said.

'Oh they'll be all right, just stick yer speakers in the corners and round the sides, it'll be all right, they'll manage.'

I started bringing my gear in. Now, like I say, usually you just set up and you might as well be the Invisible Man's skinny brother for all the attention you get. But this place was so cramped it was inevitable that the skinheads would want to give me hassle.

'What yer doing, mate?'

'I'm the singer tonight,' I said. (Keep it breezy, I thought. They're only skinheads and, after all, skinheads are just normal people except with shorter hair.) 'I'm just setting the gear up...'

'Fucking hell. Right.'

It was as though I'd said some magic word. As though they'd been hypnotised and the cue word was 'singer'.

They stopped playing pool and turned to face me, crossing their arms.

They stayed that way as I set up. I looked over at the landlord, who was chatting to someone at the bar. Not that I could expect much help there. I looked back to the skinheads, then began my set.

Sadly, I didn't know any skinhead songs. I still don't, funnily enough. Instead I started with 'Stuck On You', the Lionel Richie tune.

And as I sang, telling the skinhead pool players that I was stuck on them, and that I had a feeling down deep in my soul that I just couldn't lose, one of the biggest came over and stood right in front of the mic stand. So close to it that his huge, broad skinhead nose was almost touching the wire.

'I'm stuck on you,' I told him, adding that I'd been a fool for too long, and now it was about time that I came on home.

He had to be six foot two. Huge, built like a brick outhouse, tattoos all over his face. And don't forget, I was no Walter Wimp. At school I was the terrier; I'd face up to anyone. I don't back out of fights.

But someone who gets their face tattooed. Come on.

He had red eyes. I continued serenading him with Lionel Richie. It was almost as if his eyes were glowing with hatred.

In the end, after what felt like years of singing him Lionel Richie, the song finished, and as my tape spooled into silence I leaned around the microphone to speak to him, not wanting to antagonise him, but even so – I needed him to know I wasn't intimi-dated.

'You all right, mate?'

All of his mates were looking over at me. There was a dreadful silence. Then, at last, one of them said, 'Do you do any Elvis?'

There was another pause. I looked at them. They scowled across the room back at me.

'I do now,' I said and launched into an Elvis medley that, looking back on it, probably saved my life.

Still, I'm most likely one of the few who have serenaded a Salford skinhead with a Lionel Richie song and lived. Could have been worse, I suppose. Could have been 'Hello'.

And I'll tell you something. I often get asked about nerves. 'Did you get nervous at Wembley, Russell?' 'Were you scared performing for the Pope?'

No, not really. Because at Wembley people have paid to see me, it's not five people in a smoky, beer-smelling room who want to have a drink in peace, who I've got to impress.

And, anyway, the Pope isn't going to knee me in the bollocks for singing 'Stuck On You'.

The day after, I rang Dave Oldfield.

'Don't you ever put me in a place like that again, matey.'

'Hey, you know, it's a nice lickle pub that.'

'It wasn't a nice lickle pub,' I said, 'it was full of bloody hard men. I started singing bloody "Stuck On You", Dave, and it was a load of bloody skinheads and tattoos and pints, playing pool. That's not a nice lickle pub, is it?'

And the next night I packed my gear and went to the next nice lickle pub – fully expecting it to be nothing of the sort.

At the time, the best day of my life. Now, of course, I can't make the distinction; you love both your children just the same. But no doubt about it, then, the best thing that had happened to me so far was the birth of my first daughter, Rebecca.

We found out early 1994, and we were overjoyed. It was what we'd always imagined for ourselves, and for my part I always wanted to become a father, and I loved the pregnancy. Not sure how much Helen did, mind; it always seems a bit flippant for the bloke to go, 'Oh, I loved the pregnancy,' when his partner's throwing up every five minutes, but I did. I remember the scans, a nurse rubbing gel over Helen's baby bump then showing us this little blob growing in her stomach – this little bean.

But it wasn't all plain sailing. Rebecca was a breech birth. She was pointing in the wrong direction, in other words, feet first. We were told it would be too dangerous for Helen to give birth the regular way, so she was booked in for a Caesarean section.

The day came, and we went to hospital, the Hope Hospital in Salford, and were allocated a room where they gave us what can only be described as a cordon sectioning off Helen's top half from her bottom half. It meant we couldn't see what was going on downstairs, which was fine by me; I stayed up top, offering moral support.

When Rebecca first came out I thought she was a boy. Muggins here had mistaken the umbilical cord for something else. The nurse brought this tiny baby out, held her up and me – what an idiot – I'm going, 'It's a boy, it's a boy.'

'No, Mr Watson,' said a nurse, exasperated, 'that's the umbilical cord. You have a beautiful little girl.'

She was. Still is. (Thirteen now, of course, she turned thirteen in October. I celebrated by being carted into hospital and going into emergency surgery. 'I missed my daughter's birthday,' I wailed to photographers on the way out of the hospital.)

They let me cut the cord. I stared at her, at our new little baby, just opening her eyes for the first time. A squidge of a thing, tiny hands clasped in front of her, impossibly small legs pulled up as though she wasn't quite ready for the outside world; wanted to stay in there, warm and curled up in her mother's womb. I tried gathering my feelings, attempting to pull them together to resemble something familiar to me, but I couldn't, unable to do so because what I was feeling was so new. It was as though for years I'd been sailing around a planet called Me and all of a sudden happened upon a whole new emotion. Even now, trying to describe the moment, I can't fit the feeling into a sentence or sound bite. To do so would somehow diminish it. All I can say is, I learnt something in that moment. I learnt what it feels to know absolute, pure and unconditional love, and I felt it flooding through me as though I'd been injected with it.

As I looked at her, feeling myself fill with this new sensation, she seemed to take me in, and she appeared so calm, her eyes watchful. So calm, she never made a sound, and I thought, that's good, she's going to be a quiet little baby.

Wow, was I wrong about that.

Rebecca had colic. For the first three months we couldn't get her to sleep for more than two hours at a time and it was a nightmare. No, it was worse – at least you're asleep during a nightmare. Helen was exhausted, I was exhausted. It's not like I had the kind of job where I could take a couple of weeks' paternity leave. Rebecca was born and I went straight back to work. I had to – I had mouths to feed.

'Wah, wah.'

That was Rebecca, night after night. Often the only way we could get her to go to sleep would be by putting her in the back of the car and driving, hoping the motion would send her off. It did. It always worked. In fact, my Russell Watson top tip for getting restless babies to sleep is to stick them in a baby seat, put them in the back of a brown Austin Maestro and give them a whirl around Salford. Guaranteed shut-eye. It was with Rebecca anyway.

But then, as soon as we stopped...

'Wah, wah.'

We were like zombies, Helen and I, both of us just trying to get through each day. We tried doing shifts, but if I was working then obviously Helen would have to look after the baby. Her mum used to come round quite a lot, but it was tough, it was very tough. It wasn't as though we lived in Wadley Manor and I could get in at 2 a.m. and find a spare wing of my country pile for a few hours' kip. It was a small house. I'd arrive home in the early hours, my body screaming for sleep, and it was denied to me; Rebecca would keep us awake all night. It was hard.

Eventually, Rebecca settled, but by then we had a new problem, and this one wasn't going to go away; we couldn't put this one in the back of the car for a few hours' grace. Almost without us noticing the recession had bitten hard. Suddenly we'd be opening letters from the building society on an almost weekly basis as the interest rate climbed.

And kept on climbing.

Until it was at 19.5 per cent, and everybody was feeling not quite a pinch, more like a full-on Chinese burn, and the gigs at the nice lickle pubs had dwindled from three or four a week to one if I was lucky. In addition to Dave I'd hooked up with a guy called Mike Constantia by then, an agent who dealt with clubs. But things weren't exactly rosy in that garden, either. The clubs were feeling the Chinese burn, too. Everybody was strapped for cash. Everybody.

And the next thing you know, we had this strange bloke turning up at our door.

CHAPTER SEVENTEEN

It was leathering it down with rain when the doorbell went.

Little Rebecca was in a cot in the corner of the front room, Helen in the kitchen. I got the door, opening it to find a guy standing on our doorstep, miserable, the rain coming off him like he was being hosed down out of shot.

'Mr Watson?' he asked, sniffing. Water poured off his cap and his raincoat hung off him, saturated. The street behind him was deserted, most sensible people sheltering from the weather. Rain bounced off For Sale signs outside the houses opposite, another one had gone up that morning. Not that there would be any buyers, of course. Who could afford a mortgage? Ours was up to £450 a week and no, that's not a typo: £450 a week. I was lucky to earn that in a *month*. Houses were being repossessed, businesses were going down left, right and centre. Clubs couldn't afford to book a singer because people couldn't afford to go out to clubs and were staying home instead, sitting on their sofas and watching TV. Watching *EastEnders* and coverage of the war in Iraq and news stories about the recession that were always illustrated with the same bit of footage: a street lined with For Sale signs. A street just like ours.

'Yeah?' I said, sighing. This guy, he didn't look like a bailiff, but he was one. Helen and I already had eleven county court judgments against us. We had county court judgments for the gas, electric, water, the kitchen we couldn't afford, repayments on the car, you name it, we were into someone for money on it. We were hanging on to our home by the skin of our teeth. All we ate was beans on toast. Own-brand beans. The stuff with the white labels.

'My name's Jones, I've got a…' He held up a piece of paper that hung sodden from his fingers, a warrant of some kind. 'I've come to—'

'Hang about, mate.' I stopped him. 'I mean, bloody hell, look at you, you're drenched. Look, you better come in.'

He looked doubtful. As well he might. Even bailiffs who don't look much like bailiffs weren't used to being invited into people's homes. I'd lay odds I was the only person to willingly have him over the threshold that week.

'Are you sure?' he said, sniffing. Rain or something worse dripped from his nose.

'Yeah, course, come in.'

So he did. He shook himself in the hall, hung up his coat and cap and I brought him into the front room, Helen standing at the kitchen door with a tea towel.

'Helen, this is… sorry, mate, I didn't catch your first name?'

'It's Dennis,' said Dennis.

Coming into the warm from the cold his glasses had steamed up and he removed them now, wiping them then replacing them on his nose. Staring around he took in our front room, clearly relieved at having stepped out of the cold and wet.

I fetched him a cup of tea, watched him visibly relax as he took it and held the mug, drawing warmth from it. I sat, offering him a seat and he took it. Helen stayed in the kitchen. Dennis and I made small talk and every now and then we looked towards the window, the rain battering it like an angry mob.

Dennis blew his nose, pushed his hankie into his pocket, wiped his glasses a second time. He looked sheepish. As well he might.

'Uh... the reason I'm here, Mr Watson...'

Christ. I'd almost forgotten he'd come for a reason. *Of course* he was here for a bloody reason. For half a second I wished I'd left him out in the teeming rain.

'What it is,' he went on, 'I've got this warrant to reposs—'

'Oh, bloody hell,' I said, hearing the attack of the rain on the glass and thinking, Oh no.

I pulled myself together. 'Well, mate, you can take what you like.' I indicated the sparse front room. 'We haven't got much, and what we have got isn't worth a lot, but you know, we understand you've got a job to do...' I tailed off.

He said, 'Could you just afford £10 and I can suspend the warrant?'

My shoulders dropped. 'I can't, mate, I haven't got anything.'

(You forget. You forget what it's like to have nothing. Not even a spare tenner to keep a bailiff from the door.)

'But look,' I added, 'I've not got anything at the moment, but I'm a singer, and I've got a gig on Thursday, so I could give you a tenner on Friday. How about that?'

He looked relieved. 'Oh, that would be great, Russell, thanks. I'll come back on Friday and get a tenner off you.'

I said, 'That would be great, mate, thanks, you're a star.'

So he did. He came back on Friday, and because I'd had a gig the night before I was able to give him the tenner.

And this happened on a regular basis for the next two or three years. It got so he was half-accountant, half-bailiff. Sometimes he had a better idea of when my gigs were than I did.

'Don't forget you've got a gig on Wednesday, Russ, so I'll see you Thursday morning, all right?'

'All right, Jonesy, yeah, see you then.'

He was the silver lining, Jonesy was. Elsewhere things were looking bad. Clubs were working at a loss so they'd stopped booking entertainment – there was nobody there to buy the beer – or, worse, they were closing. Meantime, those county court judgments were piling up. We had a child, which meant the utilities couldn't cut us off and leave us without heat and water, but of course they don't let you pay by direct debit if you're behind, so instead we had to have a key meter, where you have to go down the post office, so everybody knows you're broke, because you're at the post office for one of these little blue key things that you stick in the meter, twist and it gives you a fiver's worth of gas, something like that.

Once again, I was clock-watching.

'Shall we put the gas on for a bit?'

We'd keep an eye on the numbers counting down, until, say, they got to £2 and we'd turn the gas off again, save that precious £2 for another time. It was the same with the electric. We'd feed it coins, watch the figures decrease.

I think the low point was the potato man. That was a time – perhaps the first – that I thought: That's it. You've tried the singing, mate, but it hasn't worked out. You gave it your best shot but your best shot wasn't enough. Now you've got to get a job. A proper job.

We used to have potatoes delivered every week, about 20lb of potatoes, and we used to get them from this guy because it worked out cheaper than the supermarket, and it got to the point where we owed him £5 for potatoes. One night he came round to get his money. We were a couple of weeks late but we didn't have a penny to our name, not a penny.

So we hid behind the couch. The lights were off; we were trying to save electric anyway. And when the doorbell went the pair of us dived behind the couch – just in case the potato man looked through the window.

Did I mention it to Helen? I don't remember. What I do recall is skulking in the dust behind the couch, thinking, I've got to get a job. I'm going to have to go back to the factory.

I didn't, though, and we scraped through. Just. And how we managed to hang on to that house I've no idea; we were being royally screwed by that interest rate. I think the building society ended up taking pity on us. Not just us, but on others in the same position. What was the point of repossessing someone's house? Nobody was buying them anyway. So the building societies tended to be a bit more flexible – ours was anyway. And they needed to be. We were always behind. Always. We spent years chasing our tails.

Looking back now, though, I wonder if that struggle kept Helen and me together. Sure, we used to argue during that period, too; our relationship was one you might kindly characterise as 'fiery'. But we were pulling together. We were working to keep our heads above water. When things became easier financially, when the country pulled out of the recession, as the club work increased and I got my first summer season at Blackpool, things became worse between us, and the rows would start.

My escape from the debts and watching meters tick down – then later the arguments – was music. Escape was performing. If it went well then I'd get that buzz off watching people respond to the music. Feeding off them as they fed off me.

CHAPTER EIGHTEEN

The Painted Fan was *not* one of those places where I got a buzz off performing. It was one of the places I almost got killed performing. Typical, it was another one of Dave Oldfield's nice lickle pubs, this during a period when I was playing both pubs and clubs.

On the off-chance you're not familiar with the workings of the pub and club circuit in the North West, the way it goes for performers is this: you start in pubs, you graduate to clubs, you aim for Blackpool.

Pubs are where you really learn your trade, and you learn it the hard way because getting up and singing in a pub is no Sunday afternoon walk in the park. Like I say, an audience with the Pope is a breeze compared to Saturday night at the Pig and Handcuffs. Most of the time, punters are just out for a drink. They get down to their local only to find out some guy's in there doing a bit of singing. So you, as the singer, you're like a bit of furniture, like a fruit machine or a jukebox, only you're louder and more fun to shout at. In a pub you can be playing on a Friday night to a bunch of leathered-up lunatics bouncing off the walls and you leave the place feeling lucky to be alive. In short, the punters are the entertainment in a pub. As the singer, you're just there to get them in the mood.

Club work is different. People at clubs are on a night out and they want the entertainment on a plate. It's still hard, no doubt about that, and you still have to win an audience over. But there's a concert secretary. Somebody introduces you to the stage and takes you off. And a lot of the time they'll have live musicians, so let's have a big hand, ladies and gentlemen, for Fred on drums, Bill on the keyboards. Yes, as the singer you know your place in the pecking order, and it's way behind the bingo, but it's a better environment. More receptive, more civilised. And, of course, better paid.

But you have to make the transition from one to the other. You have to pay your dues at the pubs before you can do the clubs. Plus, of course, you've got that period when you're just making the jump.

The Painted Fan was during that period.

It was in Warrington, and first of all I'd got it confused with another pub nearby, which was a bit more rural and probably genuinely was a nice pub. So when Dave told me about the booking it was that pub I pictured, and I imagined this pleasant gig, with me singing and the punters pausing from eating chicken in a basket to give me polite rounds of applause.

So I took the booking.

Mistake. Driving into the car park and double-checking my directions, I realised, with a sinking heart, that, Ah, it's *this* Painted Fan. The Painted Fan where, not two weeks ago, some poor soul got shot in the car park. *That* Painted Fan.

I popped the boot open, started getting my gear out, carrying a speaker from my car and into the pub.

There was an atmosphere. In pubs like that one, the bad pubs, it seems to start in the carpet and infect the air, a sense that something is Not Right, and if you're sensible you'll pretend you were looking for a mate who hasn't turned up yet, get out of there and go to one of the good pubs instead.

Which isn't an option if you've been booked to sing.

I eyed the blokes. They eyed me back, squinting at me through grey ropes of smoke, hands on pint glasses, fags smouldering in ashtrays.

'What yer singing this week?'

I've been asked that question a lot, never before or since with the same level of menace, though.

I met his gaze. 'Oh, I don't know, a bit of Elvis, bit of Buddy Holly, bit of this, bit of… you know, Elton John, that kind of stuff.'

Even the mention of Elton John failed to lift his spirits.

'I hope yer better than that wanker last week. He was shit.'

'Oh yeah,' I said, 'so do I.'

'We'll kill yer if yer not.'

His words sank like a stone. I was thinking of that bloke in the car park. I put my speaker down, trying to look indifferent.

The landlord was standing behind the bar, a soulless man framed by pumps and optics. I went up, took a bar seat, leaned in towards him.

'Listen, mate, I'll be honest with you, I didn't want to take this gig and I've got matey boy over there giving it the big one about how he's gonna kill me if I'm not up to scratch. I'm getting £60 for tonight and quite frankly it's not worth the aggravation, so I'm going to get the speaker and I'm going to go, because I don't want to do it, I don't want to do the gig.'

'I wouldn't recommend it,' he said, blank-eyed.

'What do you mean?'

'If they see you leaving with those speakers, they most likely will kill yer, just fer yer gear.'

'Are you serious?'

'Yeah, mate, I'm serious.'

He was. He was as serious as a heart attack, this guy. He said, 'Just get yer gear in, mate, I'll make sure yer all right.'

I did, and I did the gig. My friends spent the whole gig barracking me, and it wasn't as though anybody else in the place was particularly bowled over, so all told it was one of the worst gigs of my life, but I got through it. The landlord was as good as his word. When the gig was over I left, carting my gear to the car. And nobody bothered me. Even so, I sat in the car thinking, That's it. That's *bloody* it.

'Bloody hell, Dave,' I shouted down the phone the next morning. 'Nice lickle pub? Apart from the tiny detail of a shooting in the car park a couple of weeks prior, you know that it really isn't a nice lickle pub, is it?'

Déjà vu, this conversation

'Well, you know, I've been down there, it's a nice lickle pub,' he growled. 'You know, I always have a pint there and it's been all right.'

'No, mate,' I said, resigned. 'No, it wasn't. I think that's going to be it now, Dave, all right?' And I might have done a few bits and pieces for him after that, but that night pretty much spelled the end of my days doing the pubs. He and I parted company.

Still, I won't forget Dave Oldfield. If it hadn't been for him I might never have left the factory floor, thrown down my oily rag and left for a life of music. It was he who gave me that start; who not only gave me the confidence to do it, but who found me the work to make it a viable career choice. Sure, a lot of his nice lickle pubs turned out to be anything other than that, but the point is I got thrown in the deep end and I swam. And I can't thank him enough for that.

Whatever you do, though, never ask him to recommend you a nice little pub...

CHAPTER NINETEEN

You should have seen me when I was performing back then. I mean, you shouldn't have seen me, because I was crap. But if you had, it would have given you a chance to see how I'd come on in the meantime.

I remember the turning point well. It was at this club in Wigan, maybe two or three years after I'd chucked down my oily rag and started singing, and it was the night I learnt a vital bit of stagecraft.

If you're thinking, He took his bloody time to learn a vital bit of stagecraft, then you've got to remember: singing in the pubs I was quite literally just trying to survive, both physically and financially. I'd get in there, mumble, 'Hello, my name's Russell Watson. Now I'm going to sing you something by Buddy Holly,' then sing. That was it. No dancing or stage movements (I mean, I'm not exactly Michael Jackson these days. That's not my thing; the 'Nessun Dorma' dance connection remains unexplored for a very good reason), no interaction or banter with audience. In. Sing. Out. I was like a statue standing there, hands hugging the microphone for protection, singing into the floor. In those early days, all that I had – the sole reason for me being up there – was my voice.

I started doing the clubs and my act hadn't really developed. I was still this kid mumbling about Buddy Holly, hugging the microphone like it was threatening to leave me and go and live with another microphone. Worse, I'd started to go into what I used to call autopilot mode. I'd get up there, do my first number and then, if I could tell the audience wasn't particularly into it, just do the rest of the set like Robot Russell. Do the songs. Get off. Go home. Repeat chorus, repeat till fade.

And then one night I was at this place in Wigan and sure enough, I caught myself going into good old autopilot mode; found myself thinking, Screw 'em then. If they want to talk about *Coronation Street* why should I give a toss?

I did the first song, staring out over the club, through blue-grey smoke, seeing the backs of heads as punters chatted away, the bar staff talking among themselves, too. The whole lot of them, they didn't care; they were just waiting for the flyer (and if on the off-chance you're not familiar with pub-club life in the North West, that's the bingo). I might as well not be here.

I started into the second song of my set. Same backs of heads. Same talk of *Corrie*. Fag lighters flaring. Girl at the bar twirling her hair and chewing gum. 'When's flyer on?' 'Dunno, when turn's done, I suppose.'

Was this what you had in mind, I thought, when you started singing?

No, I thought. I wanted to sing for two reasons: because the music means something to me, and because I want to entertain people, but here I am, on autopilot. I've only been doing it a couple of years and I'm jaded, for God's sake, I'm cynical, burnt out, behaving like some sixty-year-old blue comedian, trotting out the same gags to gangs of cackling women who've heard it all before. I'm doing the exact opposite to what I intended to do. I'm not interested in them and they're not interested in me and I don't care. I've turned into exactly what I set out to escape.

I might as well have been on a lathe.

Well, bollocks to that, I thought. I'm having you lot.

So I started getting stuck into the audience, picking a punter out. A bloke, nattering loudly away to a couple of women. One of many, he was just the first bloke to catch my eye, an obvious candidate in my field of vision.

'All right, mate?' I said in between songs.

My first luckless victim, his Jack-and-Vera conversation interrupted, looking at me like, Who? Me?

'Yeah, you. What's yer name, mate?' I said. I had the advantage of the microphone. It's a weapon.

'George,' he replied.

'Am I keeping you up, George?'

'Yer what?'

'Did you come out for a quiet chat and someone built a club around you?'

The audience were tittering. I'd got their attention.

'Come on, George, come and see if you can have a go. Let's hear you sing "Sacrifice", then.'

He tried, failed. By this time the audience was in hysterics – and I had them. They were on my side. For the rest of my set there was no *Corrie* talk, no more hair twirling or wondering when the flyer was on. They listened. And because they listened I was no longer on autopilot. And because I was no longer on autopilot, they enjoyed it; they got it.

Poor old George. George, if you're reading this, you have no idea the wonders you did for my career, because from that night on I never looked back, and I learnt every trick in the book. I learnt how to communicate a song; I learnt how to gauge an audience, so I'd walk in at the beginning of the evening, take a look around and see who was in, have a chat with a few of them, get the measure of the place. I'd always make a point of going to the bar and standing there for ten minutes or so to have a chinwag with the bar staff. I'd have a natter with the landlord or the concert secretary: 'What are they into then, this lot?'

'Oh, you know, Russ, they love their ballads.'

Right. I'd plan my act accordingly, based on what I found out, based on the age of the audience and whether the place was up and bouncing or the atmosphere was a bit stale. If the place was already jumping, I'd think of starting with a slow one, just to bring it down a little bit. If it was really quiet, I'd start with something quick, try and lift it, raise the bar, get them all going.

I'd say to the concert sec, 'Who are the characters, then?' And he'd say, 'Oh, I don't know, Harry and Jim and Bill…'

'What's the script with them, then? You know, who likes a bit of a sing?'

'Oh, Jim likes a bit of a sing.'

I'd get him to point Jim out to me.

So during the gig I'd go over to Jim. I'd have my roaming microphone and I'd say: 'Jim likes a bit of a sing, come on, Jim, what do you fancy, mate?'

'Have you got any Neil Diamond?'

'Aye,' and I'd start singing a bit of Neil Diamond, then hand over to Jim who'd sing a few lines of Neil Diamond, and usually, let's face it, he'd be crap, and the audience would crack up. Nobody lost face; it was never about embarrassing George or Jim, it was about tuning into the atmosphere of whatever club I was playing and then using it to my advantage. It was about having a laugh. And I tell you what, after that first night in Wigan, when I picked on George, I rarely had another bad gig.

Stagecraft. Interaction. That's what it's all about. What some of the young acts today are missing is exactly what I'm talking about – the stagecraft, the ability to read and gauge an audience. They haven't done their apprenticeship. They come on some show and they sing all these fantastic songs and, you know what? They sing them well; a lot of these kids are great singers. But there's a big difference between a great singer and a great artist. What I am saying is, I've done my time and I know how to control an audience and do my job. And I learnt it then, in the pubs and clubs of the North West.

If I thought the punters weren't paying attention I'd tear into them until they did. If someone shouted out, 'Yer crap!' I wouldn't just ignore them and soldier on the way I had for years and years. I'd stop, find the heckler and go at them.

'What's your name, sir?'

They thought they could just shout 'Yer crap' and titter about it with their mates – have a laugh at the turn's expense. But this turn had turned.

'What's your name, sir?'

Let's call him Frank. 'Frank? Right, come on, Frank. Ladies and gentleman, Frank thinks I'm crap so I'm going to take a break for a couple of minutes while Frank gives us a tune or two. Come on, Frank, don't be shy...'

Let's-call-him-Frank has had a couple of pints of stout, so maybe he accepts my invitation. Perhaps he gets up and warbles into the microphone for a bar or two, expecting the house to come down. But the fact is, if you can't sing and you try singing down a PA, it sounds crap. It's funny for perhaps thirty seconds, but after that it's just horrible, it's just noise. After that, believe me, the audience will be howling for the turn to come back on and Let's-call-him-Frank has to sit down. But that's not the end of his go in the spotlight, because I'll return to him several times during the night.

'You all right, Frank?'

'D'you wanna have another go, Frank?'

Those nights learning my trade were some of the most important gigs, not only of my career but also of my life. Another was the famous night at the Wigan Road Working Men's Club, when the concert secretary suggested to me I sing 'Nessun Dorma'.

I say famous because it's one of those stories that's become attached to me. It's become part of the whole Russell Watson myth, to the extent that every single interview mentions it.

It's true, though, it really did happen. It was 1994 and I was playing at Wigan Road Working Men's Club, which isn't in Wigan, it's in Leigh. By this time I'd started incorporating music from the shows into my set – *The Phantom of the Opera*, *Aspects of Love*, *Les Misérables*, *Cats*, that kind of thing – and I'd just finished the first part of my set with 'Music of the Night' from *The Phantom of the Opera*, which had gone down a storm. And all of a sudden there was this apparition, the concert secretary, Gerald Scholes, himself a phantom-like figure appearing from the mists. 'I'll tell you what, Russell Watson, lad,' he said, 'that's a ruddy smashing voice you've got.'

'Thank you very much,' I replied.

'Have you ever thought of trying out any of that operatic stuff?'

Had I? 'Uh, no, not really,' I answered, truthfully.

'You should, lad, you should. I reckon that "Nesty Doormat" by Pavarotti would suit your voice right down to the ground.'

Sometimes, I read these interviews and they give you the impression that a light pinged on, and that after the break I went up on stage and belted out 'Nessun Dorma' on a whim. Well, I didn't. What I actually did was, the next day I bought a CD, *The Essential Pavarotti*. On there was a recording of the great man singing 'Nessun Dorma' – the world's most famous version – and from that I learnt the words. Phonetically – because I didn't know any Italian at the time.

I took me two or three weeks to do, and in the meantime I had a backing track made, an Ameritz special. I had a minor problem in that the original key was too high for me; I wasn't able to get As and Bs then – but that would come in time, when I had some voice coaching.

Chapter Nineteen

Three weeks later, with the phonetic pronunciation of 'Nessun Dorma' under my belt, plus a handle on how to sing it, I road-tested the song at a club. I can't for the life of me remember which club it was, all I know is that I dropped it into the end of my set, feeling the song swell from within me in a way that I hadn't quite experienced before.

And I got a standing ovation.

Wow, I've actually got something here, I thought, the club on its feet applauding. This is working. This isn't the Three Tenors at Covent Garden, Pavarotti in *Turandot* or Domingo in *La Traviata*, this is Russell Watson at Yer Local Working Men's Club and it's going down well. It's going down really well.

So now I started introducing it at the end of every set. It became my trademark number. Mostly, I used the backing tape, although I did try it once with a live pianist at a club in St Helens and, well... this guy, this pianist, he was all right at first, but...

'What are we doing tonight, mate?' he asked me.

I had sheet music and I was going through some of the stuff with him. 'We've got "Crazy" – the Patsy Cline song, you know – we've got that Wet, Wet, Wet number, that always goes down really well, a bit of Elvis, of course...' – because during my time in clubland I'd gathered a reputation as something of a copycat, and I used to get asked to do impersonations a lot, Elvis being the favourite. *Stars In Their Eyes* eat your heart out, I'm telling you – '... oh yeah, and I'm going to finish off with this one.'

At this point I produced the sheet music to 'Nessun Dorma' with a flourish.

He peered at it, placed the sheet on top of the piano, next to a pint of bitter.

As I sang my set I watched the pint of bitter become an empty glass, and it was joined by another pint, then another, then another. Until we got to the end of the set and I looked over to the pianist, who looked back at me, swaying slightly, a sloppy grin on his face, giving me the thumbs-up. I indicated the sheet music on top of his piano and he gave me a second thumbs-up, picking up the sheet and trying to focus, then starting to play.

What he played wasn't 'Nessun Dorma'. I mean, maybe to him it sounded exactly what Puccini intended, but to me, and everybody else in the place, what he was playing was a dead ringer for the theme tune to *Tales of the Unexpected*.

I'd sung the first line: 'Nessun Dorma', but it was no good trying to soldier on, not with the theme tune to *Tales of the Unexpected* tinkling away in the background. I swear: one thing I'm not precious about is classical music. From that day in Wigan Road Working Men's Club I've been on a mission to take it away from being the sole preserve of the stuffed-shirt Covent Garden brigade and take it to ordinary people – which is where it belongs in my opinion – but a *Tales of the Unexpected* accompaniment to 'Nessun Dorma'? That was maybe taking it a bit too far.

'Excuse me, mate, tell you what, I might try this a cappella tonight, is that all right?' I said.

He stopped playing, grinned a sloppy grin, gave me a thumbs-up and went back to supping his pint.

It brought the house down. Wow, it felt good. And so encouraging, too, because I wasn't even quite doing the song justice. At the time I was only hitting A flat, which isn't particularly high, it's more baritonal than tenor. But even so, audiences loved it. People were coming up to me saying, 'What's somebody like you doing singing in a place like this?' That was one of the most common comments I'd get. 'What are you doing singing in here? You should be on stage. You should be doing the West End or you should be in an opera. Why are you singing in these places?'

I added ''O Sole Mio' to my repertoire. Then 'Volare'; then a song called 'Torna a Surriento', a Neapolitan aria; then a tune called 'Vesti la Giubba' from *Pagliacci* and after that 'E Lucevan le Stelle' from *Tosca*.

This was the stuff I'd grown up listening to. The music – I gradually realised – I'd been born to sing. I became serious about my voice, using a coach, Valerie Watts, who was based in Southport. Money wasn't exactly growing on trees then but somehow I managed to scrape together enough to pay for my weekly lessons and drive from Irlam to Southport and back again, which is a good hundred-mile round trip. Mad as a hatter, she was, but she helped develop my voice, another one of those people I've met along the way – like good old George, the Let's-call-him-Franks of this world and Gerald at the Wigan Road Working Men's Club. People who helped point me in the right direction.

William Hayward, he's another. Sir Bill.

I was doing a little bit of work for a group of lads called the Three English Tenors. If one of the lads wasn't available, I'd go in and do a gig for them. A lot of the gigs were in small theatres and cathedrals, and the conductor was a man called William Hayward. It was something like a ten-piece section with an organ and Sir Bill would sometimes play keyboards and I got to know him and liked him. He's a lot older than me, extremely distinguished, with a very posh voice that I impersonate whenever I can. Sir Bill likes to talk as much as I do and it was great to chat with him about music. He'd sit there telling me about opera and music and singing and we became good friends because we had two very important things in common: we both had a love for classical music and neither of us had a pot to piss in.

Sir Bill was a very experienced professional. He trained at the Royal College of Music in London with Sir Adrian Boult, yet he didn't seem affected. He didn't have that classical snobbery that I'd come to encounter later in my career. He started giving me voice coaching, helping me with languages. He's what you call a répétiteur, so we would go through the stuff and, once I'd learnt it, I'd then go back to Sir Bill and sing it and he'd point out where I was going wrong, correct me and give me the proper pronunciation. Be it French, Spanish, Italian, German, whatever. He's fluent in a few languages. He was helping me so much it got to the point where I said, 'Bill, I can't afford to pay for this, I can't afford to do the classes any more with you because I've not got enough money...'

He said, 'Oh don't worry about it, just come down, I don't mind about the money – it's great to be working with such a fantastic voice, just come down. You can have it for free.'

I didn't forget that.

Add the Colonel to that list. I first met the Colonel and his wife, Lynne, at South Shore Cricket Club – a hop and skip away from Blackpool, and they almost didn't stick around to hear me play. The place was deserted – four or five people in – and the way the Colonel tells it, he was leaning over to Lynne, going, 'Oh, bloody hell, it's dead in here, shall we get a taxi, love?'

Next thing, he heard this music: me, sound-checking. And he said to Lynne, 'Hey up, love, listen to this bloke.' Then after I'd done my first spot they came over and started chatting to me and Helen, saying, 'Do you work here often? We'd love to come and see you again, you're absolutely brilliant. What a voice you've got, lad, it's fantastic, what are you doing in a place like this?'

Same old story.

'You know you should be up in Blackpool or something.'

I was like, 'Well, you know, it just hasn't happened yet.'

But we got talking and we kept in touch, and my relationship with the Colonel and Lynne is one of the strongest and steadiest in my life. The last three or four years of my life I've spent a lot of time in hospital beds, and Lynne's been there at my side, making sure I'm comfortable, nursing me back to health and chatting away, constantly chatting. Nobody ever had a quick word with Lynne.

Then there's the Colonel. He looks like a cross between Kenny Rogers and Steven Spielberg – so much so there was this time he and Lynne were wandering around this mega-expensive jewellery shop in Monte Carlo, and someone came up to him and asked, 'Excuse me, are you Steven Spielberg?'

'No, love,' he said, no doubt thinking of the price tags, 'but my wife thinks I am.'

When we met I was doing my Elvis impressions and he said I sounded more like Elvis than Elvis, started calling me the King. In return I began calling him the Colonel, and the name stuck.

It was through the Colonel and Lynne that I met Stuart Littlewood. At the time Stuart Littlewood was managing Tommy Cannon, of Cannon and Ball, the two comedians. And Lynne was friendly with Tommy Cannon's ex-wife, Margaret Cannon – it's funny how the world works – and she told Margaret Cannon, who told Tommy, who mentioned it to Stuart Littlewood. And Stuart Littlewood came to see me play at the Style Prison Officers' Club.

Through him I got the season with Lily Savage at Blackpool. You would've said it was my big break if it wasn't for the even bigger break that followed it: Old Trafford. One minute I was playing at Style Prison Officers' Club, the next I'm belting out 'Nessun Dorma' at the Theatre of Dreams. Warning: it all gets a bit mad after this bit.

CHAPTER TWENTY

December 25, 2007

It's Christmas Day and I've got a mate round: a massive Manchester United fan we call Red Steve. Only, we don't call him Red Steve because he's a Manchester United fan. We call him that because he really is red. Poor old Red Steve, he claims it's nothing to do with the blood pressure, but there it is: he's a Red. And he's red.

Could be worse, I suppose. He could support City.

Red Steve comes round with his wife Jackie and we cook Christmas dinner. Mostly they cook it, actually; I hang around doing what I do, which is stupid voices, wisecracks, mickey-taking. I'm on tenterhooks waiting for Rebecca and Hannah to get here.

The kids arrive and we open our presents. I don't think they're aware of it, but watching them unwrap their gifts, sitting cross-legged on the floor, I get this gush of euphoria. I suddenly remember, with pin-sharp clarity, a feeling I had in the hospital almost exactly two months ago. A feeling that I might be saying goodbye to them. But I wasn't. I lived. I got through it. I lived to be sitting here watching them open their presents, and thinking that... well, it all goes a bit soft-focus, a bit teary-eyed.

We sit down for dinner about 3 p.m., eat and tell rubbish jokes out of crackers. Afterwards, Rebecca and Hannah insist on watching a Christmassy film, so we all sit together and watch

Miracle on 34th Street, the version with Richard Attenborough in it. Snuggling up with the kids, I think back to those evenings in front of the TV at Sunningdale Drive: me, Mum, Dad, Hayley, each in separate chairs, watching *It's a Knockout* or *Top of the Pops*. Not close the way I am with my kids now. And I'm not saying it was bad or wrong back then, as though Hayley and I were neglected kids or anything, far from it – if I haven't already made it clear, let me do so now: I had a *brilliant* childhood. But that was the 1970s and things have changed since then. People are more articulate with their emotions; I'm so much closer to my kids than my parents were to theirs. Things have changed for the better in that respect.

After the film we decide to play some board games. I'd asked Victoria to get one for us before Christmas, so we dig it out.

It's *Operation*.

Memo to self: remember to thank Victoria for her oh-so-appropriate choice of board game: *Operation*. *Op*-a-bloody-*ration*.

Here's something that hasn't changed for the better. In my day, you got a game like *Operation* and it came made up. You got it out of the box and a couple of minutes later you were extracting butterflies from the stomach and watching the red nose light up. Not any more. These days you have to bloody well put it together yourself. I was there for about twenty minutes just popping bits out of plastic frames, attaching the little power pack, the works. Got the bloody thing going and the kids are bored after five minutes. 'Come on, Dad, let's have a game of *Trivial Pursuit*...'

Even so. It's a great day.

December 31, 2007

It's New Year's Eve. The kids are here again, plus the Colonel and Lynne come over.

Tomorrow will be January the first, the day before January the second, and we all know what happens then, don't we? It's nuclear reactor time.

I'm not one for feeling sorry for myself, not usually. Most times, if I've got a problem, then I find a way of dealing with it. Like most of the time I'm not thinking, Oh poor you, you've got a brain tumour. I try to get on with it, I try to keep doing what I normally do, stay focused on getting better, keep my spirits high if I start feeling a bit down or a bit sorry for myself.

But tonight. Tonight's different. Suddenly I feel – I don't know – *bitter*, I suppose. Just plain old *hacked off* about the fact that I'd gone through one operation, thought I had the all-clear then been rushed back into hospital – almost bloody died – for the same thing and now it's New Year and around me people are giving it the big one about what they're going to be doing in 2008: losing weight, giving up smoking, all that kind of thing and I think, Bugger off, Happy New Year, there's nothing bloody happy about *my* new year...

Sorry, you need the brass bands for this bit. Too much swearing. But there's no getting away from it. No glossing over and pretending I see out 2007 with a stiff upper lip and a self-deprecating quip. I don't. I fold my arms and pull a huffy face and go, 'Oh, *bollocks* to New Year.'

For a second or so, everyone looks at me, not sure if I'm joking. I'm not, as it happens, but they all start laughing anyway.

Even so, I don't feel a part of the New Year's festivities, I don't share that great-new-beginnings sentiment. If anything, I feel as if a clock is ticking down, and my eyes start to fill up. Lynne and the Colonel know. Everybody there does. They all know how I feel, and Lynne comes across to give me the hug that lets me know they're thinking of me. It helps – it helps more than they'll ever know.

I thank them. Take myself off to bed. I don't really sleep, though. It's the first day of the radiotherapy tomorrow.

This is me age seven …
believe it or not I'm still
nervous around birds! ▶

Not many people get to meet their
great-grandparents. I did, this is
my great-grandma Davis who lived
to the grand old age of 98. ▼

Always proud to
pull on the school
team kit. Look at
those legs! ▶

▲ Three generations of the Watson family: Grandma, Father and Daughter.

▲ Mum demonstrating her bicep prowess.

Me and my Gran (Crnab) in an xmas pose. ▶

◀ Proud Dad first time around. That's me with Rebecca. I was initially astounded that someone so small could make so much noise!

Proud Dad second time around. Hannah was much quieter as a baby than Rebecca, but she's certainly made up for it since. She's gifted with the Watson gab. ▶

◀ Hannah's birthday — it took me days to make that cake!

I was honoured to sing the National Anthem at the 2007 FA Cup Final — Manchester United vs Chelsea — at the new Wembley Stadium. We had a fantastic day. ▼

Watson 10 or … d'ya get it? 10 or … Tenor … clever, eh! ▶

Me with Sir Alex at Old Trafford. I was star struck for the first and only time in my life. ▼

▲ The legend that is 'The Colonel'. My best mate and one of the world's best guitarists.

◀ Red Steve and Jackie on their wedding day. He was made up: United had changed their game to Sunday!

▲ The bravest kid I know. Me and Kirsty duet at Old Trafford in front of 76,000 people.

One of my proudest moments and fondest memories: Pope John Paul II. Need I say more. ▼

▲ Meeting Her Majesty in 2001 at
The Royal Variety Show. Not bad for
a former engineer from Salford.

Me with another queen
at the same do. ▼

CHAPTER TWENTY-ONE

Autumn 1996

'Are you all right, cock?'

I'd turned up at this place. Better not name it but it was a Liberal Club, and if I'm honest I probably arrived there with a bit of an attitude on me. Thing was, I'd just finished a summer season with Lily Savage in Blackpool, I'd made huge inroads into the Blackpool club scene, I was really starting to get noticed, I'd even (whisper it) started to think in terms of a record deal. After Blackpool, it really seemed like the next possible step. After Blackpool, anything seemed possible.

But then there's this gig at the Can't-Name-it Liberal Club and it felt like a step down. Plus if there's one thing I don't like it's people calling me 'cock'. We all have our little hang-ups.

'Are you all right, cock?'

This is the concert secretary, appearing via a set of double doors through which I got a glimpse of the main room. It was small, but otherwise like a thousand club rooms I'd played over the last five or so years: stage at the back, straight-backed chairs arranged at the sides, posters of forthcoming events, the smell of stale beer and last night's fag smoke. I couldn't see it, but I knew – I knew that somewhere in that room would be a bit of Christmas tinsel clinging on somewhere that would stay up there all year round, maybe even a solitary deflated balloon taped high up and refusing to be budged. All of it seeming so tired, sad and predictable after Blackpool, which was, any way you looked at it, a huge step up for me. Blackpool North Pier, it was, a summer season with Lily Savage. For a start, I'd been working with Lily Savage. Paul O'Grady. Look, I'm not going to say nice things about Paul O'Grady just because he's got a chat show and I might be invited on to promote this book. I'm going to say nice things about Paul O'Grady because all I've got is nice things to say about him. First, he was easily the most famous person I'd ever worked with. Second, he was the best. Third, he was and is a very, very funny guy (or girl), and because he's so funny people want to see him perform, which meant we were playing to packed houses, over a thousand people every night. And I wasn't having to fight them, either. They were there to watch the show, to be entertained. So all of a sudden I'd made this massive transition from places like this, the Can't-Name-it Liberal Club, where basically they'd come out to drink beer, play bingo and chat with a friend and there's me getting in the way, to something in a higher league. I'd done the whole season, travelling to and from Blackpool, sometimes staying at the Colonel's but trying to spend as much time with my family as I could. And there was none of yer winging it during the show, either. The show was choreographed, produced and directed.

My entrance every night was for a Bryan Adams song called 'The Only Thing That Looks Good On Me Is You', with me sporting a pair of jeans and a leather jacket. This would have been all right, but you remember me saying how I'm no Fred Astaire? Right, so I really struggled with the dancing. Our choreographer was a guy called Kim Gavin who's done everyone from Take That to the Spice Girls. Even so, he still ended up having to tailor the whole routine to the Watson two left feet. One bit, I was supposed to come running on from the back to start the song and I had to skid across the stage, so they gave me kneepads that were ten sizes too big. Everyone kept asking, 'Are your knees all right, mate? Have you got something wrong with your knees, because you look like you've got bulging kneecaps there...'

And I'm like, 'No, I've got these bloody pads underneath my jeans,' so I could do this rock thing – this slide across the stage, which, if I'm totally honest, was just alien to me. The next song I did was the Bond theme, 'GoldenEye', and for that Lily was dressed in this magnificent gown, with me done up like James Bond, playing the straight man to her funny girl. We did another song, 'It Had To Be You', except this was the Lily Savage version, so some of the words were changed to swear words, and then at the end I did 'Nessun Dorma', which was my finale.

And that was it, every night of the summer season. The show had been a massive hit and I'd picked up some good reviews, plus I'd had a great time. Paul would throw some fabulous parties and obviously I didn't need much convincing to drag myself along to a couple. It was an exciting time; I'd picked up other Blackpool bookings off the back of it. Things were moving for me.

Then – bang – right back down to earth at the Liberal Club.

'I'm the artist tonight,' I told the concert secretary as he approached.

'Are ya, cock? What's yer name, lad?'

On the wall was a poster with a picture of me on it, so I pointed to that. He stopped, peered long and hard at the poster.

'Russell Watkins?'

'No, Russell Watson.'

'Right, cock, all right, cock. Well, listen, come through with me and I'll show you where you're going to set up.'

'Right, okay, great stuff.'

We walked through the double doors and he indicated the stage.

'Right, set up on stage there, we'll put you on for your first at nine p.m., cock, all right?'

(Argh, I thought, I wish he'd stop calling me 'cock'.)

'You've got to be off for half nine, because that's when we do the flyer, cock...'

(That's the bingo, remember, and if this bloke calls me 'cock' one more time...)

'...and if you're not off by nine thirty for the flyer, they'll lynch yer.'

He said it with relish, as though frustrated bingo players lynching singers was always a highlight.

'What's yer name again, cock?' he asked.

'It's Russell Watson,' I told him.

'Right, cock, right, I won't forget that.'

So I set my gear up, retreated into my dressing room where I stared at the wall, probably a bit up my own arse, if I'm honest, because there was no getting away from it – it was a bit of a come-down after Blackpool.

There was a knock. It was my mate, poking his head round the door.

'Right, are you ready, cock?' he said. I nodded yes. 'We're going to put you on now, I reckon.' He checked his watch. 'Yep, it's coming up to nine o'clock, so I'm going to put you on, all right, lad?'

'Yeah, yeah, great stuff.'

'What's your name again, cock?'

Through clenched teeth I said, 'It's Russell... Watson.'

'Right, cock.'

And I follow him, hanging back as he gets up on stage, goes to the mic stand and introduces me, saying, with one hand reaching off the stage to usher me on, 'Right, we've got a very special treat for you tonight, ladies and gentleman. He's just finished a sell-out summer season on Blackpool's North Pier, will you please give a warm welcome to... Russ Watkins.'

I trudged on, shooting him daggers that went straight over his head. The place was tiny, the audience disinterested, but I ploughed on, finishing the first part of my set with 'Music of the Night', thinking, Last week I was singing to a thousand people every night.

I came off stage, retreated dejectedly to my dressing room where there was a knock at the door. Once again it was my friend, poking his head round the door.

'Are you all right there, cock?' he said.

'Yeah, come in,' I said my heart sinking, thinking, Please, *please*, stop calling me 'cock'.

'You mind if I have a word with yer, cock?'

I finally snapped. 'You can have a word with my cock, pal, but if it answers you back, it's going in the act.'

'Right, so, the only thing is, we have the flyer on at...'

Typical. My best snappy comeback and it had gone straight over his head.

Thinking about that bloke, though, it reminds me. Club concert secretaries are a breed unto themselves, they really are. One club I recall, they had a guitarist booked to play, and shortly before he was due to go on, this guy was sitting on the edge of the stage, tuning his guitar and completely unaware that the club concert secretary was stood at the back of the room, arms folded, glaring at him. And the glaring continued. You could see the concert secretary standing there, simmering, until at last he couldn't take it any longer, striding over to the unsuspecting guitarist and demanding, 'What you doing there, lad? What are you bloody doing?'

The guitarist glanced up, gobsmacked. 'I'm... I'm tuning me guitar.'

The concert secretary almost exploded. 'Tuning your guitar?

Tuning your guitar? You've known about this bloody booking for six months...'

Another time I recall there was a woman singer on before me. She was making heavy weather of 'I Will Always Love You' and nobody in the club was taking a blind bit of notice, drinking up, chatting about the soaps, you could hardly hear this girl. Until the noise levels eventually got so high that the concert secretary strode up to the stage, grabbed the microphone off the singer and shouted, 'Come on, ladies and gentlemen, come on, let's have some order.'

Everybody in the club looked at him. 'Now come on,' he continued, 'you know she's crap, and I know she's crap, but give the poor cow a chance...'

He left, and the poor cow in question, mortified, continued with 'I Will Always Love You', the noise levels returning almost instantly to previous levels.

Onwards and upwards, though. By now I'd pretty much left the pub scene behind altogether, and those gigs I did I was lucky enough to be choosy about. One of the final nails in the coffin was a pub in Burnley that was so rough I literally turned around and walked back out again. My agent for the show was a guy called Fred Jones and I called him the next day, telling him I'd been ill.

'I don't believe you' he said, agitated. 'I don't believe you, Russell Watson.'

I said, 'No, Fred, honest, I was ill.' Doing my best ill voice down the phone.

He said, 'I don't believe you, I don't believe you. You've let me down, you have, you've let me down. I've lost that pub now, I've lost that pub.'

I said, 'What do you mean?'

'Well, the act last week didn't turn up either.'

No wonder, I thought; he probably walked in and saw the place same as I did.

'You know what, lad?' added Fred, as though about to deliver life-and-death news. 'You'll never work in Burnley again.'

Fred and I were parting ways anyway. There had been a disastrous gig where I'd been asked to sing some Tina Turner and the local Tina Turner lookalike, who was 85 if she was a day, wearing high heels, mini skirt, the whole get-up, had got on stage to dance with me.

And by now, of course, I was doing quite well. With the Blackpool season, the gigs that had come out of that, at last, I was pulling myself out of debt. And just as my relationships with agents like Fred and Dave Oldfield were coming to a close, so was my relationship with Dennis Jones, my own personal bailiff, who I'd been seeing on a weekly basis for the last three years or so. I remember vividly the last time I ever saw him – the day I finally had enough money to go in and pay off all my debts.

I went down to the offices, in Salford they were, at the end of the M602, and I waltzed in with this cheque, saying, 'Right, Jonesey, it's time to say goodbye to you, mate. I'm going to miss our cups of tea, but you know something? I'm not going to miss you turning up every week asking for money off me.'

He looked at me, took the cheque from my fingers and scrutinised it, then said, 'I'll tell you what, Russell, bloody good on you, mate. Congratulations and good luck with your career, mate.'

'Thanks a lot,' I said, and left, feeling a huge weight lift.

CHAPTER TWENTY-TWO

Not long after, I sang at an event at the Midland Hotel in Manchester. A great night, a red night, I remember red roses on the tables and on the stage, and there were tons of big names there: Jack and Vera Duckworth from *Corrie*, Ryan Giggs, Tony Wilson, loads of people from United... and I was on fire that night. I did ''O Sole Mio' 'Volare', 'Funiculì, Funiculà', and I finished with 'Nessun Dorma', which brought the house down.

Afterwards, I was standing in the lobby of the hotel and felt a tap on my shoulder. Turning round, I had one of those moments. You know when you look at somebody and you think, 'I know you,' but you don't instantly recognise them? It took a couple of seconds before it clicked. It was Martin Edwards, chairman of Manchester United.

'That was absolutely fabulous, Russell,' he said, as I was still trying to process the data that the chairman of Manchester United had just tapped me on the shoulder. 'What an amazing voice. I love that type of music – that was just amazing.'

Blinking, I said, 'Thank you.'

'We should find an occasion for you to come and sing at Old Trafford. I think you were meant to come and sing with us, weren't you, at one point, and it didn't happen.'

Yes. Eric Cantona's testimonial. I'd been booked to sing along-side Mick Hucknall but it never happened. Why? Differing reports, but let's just say there are no Simply Red records in the Watson household.

'That's right.'

He said, 'Oh, they'd love you, they'd love you, and we're trying to incorporate different things, you know, for half time and so on. I really think it would be fantastic.' I gave him my details and that was it. For that night at least.

Meantime, I watched the season coming to a close, hoping the phone would ring. But as the finale approached, United heading for the title, there was no call, and I began thinking that was that.

Then, maybe three or four days before the Tottenham game, the last game of the season, the phone rang.

'Hello.'

'Hello, Russell, my name's Ken Ramsden, I'm the secretary of Manchester United, and Martin Edwards has asked me to call you because he'd like you to come down and sing for us at Old Trafford at the last game of the season against Tottenham.'

I said, 'Right.'

There was a bit of a pause on the line. Outside on Eldon Road a car passed.

He said, 'Russell? Are you available?'

'Just let me check,' I managed, and I covered the phone, looking around my tiny living room as though to check I was still on planet earth; my mouth opening and closing, a nervous, excited feeling in the pit of my stomach, hearing in my head a memory, like an echo, a voice – Hanky's voice – saying, 'All right, Russ, do you want to come to Old Trafford with me and me dad?'

I went back on the phone to Ken Ramsden. 'Yes,' I said. 'Yes, I'm available.'

'Oh, good. That's great.'

'Actually,' I said, 'I didn't really check my availability, I've just done a couple of backflips and a cartwheel in the lounge.'

'Oh, bless you,' said Ken Ramsden.

'Just let me know when,' I said, 'I mean... I know where – I've been there enough times, but just let me know when...'

My next phone call was to my dad.

'Guess what?'

'What?'

'You're coming with me to Old Trafford for the last game of the season.'

'Oh great, are we going to watch the game?'

'No,' I said. 'I'm singing there.'

'You're bloody joking.'

'I'm not, I've been asked to sing there. They want me to sing "Nessun Dorma".'

CHAPTER TWENTY-THREE

My bass player is a guy called Trevor Barry, a cockney.

'Fack me, Rass,' he said to me one day (and like everyone else, he has to suffer me impersonating him; I can't resist doing it, not even when I'm writing it down). 'The fing that gets me abaht you is, you just facking larve the big occasions, dunchya? It's amazing watching ya, it's like you come alive or summat.'

So when people ask if I get nervous before a big concert I have to risk sounding arrogant by saying no, but the truth is, I don't get them, nerves. Not even before the Old Trafford appearance. Not even then. Excited, awestruck, overwhelmed. But not intimidated, never fearful.

Not even when I walked into the reception at Old Trafford with my dad on May 16, 1999.

Because normally when I visited Old Trafford, I pushed a turn-stile and walked up some smelly steps with a load of blokes moaning and grumbling about who was in or out of form.

This, though. This was very, very different – this was the United inner sanctum. Sat behind a desk was the receptionist, who I later got to know, a woman called Kath, who greets everybody the same, whoever you are: 'Hello, love, how are you?'

She ended up taking a bit of a liking to me, Kath did. I ended up going to Old Trafford a lot, and she was always there, she's like a fixture of the place. I used to get a hug off her. They were all great, in fact, the staff at Old Trafford. No airs or graces about them; not up their backsides just because they're working at one of the world's most famous sporting teams. I remember another bloke there, a guy called Stan who worked in the director's box. On one occasion he presented me with a box of Mario Lanza records he'd brought from home. 'Here you go, lad, I knew you were coming in and thought you might like these.' I loved that about Manchester United – about going in there. They say you should never meet your heroes because they let you down, yet I was meeting a whole football club, one that I'd idolised since I was old enough to kick a ball. And what I cherish most about the whole experience was that they didn't let me down, and never have. I'd supported them as a child, given them all my love. It's turned out that they were more than worthy of that love.

Anyway, back to that day, and collecting me and my dad from reception were secretary Ken Ramsden and the assistant secretary Ken Merrett.

'Are you ready to do a mic check?' I was asked.

'Yeah,' I said, still trying to take in the reception area and seeing my dad doing the same. It's just as you imagine it to be: pictures on the walls: Sir Matt, Bestie. I'd have more time in the future – when I came to sing at other games – to admire the pictures, but not then, because now I was being led out on onto the pitch. Or, not the pitch; I wasn't allowed on the pitch. Groundsman doesn't let anybody go onto the pitch until the game. Instead, I had to be content with standing on the touchline, seeing for the first time in my life Old Trafford from the business end, but empty. So quiet I could hear pigeons in the top stands. Thousands and thousands of empty seats. Millions of stories.

Not quiet for long. I did my mic soundcheck. I knew from experience how to make a soundcheck work in my favour and I wasn't about to change my approach for Old Trafford, even though it was the biggest PA I'd ever worked with. Biggest by far.

What I did then – and I still do it now – is I never go for the top note. I like to keep that for the real thing. Plus, there's another trick. When you do your soundcheck, you do it to an empty stadium, or concert hall, or theatre, whatever. But when the place is full it swallows up the sound a bit, so during the soundcheck I always hold the microphone quite a distance from my mouth, so they have to push the levels up, because when I sing, I want to be heard by Sputnik. I want people to feel it. So I hold the microphone down and give it about 80 per cent volume.

After the soundcheck, my dad and I were invited up to the director's box for sandwiches and drinks and I felt like Charlie in *Charlie and the Chocolate Factory*, constantly nudging my dad and talking out of the side of my mouth, 'It's Sir Bobby Charlton, Dad, it's Sir Bobby Charlton.'

'I know, I saw him. And look over there.'

'Oh my God, it's Alan bloody Shearer.'

'I know. Alan Shearer. Bloody hell.'

Martin Edwards came over. 'Russell. Lovely you could make it.'

'Yeah, you know,' I said, 'in between engagements I thought I'd pop down and give you a song.'

He grinned. And that's the thing about him, Ken Ramsden, Ken Merrett, all these guys. They're unfailingly polite – 'We're so pleased you could make it' – they'd never lord it over you, make you feel like you should have to grovel for being there, quite the reverse. But they know. They know what it means for someone like me to be standing in the director's box at Old Trafford, watching the ground slowly fill up, eating prawn sandwiches, looking over to the Scoreboard Paddock where I'd stood, man and boy, for so many years, checking over to the stand where I knew Gleavo sat.

He'd be taking his seat, Gleavo would. 'I'll be looking out for you, mate.'

Somebody from security approached, telling me I'd be needed in the players' tunnel at half past two and that someone would be sent up for me.

I waited until twenty-five past two, waiting to go down to a little room I'd been given for changing. Here, I had my pre-concert ritual. What it is, I get changed right at the last minute, so I'm literally pulling on my socks as the band go on stage. They've all gone on, I'm sat around in shorts; I make a point of it because once I put the gear on the adrenalin starts going and I'd found that if I'm sitting around in my suit for half an hour by the time I get on stage I'm almost burnt out. It's like sticking a runner in the traps and then expecting him to hang about before the gun goes. So I literally put my gear on, go out of the door and straight on stage – and that's something that's been with me since I can't remember, a long time.

Five minutes I was in my little changing room. Enough time to get my gear on, do some scales.

Then down to the stadium, coming out of one of the doors they have there, where I stood with Keith Fane, the club announcer and DJ.

'Are you all right, son?' he asked. Keith was a mate of mine. It was down to him that I'd almost sung at Eric Cantona's testimonial. The one we don't talk about, that was about to be eclipsed for all time.

I looked around the stadium. Watching it gradually fill in the director's box still hadn't prepared me for the charged atmosphere. Old Trafford's electric at the best of times, but this – this was something different. The last game of the season and we were virtually neck and neck with Arsenal. United needed to win. We *needed* to win.

'Do you want a Bovril?'

Somebody handed me a little plastic beaker of Bovril, gently steaming, and I took it, grateful for something warm to drink. Warm drinks are good, they loosen the vocal chords, although it's best to steer clear of tea – or tea with milk anyway, because dairy products are no good, they create mucus, which can play havoc with the voice, causes a blockage, particularly on the top notes, which can be catastrophic.

Especially when you need to hit the top note of 'Nessun Dorma' on the last day of the season before a packed Old Trafford.

Alcoholic drinks are bad, too, because alcohol's a diuretic, it makes you go for a wee and you don't want to be needing a wee at Old Trafford, halfway through Puccini. Tea and coffee are both diuretics, too. Bovril, that's my Russell Watson hot tip for a good pre-gig drink. Get a Bovril down you.

I stood there, sipping mine. Keith was doing announcements, reading out birthdays, stuff like that. The time ticked by, the stadium still filling. If it seemed to crackle at half past, by a quarter to three the place was charged.

I was chatting to Keith. 'Are you ready for this?' he kept asking. 'Are you ready, Russ? Are you ready, son?'

Am I ready? I thought. Beside me, my dad was staring out at the stadium, mouth half open, probably thinking, My son's got to go out there in a minute, do a bit of singing.

Am I ready?

'Yeah, yeah,' I told Keith. 'I can't wait to get out there,' checking myself like the way you check for blood after hitting your head and finding out that, *wow*, I was telling the truth. I really *could not wait* to get out there.

I looked out to the pitch. There, some of the players were warming up. Pushing one hand into my pocket and taking a sip of Bovril with the other, I was thinking, Can't mess this up, Russell, got to hit that top note. 'Nessun Dorma' is all about that last note. You need to hit it. It's like in football, all everyone cares about is the goal. You can play 90 minutes of the best football in the world but if you don't score a goal you won't get the three points.

You *need* to hit that note.

The players warming up came off. The pitch was empty, the stadium alive with expectation, camera flashes exploding in the seating; hope seemed to roll off the stands in waves.

When the guys scuttled out on to the pitch with the mic stand and the speaker, I was expecting it – I'd been told that there was a presentation on and then me. But seeing them set the gear up in the centre circle, it became that little bit more real.

'One, two. One, two,' over the PA, check it's working all right.

The presentation took about three minutes. I looked over at my dad, who gave me a 'Good luck, son' face as Keith looked at me and said, 'Are you ready, Russ?'

Only this time he didn't mean it as in: Are you prepared, can you handle this?

He meant it as in: You're going on now.

'Yeah, I'm ready,' I said. I was bouncing on my feet slightly. The presentation people were coming off, all smiles. I looked past them to the centre circle where the mic stand stood, two tiny little wedge speakers at its base.

'All right, then,' said Keith, by my side, 'I'll introduce you, then you're on.'

Right. I looked at the mic in the centre of the pitch. The stadium seemed to contract around the mic stand.

'Right,' said Keith, only now he wasn't talking to me. Now he was talking to a capacity crowd at Old Trafford, telling 55,000 people that 'we've got a special treat for you now, it's Salford's very own tenor, Russell Watson, who's going to sing Puccini's "Nessun Dorma" for you'.

I strode out to the centre circle. Around me, above me, a cavernous Old Trafford – an Old Trafford I'd only ever known as a spectator. Now, I stood at its centre, the world of the stadium settling around me.

Over the PA, my backing tape began, the first tentative strings of the aria. It's not like a normal song, you don't get an intro, the tenor comes in almost straight away.

And I did.

'Nessun Dorma.'

As I say, it's an aria. An aria from the third act of *Turandot* by Puccini, an opera set in Peking in legendary times. It's sung by an 'unknown prince' who has fallen in love with the Princess Turandot. It was love at first sight for the prince but Turandot, even though she's the honey of the era, is emotionally cold and distant. How cruel is this woman? Well, we first meet her ordering the execution of the Prince of Persia; plus, anybody who wants her hand in marriage must correctly answer three riddles. Suitors giving the wrong answers to riddles are executed – which is how the Prince of Persia met his sticky end. Our man the prince, though, is truly, deeply and madly in love with Turandot and he strikes a gong indicating that he wants a crack at solving the riddles and therefore winning Turandot's hand in marriage.

In Act II, the young prince is set his riddles by the beautiful but cruel princess. For the first, she asks: 'What is born each night and dies each dawn?'

'Hope,' says the prince, giving her the correct answer.

For the next riddle he's asked: 'What flickers red and warm like a flame, but is not fire?'

He thinks for a few moments before replying, 'Blood.'

Turandot's not happy, and she's especially displeased that the crowd are cheering for the prince, but she poses her final riddle: 'What is like ice, but burns like fire?'

He appears stumped and she takes the mickey out of him for a bit until, suddenly, he replies, 'Turandot.'

Which is the correct answer. Mortified, Turandot begs her father not to make her marry the prince. But the king says no way, you have to make good on your promise. Even so, the prince gives her a possible get-out clause, telling her that she doesn't know his name – and if she can discover it by sunrise then she has leave to execute him.

Turandot orders her staff to get to work on finding out the prince's name. If they can't discover his name by sunrise, she says, then they will die.

Meantime, the lovestruck prince, alone in the palace's moonlit gardens, passes the time by singing 'Nessun Dorma'.

The title translates as 'none shall sleep'. None shall sleep, he pledges in the song. Try as you might, he sings, my secret remains hidden.

I had a secret of my own at Old Trafford, hidden beneath my suit. And I started singing, with the crowd still settling in, a lot of noise, then gradually settling down, the hum of the place fading. About a third of the way through and the place became quiet – quiet apart from me. I knew they were listening. I had them.

Gleavo, sitting up in the stands, told me later that he heard a couple of blokes chatting behind him, going, 'Bollocks, he's never from Salford. He's not from Salford with a voice like that.'

Just before the end of the aria, the chorus comes in, Turandot's servants lamenting that they do not know the prince's name and that they will have to die as a result.

Euphoric, with the angelic, doomed voices of the chorus swelling around the stadium, I unbuttoned my jacket then dropped it to the floor. Next I removed the mic from its stand so I could move freely, turning to let the entire stadium see the Manchester United shirt I'd been hiding beneath my suit jacket. On the back it read: Watson 10 OR.

'Fucking hell,' said the one of the blokes behind Steve Gleave, 'maybe he is from Salford.'

Then comes the aria's finale. The prince calls for the night to end, saying that by daybreak, he will have victory: *Vincerò*.

Vincerò, he says. I shall win.

And I hit the note. Thank you, Bovril, I hit that note right out of the park. A sustained B note that I held for longer than I think I ever have, before or since. If there was one moment in my career, one moment that I had to say was my defining moment, it was that one.

United would go one down to Spurs. Les Ferdinand scored in the twenty-fourth minute, well against the run of play and Old Trafford held its breath.

I watched the game in the director's box, barely able to take everything in. People were approaching me, telling me how much they'd liked the performance, and I stayed wired, high on adrenalin the whole time, knowing that if United won, then it was the spring-board to them winning the treble: the championship, the FA cup and the European cup. That if United won I would, as agreed, go back out there and sing 'Barcelona'.

Beckham scored just before the break. Cole just after.

Vincerò.

As the players did their lap of honour I went back on to sing 'Barcelona'...

My childhood team had just won the championship. I'd silenced Old Trafford with a performance of 'Nessun Dorma' that even brought a tear to my dad's eye. I'd serenaded the fans with 'Barcelona'. Afterwards, Paul Hince of the *Manchester Evening News* wrote a piece about the performance, a separate story that appeared on the same spread as his ecstatic match report. He wrote, 'You know when you have just witnessed something special when even the cynical hacks in the press box rise to their feet and join in the ovation. I swear, even the pigeons on the roof of the stands flapped their wings.' It doesn't get much better than that, does it?

CHAPTER TWENTY-FOUR

January 2, 2008

The phone goes. It's Richard Thompson, my manager. He tells me to expect company at the hospital; the press will be waiting for me.

'All right, lads?' I say.

Click. I get photographed as I'm coming up the street towards the Christie. The elbow you can see in the picture belongs to Gary. That elbow's famous. Any time you see an elbow in a photograph of me, it's Gary's elbow. We should get it an agent; perhaps start thinking about a Gary's Elbow Calendar 2009.

Later, I look at the photograph of me arriving at the Christie and I look like what I am: a knackered bloke about to go for his first radiotherapy session. A bloke running on nerves and two hours' sleep.

'How are you feeling, Russell?' say reporters.

'I feel like shite. How do you think I feel, you idiot,' I reply.

Only joking. Not really. Tempting though it is, because the truth is I feel rotten. No sleep, hormones all over the shop. Just rotten. I try not to let on too much. I tell them that I've felt better, and that it's shaping up to be a memorable new year for all the wrong reasons.

There are some PR people from the Christie there and they're really nice and they've got their job to do, but they want to film something while I'm walking into the hospital. Like I say, they're very nice, but I tell them, 'Look, I don't feel comfortable striding around the hospital while there's a camera filming me. There's people in here who are really sick and I don't think it's appropriate...'

'Um,' they say, 'well, what if we take you somewhere where it's really quiet?'

We compromise. I tell them I'll do it but not through a waiting room where there's people who aren't well. It just looks big time.

Oh no it doesn't, they say.

Oh yes it does, I reply.

Christmas might be over; panto season continues.

In the end we find a little corridor with nobody in it and I'm filmed as I walk down it and then around the corner.

They want me to do it again but I've had enough. I've got an appointment with a microwave.

One good thing, though, all that palaver certainly takes my mind off the radiotherapy, so by the time I get to the machine it almost feels like I've got the difficult bit over and done with. Then the machine's there in front of me and God, I'd forgotten how big it is. Where are you reading this? If you're inside, look at the ceiling. That's how tall the machine is.

We're in the room. The room where it all happens. And the nursing staff are busy around me. There's a window in one wall of the room and behind that window the control room where everybody will retreat once the zapping begins.

They put a perspex box over my face. Suddenly I know what it feels like to be a sandwich in a Tupperware container.

'We're at ninety-eight point two on the left, how are you on your side?' I hear.

'Ninety-seven point three.'

'Great. Are you touching soup yet?'

Touching soup? What on earth does touching soup translate as? I mean, I've heard of touching cloth, but...

'Yes, I'm touching soup now.'

'Okay, great, we're just going to take him up a little bit more now.'

With the soup touched they do another calculation.

'I'm just going to put this piece of card on the top of your head,' says a nurse. 'We're just going to do a quick calculation to make sure you're in the right place.'

Then she goes back into jargon mode. 'Okay, touching soup at eighty-six point two. Are you okay your end?'

They're okay, they're touching soup. Now it's time to fit my medieval torture device-cum-mask-cum-frame. It's a nightmare, this thing. The gum-shield thing goes in my mouth, with a bracket coming out of the front. A frame keeps my head pinned to the table, a moulded headrest behind, and I can't move. It's bolted there like I'm Frankenstein's monster or something.

'Sorry about this.'

I blink as somebody reaches over and uses a felt-tip pen to put a dot on my nose. Then she's gone. Where she's dotted on my nose leaves an itch that I dare not scratch, just in case it affects the touching-soup levels.

The last person leaves the room, shuts the door behind them. I'm alone.

The machine begins to hum.

CHAPTER TWENTY-FIVE

May 1999

The phone rang. Ken Ramsden.

'What are you doing this week?' he asked, and the room seemed to freeze around me.

I didn't have plans. I mean, nothing solid. Nothing that couldn't be postponed. I was going to watch the UEFA Champions League Final on TV, that much was for sure. United were playing Bayern Munich, and they were playing for the treble, having already won the FA Cup and clinched the title. Frankly, I was still walking on air after singing 'Nessun Dorma' on the day United won the Premiership.

'What do you mean?' I said, cautiously, hardly daring to believe the conclusion my wildest imagination had already reached, like, No. Come on. He's not going to ask you to fly to Barcelona and sing at the Nou Camp for the United match. He's not going to ask you that because you've just sung at Old Trafford. He wants you to fix a leaky tap, or maybe if you're lucky sing at some function they've got planned around the Champions League Final...

'Well,' he said, 'you went down so well on Sunday, we'd like to take you out to represent Manchester United at the Nou Camp stadium for the Champions League Final.'

Turned out I was available.

It was one of the best nights of my life. And I've had some incredible experiences. My singing career has brought me adventures that most people can only ever dream of. Believe me, I never forget that for a second. Fatherhood has changed my life and that, too, has offered me some incredible experiences, but in the top five of everything I've been lucky enough to do – maybe even the top three – was that night at the Nou Camp in Barcelona.

Would it be higher up the chart than Old Trafford? Well, probably not. Old Trafford was special. It was special for reasons that stretch all the way back to that first visit with Hanky and his dad. Old Trafford was the place where I'd gone to worship the local sporting heroes and show my respects to them in the Scoreboard Paddock – and there I was, performing on that same hallowed turf years later. Old Trafford was special all right.

Even so, the Nou Camp was amazing. Before the match, I came on and sang ''O Sole Mio', 'Funiculì, Funiculà' and 'Nessun Dorma'. After me, Montserrat Caballé came on to sing 'Barcelona'. They brought her on in a chariot.

And then it was the game. Breathtaking. An incredible game of football – probably one of the best games in the history of the sport and certainly the best match I've ever been to.

For a start, me and my dad were sitting in the front row of the second tier with members of the team who won the European Cup in 1968: so me and my dad sitting next to Paddy Crerand, Wilf McGuinness, Nobby Stiles, George Best – all of them lined up along the front row of the second tier.

Then, of course, there was the game itself. Quick, potted match report for anybody who missed the game or got so drunk they don't remember what happened. Bayern Munich went ahead in the sixth minute, scoring from a free kick. This left United chasing the game, and chase they did, seeming to dominate possession but, despite some dangerous runs from Becks, plus Andy Cole crossing for Ryan Giggs, failing to create many chances.

In the second half, Bayern Munich looked dangerous and United had to work hard not to concede another goal – which would have been a complete disaster. Then, manager Sir Alex Ferguson brought on Teddy Sheringham – a fresh pair of legs – and next, with about ten minutes to go, Fergie introduced Ole Gunnar Solskjær to the game.

In the stand, sitting with the 1968 cup-winning side, I looked up and it was a beautiful clear night, stars in the sky, not a cloud in sight. And I thought, God, if you're up there, please just let us score a goal.

I felt guilty about it, to be honest with you. If there was ever some kind of day of reckoning where you discover you only get a certain amount of answered prayers then that would be a really stupid request to make. Because football isn't something you should pray about, it really isn't. At the end of the day it's a bunch of overpaid blokes kicking around an inflatable bladder and you should never forget that. It's not a matter of life and death. You shouldn't waste your prayers on it.

But I did anyway. I said to the man upstairs, 'Please let United score this goal.'

The minutes ticked past. Hope slowly began to fade. Apparently they'd even put the Bayern Munich ribbons on the cup and were carting it down to the podium ready for the presentations. Along our row of champions, George Best got up and left...

Which meant he missed it when Teddy Sheringham got the equaliser.

The story goes that Bestie got outside the stadium and heard the roar, tried to get back in the stadium but they wouldn't let him, so he headed for the nearest bar to watch the rest of the game from there. I doubt he made it, though. Sheringham scored in injury time. We're talking the dying seconds of the game here. The score was one all and we were going mad. Oh my God, I was jumping all over my dad and Paddy Crerand was next to me, rubbing my head like, 'Come on, son!' And like everyone else in the ground or watching at home we were still going mad about the equaliser when United scored again to make it 2–1. It was Solskjær this time, literally thirty seconds after the restart.

For a moment or so it wasn't real. These things don't happen, not in real life. They happened in my *Roy of the Rovers* comics; in the Super Striker games we used to play in my mum and dad's garage. But they didn't happen in real life.

Only they did. They had. And for a second, time seemed to stand still as the stadium absorbed the goal. Thousands upon thousands of fans who, like me, couldn't quite believe what they'd just seen. The winning goal.

And then, the place went mental. We were jumping up and down, screaming. Pent-up emotion flooding the place. The feeling, pure ecstasy. Years and years of following United. All that bottled-up hope escaping in one blast of pure, ecstatic celebration.

And that was it. I think play did restart for a few seconds, but most of the Bayern Munich players couldn't even get off the floor. These guys – you've got to feel sorry for them – they were gutted. And I can understand why. Football was like life or death that night. It just seemed so relevant, so important.

And there was me, somehow in the middle of it all. How on earth did that happen?

CHAPTER TWENTY-SIX

I'd had dreams, bad dreams, since I was a kid. I had one where I was lying in the dormer of the bungalow on Sunningdale Drive and I'd hear a tap at the window.

Can you believe that? A tap at the window. Like in an old horror movie. Just shows, though – shows how universal that dread can be.

In the dream I'd pull the covers aside and get out of bed, go to the window and peer out into blackness. See nothing – nothing but pitch black, my own reflection squinting back at me. And I'd focus and peer, trying to look through my reflection, trying to look into the darkness to see what lay out there, until, gradually, she became clear – the witch standing outside my window. She stood stock still, her head tilted to one side. She wore no hat. Not a cartoon witch, this one; not a Halloween caricature. Instead she had long, grey – almost white – hair that hung straight, almost covering her face. Her eyes seemed dead and sightless, though I felt almost transfixed by her gaze. As I watched, she raised one arm, fingers little more than brittle flesh over bone, crooked nails like talons, dragging, nails scraping down the glass of my bedroom window…

I'd run back to my bed, get in, swaddling myself in covers as though they might offer protection from the witch. Knowing they would not.

And then I'd wake up from the nightmare. I'd awake with dream world and reality intertwined like laundry that I had to separate and sort, taking what felt like ages to work out that it was a dream, just a dream; that there was no witch outside the window. No fingernails tapping on the glass.

I had another dream where I was on a fairground ride, except it was a boat – a Tunnel of Love-type thing. There was just me in the boat and then everything would go dark in the tunnel. I could sense shadows and see the water moving, oily, thick and black; a dark sheen, a nasty hypnotic gleam on the water. Then, suddenly I'd look behind myself to see a shadow, something in the back of the boat, a figure looking down at me...

...and I'd wake up, scared; whimpering, often, when I first used to get the dream, until I learnt to expect the dark figure in the back of the boat.

I used to get that one a lot when I was a kid.

As I grew up, though, these recurring dreams stopped and were replaced by another one. One that was part dream, part premonition. A dreamlike vision I used to have frequently, once every fortnight or so.

In it, things used to detonate in my head. I dreamt images of huge explosions in my brain and I always woke up with the same eerie feeling – a feeling that I wouldn't make forty.

CHAPTER TWENTY-SEVEN

Here's somebody else to add to that list, the one with the Colonel and Lynne, and Gerald Scholes and 'George' and 'Frank' on it.

It's the person who sent my CD to Cliff Richard. What I used to do was sing for a gathering of Italian restaurateurs called Ciao Italia and I'd sell CDs in the restaurants. Someone who saw me sing bought a CD and sent it to Cliff Richard's manager, David Bryce. There was a picture of me on the CD, one of the many things the Colonel had helped me with, and I was invited to a meeting at a recording studio in London, a church conversion, a beautiful place.

There, I met David Bryce. 'I just had to check,' he said, bemused, looking from me to the CD box in his hand. 'I receive this CD in the post and it's got a picture of this young chap on the front, so I play the CD and there's this... *voice*. I just had to check. I mean, this is the kind of noise you associate with bearded blokes weighing twenty-five stone, not...' He waved at me. 'Is it studio trickery?'

We were sitting in an office, either side of a desk. 'You know what?' I said. 'The sound looks like it might be good in there,' and we walked through into the main church, into the centre of the space, where I stopped, spread my hands and began singing "O Sole Mio'. I was right about the sound. It seemed to fill the room, rich and deep. I couldn't have asked for a better demonstration space.

'Okay,' said David Bryce when I'd finished. He was grinning. 'That's amazing. You've got to meet Cliff.'

Cliff Richard. A favourite on the Sunningdale Drive radiogram. My mum was a huge fan. *Cliff Richard*. Everybody grew up listening to Cliff.

I met him at Bray Studios. I'd been told there was a spot on his show, the Route of Kings, a series of open-air concerts on Hyde Park, expected attendance: 25,000 per show. Cliff had his rig set up at Bray; he was rehearsing for the show, and with the backing of his band I performed 'Nessun Dorma' for him.

'It's going to be great working with you, mate,' he said when I was done, total Cliff.

And I was on the show.

Six nights at Hyde Park. I sang a song with Cliff, a duet called 'Vita Mia', after which Cliff would address the crowd, saying, 'Russell has kindly agreed to stay and sing another song for us, haven't you, Russell?'

'Yes, Cliff.'

'I think you're going to like this one, it's called "Nessun Dorma".'

It was an incredible experience, not only for the opportunity to play in front of such huge crowds, but for the exposure; plus, of course, to learn from one of the biggest names in the business.

One day during rehearsals, the second day it was, I walked into the studio and Cliff was on stage, saw me crossing the floor and called out, 'Oh, hi, Russell.'

'Hi, Cliff,' I replied.

He said, 'Listen, Russell, I was out with some friends last night, and we were chatting over dinner, and I said to them that I thought it would be a great idea if you changed your name.'

Oh no.

I smiled – the way you might smile if Sir Cliff Richard has just suggested you change your name.

'Oh, right,' I said, smiling.

'Yuh, and we were thinking, and we came up with this name.

How about something like *Watson… Russo*? I think it's got a real kind of Mediterranean… twang to it. What do you think?'

'Right, Cliff,' I said, careful to keep the smile stitched on. 'Thanks, yeah, that's great.'

'Great,' he said, and motioned to the band, who struck up to continue the rehearsal, me walking off, thinking, Oh no. Because bless him. I mean, it was sweet of him. But *Watson Russo*? It just wasn't what I'm about.

Anyway, he seemed to drop the idea, and it didn't come up again, apart from the next day when I turned up for rehearsals and, as before, Cliff was on stage, calling to me as I arrived: 'Hi,' he said. 'Hi… Watson.'

He's a great bloke, though, Cliff. He sent me bouquets of lilies both times I was in hospital. Even used my real name.

Meanwhile, at the same time as the Route of Kings stuff was happening, I was getting a reputation as the go-to guy for big sporting events. I was singing at the rugby, I'd done the Wembley Horse of the Year show (singing 'The Toreador Song' from *Carmen* on the back of a chariot – not easy) and the FA had been in touch for England, asking me to do the Euro 2000 qualifiers. One match in particular was the Sweden game, where I had to sing both national anthems. The English national anthem I knew, obviously, but I had to learn the Swedish anthem phonetically, so I wrote it out on a piece of paper. The night before the game I was boozing in Covent Garden, a few of us were there, one of them was Keith Fane, so it was a right crowd, and by about two in the morning we were well oiled, me singing opera in the middle of the piazza, when these guys, wandering past, heard me.

Next thing you know they were singing too, joining in then coming over to speak to me, saying how much they'd enjoyed the singing. Turns out they were Swedish.

'Really? I'm singing at the game tomorrow,' I told them.

'Are you serious?' Needless to say they spoke great English. 'No, you are joking. You are pulling our legs.'

'No, really,' I said, 'I'm dead serious. I'm singing your national anthem.'

One of them thumped a proud hand to his chest. 'The Swedish national anthem? Is this true? You *know* our national anthem?'

A lightbulb pinged on above my head. 'Ah,' I said, 'sort of,' and then I was rummaging in my pockets for my piece of paper, the one with the Swedish national anthem written out. Then, I started singing it to them.

Any suspicions that they were on receiving end of a piss-take evaporated, replaced by sheer amazement at having wandered through Covent Garden only to end up in a singing competition with the following day's pre-match entertainment.

A pretty happy accident for me, too. We spent a merry hour or so, with the lads from Sweden teaching the bloke from Salford how to sing the Swedish national anthem. In Covent Garden. The night before the big match at Wembley. And when it came to the performance, I sang safe in the knowledge that I'd been given the correct pronunciation straight from the horse's mouth.

It still cracks me up to think of that night. My life, at that time, was just full of that kind of brilliant strangeness. It's never really settled down since, come to think of it, even if some of the strangeness hasn't been quite so brilliant.

Anyway, there's a postscript to that story. A couple of years later I got invited to sing on the Swedish National Lottery and turned up only to discover that the TV company had tracked down the original fans who helped me learn the song, so I got to meet them again – although we were all sober this time.

While all the sporting events were taking place, my deal with Decca was brewing. It came through the Cliff connection. David Bryce knew a guy, a music entrepreneur called Rick Blaskey, who had contacts in Decca. Rick Blaskey and I went for a meeting at Decca.

That meeting and the subsequent deal – they still talk about it today.

I met Rick for the first time outside the building. 'Great to meet you,' he said, then adopted a serious tone. 'Listen,' he said, 'what I'm going to say now isn't supposed to be negative, but the fact is, record companies aren't signing artists at the moment. There's not the same money floating around now that there was ten years ago, and they're not signing artists. So what I'm saying is, to get deals, it can take months, and even then, at the end of months of negotiations, you're not guaranteed that you're going to get the deal. So I'm just letting you know, okay? This will be the first of probably what's going to be a lot of meetings. Don't get your hopes up.'

Going up in the lift I had other ideas. I was a headstrong bloke at that time – what am I saying? I still am – and I was full of confidence, determined not to let this chance pass me by. I knew that Charlotte Church had just been signed to Sony, and that it was a big deal making Sony a lot of money, and I was mulling that over as the lift rose, thinking, I'm going to get this deal. I don't want to wait six or seven months, I want it now.

And if all that makes me sound more like a contestant on *The Apprentice* than a singer, I'll tell you why I was thinking that way. It was because with everything that was happening – the sporting events, the Cliff show – it felt like my time.

And in six or seven months it might not be my time any more.

'We need to just be cool and not get too carried away,' said Rick as we stepped out of the lift then were shown to a huge office. There we walked in to see Decca bigwigs suited and booted and sitting round a massive table. There were framed discs on the walls, a stereo at the back, a big potted plant in the corner. Mark Cavell was there, the head of the label; Costa Pilavachi, the man who signed Bocelli to Philips, five or six others.

And I remember thinking, That's a good sign. There wouldn't be so many of them here if they weren't so serious.

Introductions over, we sat down. I smiled at them. They smiled back at me.

'Okay, Russell,' started Costa, 'have you brought a CD with you that we can have a listen to, that I could play to the gentlemen?'

He swept an arm around the table, indicating the expectant Decca execs, who looked back at me.

'No,' I said.

'Ah, okay... have you brought any TV footage of you? Anything like that at all?'

'No,' I replied.

Beside me, Rick cleared his throat and shifted slightly in his chair.

'Okay,' said Costa, 'then have you brought any press or anything we can show the gentlemen?'

'No,' I said, 'but I've brought my voice with me.' There was laughter from the assembled execs. 'And I can give you a little blast if you like,' I added.

They looked at me. Costa spread his arms, shrugging, *Why not?*, and I stood from my chair, stepped up onto the boardroom table and did my party piece: I sang them ''O Sole Mio'.

I watched their faces as I sang. They wore the sort of expressions I was getting used to by now. Expressions that said, this little northern guy, he opens his mouth and it sounds like...

Tony Wilson once said something about me. This is Tony Wilson the Manchester music legend I'm talking about, who founded Factory records. He was a bit of a fan and came to see me a few times. For a documentary he was asked to sum me up in one sentence, and he'd said, 'Russell Watson? Baseball cap, voice like God.'

He was fond of exaggerating, was Tony Wilson. Simply 'a big voice' would have been enough, and I wasn't wearing a baseball cap for my meeting at Decca, but you know what I mean. It's the gulf between what people see and what they hear – that was what it was all about back then; that's the story the looks on their faces told.

I finished and stepped back down from the table, grateful to reach terra firma without falling on my arse and shattering the effect.

'Well,' I said, 'what do you think?'

Costa was first to reply. 'Well,' he said, 'that was amazing.' He looked around the table for assent. 'I don't think we've ever seen anything like that before. Ever.'

I leaned forward and said, 'Listen. If you're looking for a highly polished, sophisticated, school-trained Sebastian Fotherington-Smythe, then I might as well walk out of the office, because I'm not your man. But if you're looking for somebody who knows – because I've been doing it for ten years – who *knows* that they can take this music into a different place in the market and make it accessible to the man on the street, because I know, because I've been singing it to them for years and they've been loving it, and take it to a younger market as well, and give you an audience that you've not had before, then I'm your man.'

Like I say, they still talk about it now. Not just the meeting but the speed of the deal. Because when I got back to Manchester after leaving Decca there was a fax waiting for me, a five-album deal.

Leaving the Decca office, everybody on brilliant terms, I said to Costa, 'Hey, let's have a bit of a laugh before we go.'

'Why? What are you going to do?'

We were standing in the doorway of the meeting room, outside was a huge open-plan office, the hub of Universal, people going about their business, at computers, on phones, standing chatting with cups of coffee.

'Here, you go like this, we'll pretend it's you singing.'

'You're crazy,' he said but stood there anyway, throwing out his arm and pretending to sing as I hid behind him and opened up.

Coming out from behind him, I saw the entire office looking our way. People on phones standing open-mouthed.

'It's not him,' I said, 'it was me,' and Rick and I left, a round of applause taking us to the lift.

'Well,' said Rick, 'I really didn't expect that. You, mate, you're bloody mad, you are.'

Worked, though, didn't it!

CHAPTER TWENTY-EIGHT

The first fruit of my deal with Decca was a single to tie in with the rugby: 'Swing Low 99', the official song of the England team in that year's Rugby Union World Cup. My fortunes were linked to those of the team, though, and it got no higher than number 30. Next, I was featured on a compilation, *Land of My Fathers*, which was the official album of the Rugby World Cup and saw me in the company of Bryn Terfel and Shirley Bassey – *Dame* Shirley Bassey. It went gold, selling over 200,000, the first gold disc on my wall. Meanwhile, we started preparing for what would be my debut album, *The Voice*, and the single that would come out beforehand. We had this idea that we wanted to stamp my identity on the public right from the start, so we came up with a plan: a duet with the Happy Mondays singer and legendary hellraiser Shaun Ryder; me and Shaun singing 'Barcelona'. It was an idea dreamt up by me and my then-manager, and the point of it was to stick an immediate two fingers up at the classical music establishment.

It certainly did that. The classical music establishment, whoever they are, never exactly welcomed me with open arms, and I'm still not really accepted. So maybe I burnt my bridges a bit there. The public, though, loved it.

We're completely different, Shaun and I. He's a pint-of-beer bloke, I like a glass of wine; he'll smoke a fag, I go to the gym; famously, he was a crack addict for years and my attitude to drugs is that I've never been interested in putting chemicals in my body when I don't have a fairly good idea what the outcome will be – or what the long-term effect will be. About as rock and roll as I've ever got is having the odd cigar. Shaun, though. He's mister rock and roll, he's been there.

'Fookin' 'ell,' he said to me when we first met (and believe me, you need the brass bands for whenever Shaun's about). 'Fookin' 'ell, I can't believe a fookin' proper singer wants to fookin' sing with me.' He brought a bunch of his homies with him, guys like him in hats and baggy sportswear, plenty of hard living between them, and we all had a Chinese. He's a lovely bloke, but you wouldn't want to get on the wrong side of him. I saw him tear into a director at *TFI Friday* when we appeared to play the song (the show was live but we had to pre-record it because Shaun was banned from doing live telly with Channel Four. Reason? Swearing so much on previous occasions). He just exploded: 'Where are me fookin' monitors?' he was screaming at this woman. 'I can't fookin' see me fookin' monitors.'

'Hey, Russell,' he said to me on the first day of recording. He slouched into the studio, peering at us from under the brim of his hat, a vision in Adidas. I was there making *The Voice* with my producer, Nick Patrick, who's become a very good friend of mine over the years, and Pete Schweer, both of them very southern and very posh. Immediately they opened their mouths I could see Shaun's face. Thunder.

'You all right, Shaun?' I asked.

'Yeah,' he drawled, 'I'm all right, like, but I'm not too fookin' sure about the two Wrangler-wearing public school boys you've got here.'

What am I supposed to do? Get them to change, not only their genes, but their jeans? I tried to defuse a potentially nasty situation, introducing them, Shaun scowling but just about polite. As it was, though, he only stayed a couple of hours, during which time he sang some lines that were frankly unusable, then buggered off to the pub.

Now, I don't know if you've heard 'Barcelona', the Russell and Shaun version, but its structure is that I sing the first verse of the song, then a breakbeat comes in, after which you get Shaun singing the second verse, then we both sing the chorus with Shaun taking the 'Barcelona' part.

Now, Shaun has got an amazing voice. You hear it, you instantly know it's him. But it's not... how can I put this? It's not the most disciplined voice in the world. So when he left the studio for the boozer, the material we had in the can... Well, it needed work.

So I re-sang some of Shaun's bits. What had happened was, his lines tended to tail off instead of ending where they should. He had a habit of extending the note way beyond where it should go. And we'd been told by his management that once we had our two hours, that was it, we had to work with what we had. But we couldn't. We tried doing it in Pro Tools but no joy. In the end, I sat down, practised my best Shaun Ryder impression, which wasn't bad if I say so myself, and sang some of the ends of his lines, ending the note correctly so it could be dropped in at the end of Shaun's lines. Some of the harmonies at the end of the song are mine, too. Funny, in my club days I used to do a version of the Nat King Cole and Natalie Cole duet 'Unforgettable', where I would sing both parts of the duet, impersonating both Nat King Cole and his daughter. It was one of those numbers where I'd have people shouting out from the audience, 'Oi. He's miming to a backing track.' Grinning, I used to take the microphone away from my mouth to prove I wasn't miming (although even that wasn't enough for one punter once, who screeched, 'See? I told you he was miming.'). With that single, I'd gone from being Nat

King Cole and Natalie Cole to being Russell Watson and Shaun Ryder.

We made a video after that. I guess there's only one place you can really film a video to 'Barcelona', so that's where we went. Any money left over went on hiring a stunning model for me to fall in love with – but just for the purposes of the video, mind – and we had a right laugh making it. Promoting it after that we did *TFI Friday*, plus there was an appearance on the *Jim Davidson Show*, which also featured a very young Atomic Kitten, right at the beginning of their career. Jim Davidson: now there's another guy who's not exactly tactful, not if my experience of him then was anything to go by. Poor old Atomic Kitten were rehearsing on stage, and in walks Jim.

'Who the facking hell are these, then?' he demanded to know at the top of his voice, Atomic Kitten singing away.

'Atomic Kitten,' replied a stagehand.

'Tonic Kitten. Who the facking hell are they, then?'

By this time the Kittens were standing looking uncomfortable, aware that they were the subject of Jim's attention.

'You booked them, Jim.'

'Did I?' he bawled, apparently oblivious to the fact that they were a few feet away. 'Jesus. They can't facking sing.'

During the performance itself, Shaun came on way before his cue, then sang all my bits. A complete fiasco, but a lot of fun. Another time we did an MTV interview, complete with the standard stunning MTV host, and Shaun was leaning over to her in between questions, saying, 'My mate wants to shag you. Do yer fancy a shag, love?'

Like I say, he was quite a handful.

Recording that first album, I knew exactly what I wanted. It wasn't hard; I'd gone into Decca with the idea of who I was going to be, so it was just a case of finding the right balance between the classical stuff and the more poppy numbers. Most of the stuff on that first record I'd been singing for years in the clubs, no surprises there: 'Nessun Dorma', obviously. ''O Sole Mio', of course. Then I chose a few poppier numbers. I've always fancied singing: 'Bridge Over Troubled Water' and 'Vienna'. During the promotional process somebody said to me, 'How did you go about choosing what goes on your record?' I said, well, you know, my manager puts his ideas in, the concept producer put some of his ideas in, the record company came up with some ideas and the A&R person came up with some ideas... and then we did what I wanted. And if this sounds like I'm being Billy Big-Head, you've got to remember that most of the ideas these people come up with are crap. Believe me. I'll give you an example. An old manager of mine once said to me, 'Russell,' he says, 'I've had this great idea about a song for you.'

'Right, yeah, what is it?'

He said, 'Well, you know "'O Sole Mio"?'

'Yes.'

'How about, right, we put English words to it and turn it into, like, a pop song?'

'Yeah, well, it's a great idea, mate, but Elvis beat us to it with "It's Now or Never" forty years ago.'

'Oh.'

See? Clueless. Completely clueless.

A&R. Supposed to be artist and repertoire, although I call them alcohol and restaurants. They're another lot forever coming to you with blindingly obvious ideas. Let's do an album of Elvis covers, Russell. Yeah, mate, cheers. Oh, look, an open bottle of Sauvignon Blanc. Quick, run while his attention's diverted.

Fortunately for me, I wasn't too intimidated by the studio, either. My time doing stuff for Ameritz had given me a bit of experience on that front. One thing that really turned my head, though, was the fact that we were going to be recording at Air Lyndhurst, the studio owned by George Martin. That news stopped me in my tracks. Not only that, but we'd be using the Royal Philharmonic Orchestra. And that news stopped me in my tracks, too. *And* they were going to give me such and such a big-name conductor to conduct the Royal Philharmonic Orchestra ...

Ah, no, I said.

Actually. I've got my own conductor who I use for the core classical stuff.

And they said, 'Well, no, we use this guy.'

'But he knows my stuff,' I told them. 'He knows how I sing. He's the guy I always use. Sorry, but I'm going to use him.'

'Oh, Russell, lovely to hear from you,' said Bill, when I rang him. 'How's it all going?'

I said, 'Yeah, it's going really well, mate,' which was the understatement of the century. I hadn't seen Bill in about a year: a year in which I'd sung at Old Trafford, at the Nou Camp, at Hyde Park with Cliff Richard, got a deal with Decca, and was now recording my first album.

'I've got a gig for you,' I said.

'Oh, lovely, what's that then?'

I said, 'I want you to come down to Air Lyndhurst and record the Royal Philharmonic Orchestra with me.'

There was a pause on the line. I thought back to all those times we'd sat around together, him telling me how he dreamt that one day he'd get to conduct the Royal Philharmonic. I thought back to the time I told him I couldn't afford to pay for the voice coaching and he told me not to worry, to come anyway.

'You're joking?' he said at last.

'No, mate, deadly serious.'

'Well, bugger me, I don't bloody believe it. Why me?'

I said, 'Well, 'cos I love you, you know, you're the man.'

'Yeah? Ha, well, I don't bloody believe it, bloody hell. Oh, that's bloody fantastic, what a great opportunity, thank you so much.'

And hearing the trace of an emotional sniff down the phone, I left him to it. It felt good, that phone call.

Not long later, I was watching them file into the huge studio at Air Lyndhurst. A 72-piece orchestra, the Royal Philharmonic, sitting down waiting for Sir Bill to conduct them. I remember watching them as they waited. A couple of the players retrieved knitting from bags. One or two read newspapers or paperback books, another did the crossword…

We did 'Saylon Dola', 'Non Ti Scordar Di Me', 'Bridge Over Troubled Water', 'Vienna', me leading the orchestra, my chest full of the sound of one of the world's best orchestras as it swelled and blossomed through the studio. It was amazing, absolutely incredible, and there wasn't a second where I forgot where I'd come from; that just over a year ago it was a half-drunk bloke on keyboards and the *Tales of the Unexpected* theme tune instead of 'Nessun Dorma' – and look where I was now.

I remember thinking, Wow, this is it, this is the pinnacle. It doesn't get any better than this. Here I am commanding the Royal Philharmonic Orchestra on my first record. This isn't too shabby.

It was during recording that my nickname first came about – and a title for the record was born.

Imagine my day at work then. I had a flat in London for the recording and I'd get up in the morning; the first person I'd see would be my manager.

'All right, mate,' he'd say, 'how's the voice this morning?'

'It's all right, yeah.'

In the kitchen Bill might be eating a bowl of cornflakes.

'Oh, good morning, Russell, how's the voice?'

'Yes, it's not bad, it's all right, thank you.'

Jump in the car, over to the studio and my producer, Nick Patrick, would be there saying, 'Mate, how's the voice today?'

'It's all right, thanks.'

Then one of the record-company guys would come over, Mark Cavell usually, saying, 'Hello, Russ, how's it going, how's the recording going, mate?'

'Yeah, yeah, not bad, Mark.'

'How's the voice?'

'The voice is all right, but when's somebody going to ask how I am?'

It became as though the voice was disconnected from me; some kind of separate entity. I was just the guy who carried it around. The nickname stuck – plus we had a title for the first album: *The Voice*.

Next the record came out, of course, and that's when the fun really started.

CHAPTER TWENTY-NINE

January 9, 2008

I can smell burning flesh.

'Hm,' I say to myself, in my best Homer Simpson voice, 'burning flesh.'

But I'm used to it by now, the smell of burning flesh. I'm used to the sheer size of this machine. I'm used to the deafening volume of the thing as it makes its way around my poor, battered head.

It's like a big dome thing suspended on an arm, and it moves around in different directions. The first treatment is to the left and then to the right, then on top. At each stage it shoots a beam into my head. It's loud, there's that smell. Each session a fresh assault on already assaulted senses.

It's not actually burning flesh, thank goodness, but that's the way it smells. A seared, metallic scent. And even though I can't feel the laser, I get a very strong sense of it being there. It's more like a feeling, really. An impression. A nagging sensation that something is boring into my skull.

It zaps one side, then the other. Next, it's the bed's turn to move. It rotates 90 degrees, so the dome first does the back of my head then moves over to do the front. In all, there are four zap points.

First couple of days I felt very tired and nauseous. We were laughing because they asked me, 'How are you feeling?'

'Okay, but I've been feeling a bit sick.'

'Ah, well, we've got some tablets for sickness.'

'Right,' I said, imagining a fresh lot of pills for Gary and Victoria to dispense. Any more pills and we'd have to buy a wheel-barrow. 'Have you got any tablets for people who are sick of taking sickness tablets, or just sick of taking tablets in general?'

They laughed: 'Yeah, we probably have.'

My taste has gone, that's another by-product of the radio-therapy. I've got a constant metallic taste in my mouth, which isn't nice, so things that I usually enjoy, like wine, now taste like I'm drinking soapy water.

'What did you wash this glass with, Gary?' I said the first time, pulling a face.

'Er, usual, Russ,' he replied, and it clicked that it was just a side effect. Tell you what, though, my hair's still hanging on. Go, hair!

Meantime, it's the same. Every day. The medieval torture device. The felt-tip pen. Touching soup.

Then, the other day, reality seemed to pierce the routine. I could feel the tension in the back of my neck, feel myself becoming more rigid. And that overpowering mechanical noise. Normally I can zone it out, but suddenly it wouldn't fade into the background, this noise that seemed to push in on my head. The smell.

Oh my God, I was thinking, what's it doing to my head, this thing? I could feel the medieval device seem to tighten round my skull. The gum piece in my mouth felt as though it was expanding, filling my mouth, constricting my tongue, and I was wanting to gag, trying to pull myself together, thinking, Just go to your usual place; the place where you disconnect yourself from the room and think about a game of pool with Gary or what you'll do with the kids this weekend, or anything but this...

Noise.

They give you a thing to hold, like a panic button, except it's a pull-cord. My fingers tighten around it. One pull and it would grind to a halt. Emergency stop. Penalty for improper use, one extra radiotherapy session.

I don't. I pull myself together, thinking, *Don't be so bloody soft.*

And soon, it's over.

I'm telling the nurse about it as she comes to get me out of the machine, but what she hears must sound like, 'Hmfrhphrfh,' because she grins at me.

'The other nurses have been telling me you never shut up,' she says.

'Hthrmph?' I say.

'Apparently you're the only person who ever tries to talk with the mouthpiece in.'

'Hfrthrymp.'

Six down, though, nineteen to go.

Meantime, I keep taking my pills, working out to stay strong, knocking around the house growling at Gary and Victoria one minute, making them laugh the next. I still have my hair and to be honest the side effects aren't too bad. What's a tastebud between friends? They tell me it gets worse, though; they'll start soon. It continues way after the radiotherapy course has finished as well. Sickness, lethargy, mood swings. Got that to look forward to. And I watch films, play on the PlayStation. I haven't tried my vocal scales in a while. Don't seem to have the energy.

September 2000

The Voice came out on September 23, and I remember that despite all my confidence my expectations for it were actually quite low, certainly nowhere near the level of sales we eventually achieved. But it built and built, and at the time of writing it's still selling. It's the biggest-selling classical record of all time in the UK.

And the sales took us all by surprise. Sales drive a promotional campaign. You do some promotion and if the record sells you do some more, until the record's selling well, and suddenly you're not promoting the record any more, you're responding to a demand – a demand created by the sales, which, you hope, are driven up by the promotion you do.

Make sense? What it means is that you promote the arse out of the record and if you do your job successfully then you stay promoting it till it stops selling. It's now not far off triple platinum. I mean, most classical artists can expect around 40,000, and we hoped to do better than that as we felt it had broader appeal, so when it went gold at 100,000 that was like the dizzy heights for us. Then it just took on a life of its own; it went through the roof. People connected with the music and with my factory-floor-to-bestselling-singer story, which I'd go on to tell thousands of times over the next five years or so. Then, later, there was the business with David Mellor, the 'dumbing down' debate in all the papers, which, again, believe it or not, helped sales.

The period of promotion went for – what? – three years? For two more albums, anyway. And in that time I didn't stop, my feet hardly touched the ground.

It went so, say I was doing a regional tour. I'd be in the UK for a period of about a week doing what they call a regional tour, which means travelling the length and breadth of the country visiting regional radio stations, going into the station, plugging the record, doing an interview, singing a couple of songs, jumping back into the radio plugger's car, then driving 40 miles down the road to, say, Newcastle, where I'd get to the radio station, do a quick interview, back in the car, flit off down the road to, say, Sunderland, quick interview there at the BBC, chat, then, seven or eight stations later, we'd be in the car on our way to London.

'You're doing *GMTV* first thing in the morning.'

Get to London at 2 a.m., check into the hotel, attempt to wind down and sleep. Can't sleep, hectic day, better drink a bottle of wine. Bed at 3 a.m., semi-cooked, alarm goes at six, into *GMTV* for eight because I've got to do a rehearsal before my appearance at nine. Do a quick rehearsal: 'One, two, one, two.' Do the show, sing a song, quick interview ('So, just a year ago you were playing working men's clubs in Salford, Russell?' 'Yes, that's right, Lorraine...'), back in the car and we're doing the such-and-such interview this afternoon at the BBC. Down to the BBC, do the interview ('So, just a year ago you were playing working men's clubs in Salford, Russell?' 'Yes, that's right, Such-and-such...'), then maybe do a couple of radio stations in London for what we call ISDNs. That's when you go to a BBC studio and they hook you up on a high-quality digital link so you can do an interview with a radio station in Scotland and it sounds as though you're right there in the studio with them. But we're not, of course. We don't have the time to go to Scotland, next stop *The Des O'Connor Christmas Special*. They're filming it early this year. Get to the studio.

'What suit are you wearing?'

'Well, I'm wearing this one.'

'That one?'

'Yes, this one.'

'Right, let's have a look for the cameras... Okay, yeah, that's cool...'

Stage manager comes in: 'What we're going to do, Des is going to walk on here and *blah blah blah,* and you stand here, *blah, blah, blah,* and if Des asks you a question you answer it, *blah blah...*'

Do you remember that teacher in *Peanuts*? All you ever heard of his voice was that *blah, blah* sound, which is what I hear from the stage manager, me thinking, Right, so if Des asks me a question I should go ahead and reply, should I, not just ignore him? Thanks for the advice. Oh, and I have to stand here, do I? This 'stage' area? Good advice. Thanks for that.

I feel annoyed and put it down to lack of sleep that I never catch up on. I do the performance, sing the song, remember to answer Des when he asks me a question ('So, just a year ago you were playing working men's clubs in Salford, Russell?' 'Yes, that's right, Des...'), remember to stand in the 'stage' area with all the cameras pointing at it and not out in the audience, go back for drinks after-wards, jump in a car and get back to the hotel at midnight. But can I sleep? No, hectic day, better drink a bottle of wine. Bed at 3 a.m., semi-cooked, alarm goes at 5 a.m., we're off to New York. Get on an aeroplane, over to America, and America is hard work because you're jetlagged as well, so when the alarm goes at 5 a.m. because I'm doing *Good Morning America* and they've got to do the soundcheck before the show goes on air at seven, my body is insisting it's the middle of the night. It's in protest. Bugger off and let me sleep, it's saying. But time's precious, so I'm up with the alarm, getting myself ready, rubbing my poor head because I went to bed semi-cooked last night, get down to the studio at six and do my soundcheck between six and seven, 'One, two, one, two', to do *Good Morning America*. ('So, just a year ago you were playing, uh, "working men's clubs" in...uh Manchestire, Russell?' 'Yes, that's right, Diane...') I'm jetlagged to buggery at this point, but anyway, I do it, and then, next day, the same thing again, only somewhere different. Press, radio, TV. From America to New Zealand. From New Zealand to Australia. Australia to Japan. Japan to Portugal. Portugal back to the UK for a regional tour, then back to America, because the TV companies would be saying, Hey, we loved having Russell on, we'd like him back. I did *Good Morning America* five times in 2002. And there weren't breaks. There weren't holidays. If time off was pencilled in, then something always seemed to crop up.

'We're going to Spain, Russ.'

'Oh, what? I thought I was having three days off.'

'Well, it's come in, it's a last-minute thing...' and it was always a last-minute thing according to management and the label. Always can't miss this show because it's such a great opportunity and if you pass up this opportunity it'll be the end of your career.

And I was missing the kids: Rebecca and baby Hannah. How I missed them. I phoned them every day, a life of snatched moments on the phone: 'Hello, darling, how are you? Me? Well, I'm in America and it's very late at night here.'

Birthdays. The family gets a phone call. Me in the middle of the night in some hotel room, croaking 'Happy Birthday' down the phone to them. 'Hi, Mum, I'm in Japan.' Take a look at the cover of the second record, *Encore*. It's a picture of me on an airport walkway. It was the only place we could do the shoot.

And I was getting no time at home. I loved what I was doing but I never had a chance to enjoy the rewards because everything was focused around work; everything, my whole life was just a plane trip, and I don't want to moan – I was leading a life many people dream of, and believe me, I never forget that – but it's hard. It's hard when you never see your friends and your family or even sleep in your own bed. I remember going home to my house and not even recognising the place, going through the door and literally not recognising it. I'd forgotten what my own bed felt like. And it's not like you can opt out. Doing all that, it's a part of your job. The singing bit, that's the good bit. The slogging around the world – and it quickly does become a slog – that's the hard part.

I remember my first-ever TV. It was around the time of the Old Trafford performance and I was on *Granada Tonight*. I was nervous, which was a first. Probably because it was such an alien environment to me: all those cameras, and the studio floor a blank, wire-tangled space where I was used to seeing an audience. I walked into the studio, saw four television cameras and I remember looking from one to the other wondering which one I was supposed to direct my singing towards. Where do I look? What do I do? There could be a million people watching me tonight…

I was introduced to the presenter, Lucy Meacock. 'What are you likely to ask me?' I said. 'Do you know what the first question will be?'

'Right,' she said, 'well, we'll probably ask you something along the lines of when you started singing, then, who have been your greatest inspirations. How does that sound?'

'Fine.'

I thought, Right. And I mulled over some answers until I had what I thought were suitable responses. When did I first start singing? In the dormer at Sunningdale Drive, strumming along with my Beatles songbook. Greatest inspiration? That would be Luciano, not forgetting Mario Lanza.

Then came the performance. I sang 'Nessun Dorma', still not quite sure which camera to look at, but it went off all right. When I'd finished, Lucy moved over to ask me some questions, me thinking, Beatles songbook. Luciano Pavarotti. My prepared answers to the questions she'd said she would ask.

'So, Russell,' she said.

'Yes,' I said, my prepared answer coiled behind my gums.

'Where does that voice come from?'

What? Where does that voice come from?

'Uh...' I said, thinking, Never mind where the voice comes from. Where the bloody hell was the question she was supposed to ask? 'Uh...' I stammered. 'Out of my mouth?'

I learnt three things from that appearance. First, never prepare your answers. Don't even find out what the interviewer's going to ask. You lose spontaneity that way; you make a balls-up when things don't go according to plan.

Second, don't worry about the cameras. Just do what you do and they'll follow you. Those guys standing behind them with headphones on? That's their job. Third, when you're on TV, don't think of the millions of people who might be watching. Or, rather, don't think of them as a million people all glued to their screens that very second. Think about your uncle John at home, scratching his arse while he's having a cup of tea and a bun, not really paying attention to the telly. Think about the kids running round the room and tripping over, and Mum saying, 'You've got that felt tip all over my white carpet.'

They're the lessons I took onto the treadmill. They're how I got through what became hundreds, maybe even thousands, of TV appearances over the next few years. It didn't take long before nothing could faze me. Nothing could put me off my stride. TV appearances went from being something I was nervous about, learning the ropes and picking up the tricks of the trade, to something exciting, 'I'm going to be on TV. People will recognise me in the street', to something commonplace, just another day at the office.

But nobody gets away without putting the work in. I did them all: all the daytime TV shows, *Richard and Judy*, *GMTV*, loads of big Christmas Specials, *Children In Need*, *The Royal Variety Show* – the lot. And it was crazy.

One or two, like the Rolling Stones or Elton, they can achieve all that exposure from a tour. You won't see the Stones doing daytime TV because frankly they don't need to. Everybody else, they're either about to go on the treadmill, they're on the treadmill or in rehab because they couldn't handle the pressure of the treadmill. After a couple of years, people start talking about burnout. I remember somebody saying to me, 'Mate, if you carry on like this you'll be burnt out in five years.'

I thought then, But that's in three years' time. Plenty of opportunity to have a rest between now and then.

But there isn't. Sales of the first record were massive – it wasn't far off gold. There was talk of me breaking America, which meant going back and forth to the States – at one point I was number one in the classical charts in both the UK and the US. So, when it came to making the second record it seemed like a good idea to set up camp in the States.

Plus, of course, things were going badly at home and I suddenly found myself needing to let the dust settle. In the space of what felt like months I'd gone from being the cheeky chappie, loveable chap from Irlam to the latest tabloid love rat.

My marriage had gone to the wall.

CHAPTER THIRTY-ONE

Hannah was born on November 13, 2000, just two months after *The Voice* was released. She was born at Park Hospital, and once again I found myself in a room with a cordon, seeing little Hannah for the first time and feeling love flower and bloom through me.

Shortly after that, Helen and I split up. In the papers, the theme of the story was that I was a heartless pig. You know the kind of thing: changed by fame, Russell Watson leaves the wife who supported him through the hard times. There were quite a few stories about it, but I took the decision not to say a word to the press in return. I left them to it and I kept it buttoned, because it wasn't worth it. My thoughts were with Rebecca and Hannah. It was them I missed when I was away; they, who, no matter what happened between Helen and me, will always be the most important things in my life.

I thought, Okay, say what you want about me, slag me off as much as you like, but I've got two lovely, healthy kids and there's nothing I'm going to do to jeopardise the relationship I have with them, not just for a bit of titillation over the cornflakes.

Even if I'd wanted to hit back, there would have been no point because there's nothing more difficult to untangle than a divorce. For a start, the roots of the break-up – because that's what it was, a break-up, I didn't *leave* Helen – went back years. Years that we'd spent arguing like cat and dog. For the sake of diplomacy I'll fully admit it was six of one and half a dozen of the other, but this belief that fame stepped in, swelled my head and made me leave Helen in the lurch isn't really true. We were a warring couple, no different from millions of other warring couples. We argued about the same things that every other unhappy couple does: the kids, money, family, my job. And we split up because that's how it always ends. Something has to give, it has to break.

And that's what happened. Any other details, like I say, they're just tabloid titillation; they'd simply be raking over old ground.

And you know what? I'm glad I decided to play it that way. No, things didn't work out with Helen; we went our separate ways and it got a bit unpleasant at the time. But the relationship is on an even keel these days. We get on well these days, and she's been great about bringing the kids to the hospital when I've been ill. So, yes, I'm glad I kept quiet.

I did the same when I later had problems with my managers. Because apart from being branded a love rat in the press, I was also being painted as a heartless exploitation artist, leaving loyal managers in my greedy wake.

There was a court case that lasted from 1999 to 2003, and believe me, there were two sets of winners in that one: their lawyers and my lawyers. Another manager went to the press for an extra lot of Russell-Watson-changed-and-dropped-me-like-a-stone stories. He was going to sue, he said, as was a third manager. So, to the casual newspaper reader, I must have looked like a real baddie. In the end, though, two of the three courts cases simply never happened. Why? Well, because the truth was a bit more complicated than me getting a big head and walking out on them.

It didn't stop it going in the papers, though; didn't stop people believing the worst of me. That's a lesson you learn the hard way.

CHAPTER THIRTY-TWO

And all this madness was happening at the same time. Marriage break-up, management stuff, relentless promotion: 'We're going to New York to record the second album.' The treadmill never stops. I really wasn't joking when I told George Bush that I didn't have time to play for him on Air Force One. He didn't mind, though, old George; he had me back to play at the White House, on the West Lawn. And this is going forward a bit now, July 4, 2003, Independence Day. I was on to sing 'God Bless America', plus Aretha Franklin was on, too, and what a great diva she turned out to be.

To be honest I'm always a bit disappointed when the legends you meet are too humble and down-to-earth. The more eccentric and diva-esque the behaviour the better as far as I'm concerned, so you can imagine how cool it was to see Aretha Franklin throwing a fit at TV producers on the White House lawn. Remember before, how I was saying that TV people would test the patience of a saint, telling you to answer when Des O'Connor asks you a question and make sure you don't accidentally leave the building, that kind of thing? Well, most people just grit their teeth and put up with it. I did, anyway, especially at the beginning of my career. Not the Arethas of this world. For a start, she wouldn't do rehearsals, snapping, 'What do you mean, rehearsal? I've been doing this for forty years, I don't *need* no rehearsal.'

'Right, Aretha, okay.'

And she's a big lady now, Aretha, she doesn't get around too easily. So you can imagine, she doesn't take it all that well when people start giving her stage directions. One guy tried: 'Okay, Aretha, you're going to come on over here and then we want you to walk to the middle and then over to the left, maybe over to the right and walk forward to the front of the stage...'

As he'd been talking she'd been giving him a look that would freeze heat, staring at him as though he had taken leave of his senses, until he eventually dried up, his sentence tailing off.

'What?' she snapped, and he visibly paled. 'Let me tell you something, honey,' said Aretha. 'I come on stage, I sing a song and then I leave the stage. You *got* that, honey?'

He got the point. Aretha did it her way and brought the house down, of course.

That same year, I did a First Lady Luncheon for Laura Bush, something I did in my capacity as an official United Nations Goodwill Ambassador. There I had my picture taken with Laura Bush, Cherie Blair and Lynn Cheney, the wife of vice-president Dick Cheney. And I tell you what, I never once pointed to a copy of that picture, put on my best pimp voice and said, 'Hey, here's a picture of me and my laydeez.' No, never did that once. Scout's honour.

But it was two years earlier, again in Washington, that I first got to meet the President and his wife. This time because they were attending an event called the ABC Gala: An American Celebration at Ford's Theatre, which is known as America's most famous theatre, mainly because that's where Lincoln had been assassinated.

Even for that time – where I seemed to be doing monumental stuff on an almost daily basis – it was a huge gig for me, and the Colonel flew over to Washington with me, which was great. Only problem was, I was ill; I'd developed a throat infection. Arriving in Washington the infection was so bad I had to go straight to bed, lying in the hotel, fretting about the gig the next day – I was supposed to be singing for the President of the United States, one of the biggest gigs of my life – croaking at people, 'My throat hurts.' Sounding like a whispering Donald Duck. 'I can't believe my bloody throat hurts and I've got to sing for George Bush, tomorrow, live on United States network TV.'

Ten years of performing in smoke-filled pubs and clubs and barely a sore throat. Now I had the leader of the free world to entertain, suddenly I'm laid up. Brilliant.

The Colonel organised for a doctor to come and see me and the guy came in, had a look, straightened and said, 'Oh dear, it's all looking rather bleak, I'm afraid.'

The Colonel and I looked at one another, each imagining the headlines: *Russell Watson Cancels Prez For Saucy Night With Stripper.* Something like that, anyway.

'But,' said the doctor, throwing us a lifeline, 'there is one thing we can do...'

He prescribed some special American all-singing, all-dancing tablets, warning me that 'they're very strong', and at the same time giving me an injection, a high-concentration dose of vitamin B12. I was told it would give me a bit of energy.

The next day – the day of the gig, this was – I woke up feeling better and went along for rehearsals.

The security there, you wouldn't have believed it. Maybe it's like the Ford's Theatre is a sore point for the Secret Service after that major security breach of 1865 or something, but they were taking no chances. The full works: guys in shades with earpieces talking into their sleeves. Cops in mirrored sunglasses straddling CHiPs-style bikes, chewing gum and staring at you like they were deciding whether or not to open fire. We were given passes, shuffling laminates to show to security guards, passing bags through scanners, more searches as we moved through one security checkpoint to the next, until at last we came in on the main theatre, where the conductor was shouting at his orchestra.

'I'm just not feeling this, guys. I'm not feeling it. I need a little breeze here.'

Did I tell you that the first film I ever saw at the cinema was *Rocky*? It was, and like most people, the scene that stayed with me was the one where Rocky goes out for an early morning run and runs up the steps of the Philadelphia Museum of Art. It's the music that really makes that scene, of course; the composer Bill Conti was nominated for an Oscar for it.

And here he was, the very same Bill Conti, standing in the middle of Ford's Theatre giving his orchestra a bollocking, the concert just hours away. I was used to English conductors, who never raise their voice, and if they need to bollock a member of the orchestra they do it *nicely*: 'Well, that was jolly good, but I wonder if next time we might give it just a little bit more power, if that would be all right with you? I mean, if that's okay?'

But this guy was different. Conti had a hold of these people and he was squeezing them; he was making sure they were giving him everything they had. He was mental. Absolutely mental. But I could see what he was doing, and I could see that it would get results because a good conductor can make all the difference – all the difference between an orchestra sounding okay or a bit indifferent; to it sounding great or amazing. Sure, a lot of conductors can just roll up, wave their batons, turn around every now and then and flash a grin at the audience and everything will sound fine. Technically, the orchestra will play well. But you get a guy up there who's passionate and enthusiastic about it and the orchestra will respond to that. The noise they make is just better. I've only met a few like it, and Bill Conti was one of those.

'Horns. Hey, horns over there,' he bawled at a frightened-looking brass section, 'I want you to knock me off this stage, I want to feel this.

'Tiger, tiger. Yeah, you on the strings. I want to see those strings bowing. I want it, I want it.'

Never rude, exactly, but you were in no doubt what he wanted, and that he was going to get it, with you, or without you. And you know what? When the music struck up again, those violins were bowing, and we were all feeling the breeze.

We were introduced and I could see him looking at me, probably thinking, God, who's this guy? *This guy* is going to sing 'Nessun Dorma'?

Getting up on stage for my rehearsal, I watched him. The orchestra started and I sang the beginning of 'Nessun Dorma', but not really singing it properly, just marking the music, really. And I could see Conti looking round at me, his face dropping, probably already composing the speech he was about to make. The one about this limey who can't sing. So I waited until the middle section of the song and then I let rip, all guns blazing, the whole lot.

'Fuck me,' he shouted when the song was done. 'Was that you?'

'Yeah,' I laughed.

'Fuck. Me.'

I love that reaction. I love doing that to people. It used to happen a lot, especially in that mad period I'm talking about when I was promoting the early records, and particularly in America. I'd walk into a station and they'd have no idea who I was; I'd often turn up in a tracksuit and baseball cap because that's the kind of gear I usually wear. Stations would be like, 'Okay, uh, you're Russell, are you? Okay, if you say so. We're ready for you now, just want to do a quick soundcheck.'

I'd do the soundcheck and the same guys would come up to me afterwards: 'Hey, man, looking like that I thought you were going to be a rapper or something, then this goddamn opera comes out your mouth.'

I remember doing *Good Morning America* for the first time and

Diane Sawyer, who was main anchorwoman, saying to me, 'It's unbelievable. You just don't look the way you sound.' And I loved doing it. Again, it may be another reason I've never truly been accepted by the classical music mafia in this country. It's because I don't live up to a stereotype.

I did the gig. I was running on vitamins, these super-strength throat tablets and a healthy dose of adrenalin. Walking on stage to sing 'Nessun Dorma', I caught sight of President Bush and his wife Laura in the front row and winked at them.

I did the song and despite the throat problems hit the note at the end. Afterwards, I met President Bush and his wife, Laura, and I had a weird moment where my head tried to make sense of the two President Bushes: the President Bush I'd seen on TV thousands of times, 'Dubya', and the one standing right here in front of me. It was as though he'd stepped down out of the TV; he was exactly the same in the flesh as he is standing front of the cameras. Polite, firm, kind of bemused-looking.

'It's good to meet you, Russell,' he said.

We got talking. I asked him what he was doing at the moment. 'Well,' he said, 'we're just about to go over to Europe actually. We're going over to Holland and then from there we're going to Belgium.'

'Oh, fantastic,' I said.

'You know, you should come and sing for us on Air Force One,' he suggested.

'I'm sorry,' I said. 'I'm a bit busy myself at the moment.'

He laughed. They both did. I think I must have been a hit with Laura because like I say she invited me back for the ladies' luncheon. 'What is it you say in the UK?' said President Bush. 'You're cheeky. You're a cheeky man.'

I suppose it was a bit cheeky. Too busy to sing on Air Force One. True, though...

CHAPTER THIRTY-THREE

Still taking the tablets to ward off the throat infection, I jumped on a flight from Washington to New York because I was doing the morning show on CBS the following day. After that I had a rare night off that I was due to spend with Kevin Gore from Universal. The CBS thing went well, and the night out with Kevin began. My manager was there, too, plus we'd been joined by Sir Bill. Kevin was being very generous with the champagne in the restaurant. Gradually, a civilised American meal out had started creeping into not-so-civilised good-old-English-piss-up territory.

And here's where it all goes a bit hazy. The first thing I remember is feeling odd, very odd. Spaced out and dizzy. As though normal Russell had been called in by his mum for tea and bad Russell had stayed out to play.

The next thing was laying into Kevin Gore. I seem to recall saying he was 'bloody useless' at some point, but useless at what, I don't remember. Subbuteo, perhaps? Sorry, Kevin. If you ever read this, I really don't know what came over me. Well, I do, actually. It was super-strength throat infection tablets and Krug.

After that, we took our leave and I found myself in the back of a record-company limo with Sir Bill, being driven back to our hotel. Next thing you know, Bill and I are *wrestling* in the back of the limo, in blissful ignorance of the fact that the limo had pulled up to the Trump International, and a porter was reaching to open the door.

Sir Bill and I fell out of the limo. We *literally* fell out of the limo, rolling out onto the pavement outside the Trump, porters and God knows whoever else just open-mouthed, staring at us, me in my mid-thirties, Bill in his sixties, rolling around on the pavement giggling like kids. It was like a scene from *Arthur*.

'Everything okay there, sir?' said a porter, peering down at us.

Have you seen that film *The Mask*, where Jim Carrey puts on the mask and the repressed part of his personality comes out? He becomes this party-loving wild man? That was me that night.

Strolling into reception at the Trump, off my face on champagne and throat tablets, I told my manager and Sir Bill, 'Right, we're going to a party.'

'We're not going to a party, you're going to bed,' said my manager. 'You're wasted.'

Bill agreed. 'I think it's probably time that you went to bed now, Russell, you're getting a bit out of hand.'

But I was on a mission, leading them in the direction of a ballroom just off reception from where I could hear music. The sound of... a party.

We let ourselves in and were approached by a waiter, who said, 'Sir, are you a guest of Mr Clinton's?'

I didn't miss a beat.

'Yes,' I said, 'me and Bill are like that,' crossing my fingers. 'In fact, where is Bill?'

'I think he's left, sir,' replied the waiter.

'Ah, in that case, let's have a bottle of Dom Perignon then, please.'

He brought us a tray with glasses and a bottle of Dom Perignon, while around us friends of Bill Clinton's enjoyed the tail-end of what had obviously been an extremely lavish event.

Another bottle of Dom Perignon came, Mask-wearing Russell still in full effect as gradually I became aware of the band. They were on a stage, playing background music you could barely hear over the chatter coming from the tables, so I stood up, walked over and went up to speak to the piano player, tapping him on the shoulder.

'Sorry to interrupt,' I said, 'but we're personal guests of Mr Clinton's and he wants us to do a little number.'

'Sorry?'

'Yes, he'd like us to do a little number. My pianist is here. This is the world-renowned Sir William Hayward.'

'Oh, okay.'

He gestured to the rest of the band, who stopped as I gathered Sir Bill and we took our places.

Definitely an ''O Sole Mio' moment.

There must have been five hundred people in the room and all of them turned to look at me as I started singing, calling a sudden end to the polite background music they'd been accustomed to. All, it seemed, apart from a group at the back, chatting, and as the song came to its climax, I stopped, said, 'Bill, just a minute,' and he stopped too as I drunkenly addressed the crowd at the back.

'Excuse me,' I called. They all looked around, all of them stopped chatting, and I swear it was like a re-run of that night in Wigan, just five years ago, when I stopped going into autopilot. I couldn't help myself. It was the club singer in me, only instead of talking to a few people at Batley Conservative Club, it was to a bunch of Bill Clinton's friends in a ballroom of the Trump International, in New York. 'Yeah, that's right, I mean you.' I had their attention. 'So, you know next week, when you're sat at your desks at work and you're in your office and you're trying to concentrate on what you're doing?' I said. 'You know what I'm going to do? I'm going to come in and start having a conversation with my friends. Right in front of you.'

It was something like that anyway. I must have put it a bit more politely than that, come to think of it, because in the next moment they were all laughing, the whole room was laughing, and I went back into the song, into the final note, which I hit and sustained – amazing, considering my current state.

Even after all that, *Mask*-Russell wasn't satisfied, and I spent the rest of the evening either being – how shall I put this? – 'mischievous' with ladies I spoke to or offending my manager and Sir Bill.

'What's the matter with you two?' I said the next morning, rubbing my head, a blank space where the memory of last night should have been. And they stared balefully back at me.

'Oh, nothing,' said Sir Bill, 'but the drunken man talks the truth, though, doesn't he, Russell?'

'What? What did I say?'

I looked at the bottle of tablets later and the reasons for my behaviour hit me. There was a warning. Something along the lines of 'NEVER take with alcohol'. Suddenly I understood. And looking back on it now, that night, it's weird because in a way I wish I could have had more nights like it. As in *The Mask*, it brought out a side of me I know is in there, but that I rarely let out. For a start, I tend never to drink in public, not unless it's an environment with people I know and trust, and we can get dressed up in costumes and play bar football.

Yes, you did read that correctly. Even as a grown man of over forty I'm still organising the equivalent of Super Striker tournaments – except now it's with bar football. I invite a bunch of mates along to the house and we have mad tournaments that go on long into the night and next morning. Everyone has their own teams (mine's Watland Town of course, Alistair has Ally's Academicals, Trevor has Queen of the South), we wear stupid wigs and duke it out on the bar football. We film it, too, and managers have to give tongue-in-cheek post-match interviews, complete with daft wig. God help us if it ever gets on YouTube…

Chapter Thirty-three

So I don't drink out in public, plus I've never been one of those who goes out 'round the town' being the big-time Charlie. Russell Watson lamping photographers outside China White on a Saturday night, Mystery Blonde bringing up the rear. It's just not a scene I'm into. He must be in there, though, the bloke who likes all that. He certainly came out to play that night.

CHAPTER THIRTY-FOUR

There's no time for hangovers. There wasn't for me in 2001, anyway. In June, which was the same month I performed for George W. Bush and missus one night and Bill Clinton's mates the next, I was nominated for two awards at the Classical Brit Awards, so came back for the ceremony.

I won two, Album of the Year and Best-Selling Debut, both for *The Voice*. The following year, this time with *Encore* under my belt, I went back and won another two. I remember I was presented with the awards by Lulu, who I'd recorded with – a song called 'The Prayer' on the new album – and Mohamed Al-Fayed, who turned out to be a big fan. My mum and dad were sitting in the audience – and who doesn't want that, eh? Making their mum and dad proud like that? So it was fantastic, the first industry recognition that I'd had, which is important no matter what anyone says. I mean, it goes without saying that it's recognition from the public that really gets you going because that's the ultimate accolade: you're liked; you're liked enough for people to buy your albums and get tickets to your concerts. But getting the respect of your peers brings with it a different kind of satisfaction.

Turns out you can't have both, though. I felt I was on a crest of a wave with those awards, and in one sense I was, but around the time of that second Brit awards ceremony there was a debate in the classical music world about 'dumbing down'. Sir Thomas Allen, one of the top opera singers in the country, went public with remarks about the crossover artists who make the jump from the classical charts to the pop charts: Vanessa Mae was one of his targets, the violin quartet Bond another. Plus, of course, yours truly.

'The recording business is in decline and seeking a way to sustain itself,' blustered Sir Tom, 'so it produces all these gimmicks, the wet T-shirts and pubescence, and we're looking at a diminution of quality.'

He didn't stop there. Wet T-shirts sent him all of a lather, because the idea of people in wet T-shirts 'where once there had been Amadeus', had him 'reaching for the sea-sick pills, or even just retching', he said. And if you're wondering just where that comes from – all that about wet T-shirts – well, you're not alone. If Bond ever wore wet T-shirts, then sadly I missed that issue. Me, I tend to wear dry T-shirts. I virtually insist upon them.

Next, David Mellor laid into me on Classic FM, plus he had a newspaper column and he used to enjoy the odd dig there, too. Constantly, it seemed, critics would be having a go, and not just for the quality of the album – because that's subjective and everyone's entitled to their opinion about that – but talking as though I were *damaging* classical music in some way.

Sorry, but how could I be doing that? How could I, or Charlotte, or Bond – whoever – be hurting classical music? For a start, I was having big-selling records. Those records were making money for my record company, which is Decca, the classical arm of Universal. So any money I made for Decca was going right back into classical music. How could I be hurting classical music? I was helping it.

Secondly, thanks to me and Charlotte and Bond and the like, more and more people were listening to classical music. Sir Thomas Allen would of course have said that we were introducing people to the easy bits of classical music. Our wet T-shirt aficionado spoke of 'sugar-coated programming' and 'easy listening'. But even if you think that 'difficult' music somehow has more value – which I don't – so what? Isn't that how people are introduced to classical music? When I first got into classical music in my mum's kitchen it wasn't because she was playing hard-to-digest 15-minute movements of Mahler symphonies. It was because she was playing songs and melodies that stuck in my head and made me want to hear more. That'll be the easy bits, then. How many people have heard classical music used on TV and films and been inspired to investigate further? Yes, and why? Because it's good music and it's been presented to them in a way they understand. Maybe it's dumbing down to watch *Platoon* or *2001: A Space Odyssey* then go to the shop and buy the music. Maybe that's wet T-shirt music in Sir Tim Allen's opinion.

The result of all this sniping was that just at a period when it seemed I was able to combine sales with the respect of my peers, suddenly the drawbridge came up: the classical music establishment just didn't want to know. For a start, I was never invited to another Brit awards. Having begun my romance with them and winning two awards in two consecutive years, suddenly I wasn't invited back. In fact, at the time of writing I've yet to even be invited to another Classical Brit Awards ceremony. I've never been asked to perform at the Proms, either. Plus, there's a marked difference between the way I'm treated by big-name orchestras in this country and the way I'm treated by big-name orchestras in other countries.

As always, I kept schtum. Well, *almost*. Asked what I'd say to David Mellor if I bumped into him, I replied, darkly, 'If I bumped into David Mellor, then I'd bump into David Mellor...'

I shouldn't have said that, I suppose. It's the kind of response that doesn't exactly help matters. But come on. In a review of *The*

Voice, he'd said, 'To succeed, you need training and taste, and thus far [Russell Watson] has not been blessed with an abundance of either.'

This about an album that had already gone gold. And what did he know about my training? As it turned out, nowt.

Certainly, I played up to the 'us and them' environment that some of the comments created. I know the public picked up on it, too, and they liked it; they thought, 'Yeah, good for him, he's one of us,' and if anything it drew more people in. It may have been that the opera mafia didn't like it that I'd made my name singing classical music in pubs and clubs, but as more and more of the public became aware of my roots there, the more support I got. They'd been listening to classical music on football programmes for years (perhaps the Three Tenors also incurred Sir Tim's wrath for dumbing down, although I must have missed him slagging them off), so the idea of bringing classical music out of Covent Garden and into people's everyday lives wasn't new. Me taking it into the clubs and up the pop charts, that was new. And people liked it.

There were mistakes my end, of course. I'm not entirely blameless. There was an incident when my manager rang Classic FM and demanded all my CDs back. They complied, keeping one for their library. Looking back, it wasn't the best move in the world and I guess if I ever did have problems with Classic FM then I need look no further than that incident. Not good, I accept that. After that little PR coup my manager went on to suggest that Classic FM should rename themselves 'Class FM', trying to turn it into a class issue and making cracks about me not going to the right school or wearing the right tie. Again, unhelpful in the climate. I cringe, sometimes, to think of it.

Then, of course, there was this enduring misconception that mine is an untrained voice. This was another piece of propaganda likely to get the establishment's back up because training and discipline is what they're all about. Anybody who looks like they've gone a different route, well, you're seen as not quite paying your dues. I can understand that, and I am guilty of playing up the untrained voice thing, but the truth is, *of course* I've had training. Virtually from the day I decided to start singing classical, from the night of the 'Nesty Doormat' suggestion – I've been getting coaching for my voice. I'm a factory worker from Salford, for pity's sake. Yes, I had the raw materials, but I needed someone to show me how to use them. So first there was Valerie Watts. After her was the esteemed composer and vocal coach David Dubery, who was vocal coach for the Northern Ballet for sixteen years. After him, of course, Sir Bill, who's now my musical director and conductor. He loves to tell it like this, and I often trot out my Sir Bill impression to recall him saying, 'Yes, when I first met Russell he was a little bit like a learner driver at the wheel of a Ferrari, lots of power, but very little control,' and it was Sir Bill who helped me find some of that control as well as teaching me about classical music. It may have been my mum who inspired a love of classical music, but it was Sir Bill who gave me a lot of the knowledge I have; who helped with the operas and with the language. I used to spend hours with him, watching operas, leaning over, asking him questions: 'What's he singing now? What's going on in this bit?' Thank God for his patience, eh?

These days I use a coach called Patrick McGuigan who's trained a lot of the singers from the Met, New York – that's the Metropolitan Opera – so yes, it's a common misconception, partly, I must say, created by the Russell Watson myth-making machine that I haven't had any coaching. I have. I've put a massive amount of work into coaching my voice, it's just that I don't have any certificates to prove it and I never tend to speak about it in public either. Interviewers are all too happy to ask about the story of how I graduated from singing in the clubs to singing for the Pope; I'm only too happy to give it to them. What else do you do? Say, 'Well, let me just stop you there, Des, in fact the truth is a lot more boring...'?

Fact is, I didn't just wake up one morning, start singing like this, and think, Hey I could make an international career out of this. I had to work at it, same as everyone else.

CHAPTER THIRTY-FIVE

Looking back on the Pavarotti concert it's not dark, gloomy and cold. Oh no. It's sunny. It's bright.

It was summer, 2001, slap-bang in the middle of what must be the busiest, most turbulent year of my life. Pavarotti at Hyde Park. The event was called Picnic with Pavarotti and there was a crowd of 70,000. In all it helped raise over £500,000 for the Prince's Trust. I was on the bill, so was Charlotte, so was Vanessa Mae, each of us doing a solo set, before going on to do a song with Pavarotti, which was to form the climax of his headline set.

It was good to see Charlotte again. I find her mother hard work, but Charlotte herself is great company, always really nice and friendly, and very much what-you-see-is-what-you-get. I always connected with her.

Anyway… so we're at Hyde Park, and although it had been raining early in the morning the sun came out and it was a beautiful day, absolutely magnificent. I'd already done the Cliff Richard concert so I wasn't intimidated by the venue, if you can call it that, just really looking forward to doing my set. The only thing I was slightly nervous about was this duet, this song we were going to be singing with Luciano, 'Libiamo ne' lieti calici', otherwise known as the 'Drinking Song' from *La Traviata*. It's one of the great tenor workouts and I was relishing the chance to perform it with, well, one of the great tenors.

First, of course, we needed to rehearse it with him. Initially we were told that the rehearsal would be at midday, but midday came and there was no rehearsal. Then we were told the rehearsal would be at 1 p.m. By 1 p.m. the gates had opened and the crowd were pouring in, but there was still no sign of any rehearsal. Then 2 p.m., no rehearsal. Next, 2.30 p.m. and still no rehearsal, by which time I was getting psyched up for my own performance, which started at three.

The time came and I went out to do my five numbers. I didn't do 'Nessun Dorma', thought I'd best leave that one to the boss, but one of my numbers was 'Vienna', the Ultravox song I'd covered on my first record. I'd managed to entice Midge Ure down to sing it with me and it was a real treat, a brilliant success. In fact, we ended up getting on so well that he invited me to come and sing with him, and I joined him on stage at the Hammersmith Odeon to sing in front of his fans, which was cool.

So anyway. I came off stage having done my set, then went to my dressing room to wait. Me and Charlotte were still hoping the rehearsal would happen, but then it was her turn to do a set, and Vanessa Mae was on next and time crept on, and I started to think, Hang on, we're not going to get a rehearsal here. Pavarotti's on at 6 p.m. What's going on? I was still there in my room when there was a knock at the door and a bloke appeared. Slim, he wore a suit and his jet-black hair was slicked back. A moustache twitched slightly as he spoke.

And he spoke very, very quietly, whispering, 'Meester Pavuh... *wuh wuh wuh.*'

'Sorry?' I said.

'I said, Meester Pavuh... is now ready for his rehearsal with you and the young lady. If you would like to follow me.'

Along the way we stopped off at Charlotte's dressing room. I stood by as he knocked then poked his head round the door, saying, 'Meester Pavarotti is now ready for his rehearsal with you and *signor* Watson.'

Pavarotti's dressing room was in a whole new league. He had a dressing room with its own waiting room. We stood in this palatial antechamber, each of us fighting our nerves, waiting for our next instructions.

'Please wait here while I go to see Meester Pavarotti,' said our guide. 'I shall see whether he is ready for you to do the rehearsal.'

Charlotte fixed him with one of her famous dazzling smiles, opened her gob. 'All right, mate. We'll wait here.'

And we sat.

Silence. Just, from what felt like miles away, the sound of music, coming from the huge stage overlooking Hyde Park. A couple of hours ago I'd performed on that stage, but somehow it seemed light years away. Charlotte sat on her hands, swinging her feet slightly. I cleared my throat.

No sign of Pavarotti. Nor of our friend with the small voice.

'It's like waiting to meet Father Christmas, isn't it?' I said at last and Charlotte was laughing at that, trying to stifle her giggles.

'What are we doing here?' she said.

'I don't know.'

'Maybe this is the rehearsal,' said Charlotte. By now we were both cracking up. 'Maybe we're rehearsing how to sit down.'

The two of us were in fits when the guy came out again – a good ten minutes later.

'Meester Pavuh... *wuh wuh*...' he whispered.

Charlotte unleashed yet another of those legendary smiles. 'You what, mate?'

'I say Meester Pavarotti is ready to see you now for the rehearsal.'

Right. We pulled ourselves together, followed Little Voice into Pavarotti's dressing room. I'm not sure about Charlotte – I mean, maybe she didn't have quite the same history with Pavarotti that I did – but I was holding my breath; I was thinking of buying *The Essential Pavarotti* and learning 'Nessun Dorma' phonetically at Eldon Road. I was thinking this is *the* Pavarotti. This is the man.

His changing room was vast. It had the look and feel of a Turkish sauna, complete with, in the middle, sitting on a bench and swathed in bath towels, the world's most famous opera singer.

White bath towels were swathed around his legs, around his middle, all around his neck and bunched up around his face. In shocking contrast to the pristine white of the towels was his beard, his hair. Pavarotti's beard and hair were something to behold. I distinctly remember standing there, Charlotte Church by my side, half dying of awe, thinking, I've never seen a beard like it. I've never seen hair like it. I sometimes get asked if I've ever been over-awed by anybody I've met, and the stock answer's No, not usually. Two people I've met though, I've had to drag my jaw off the floor. Sir Alex Ferguson was one. We'd won the treble and I remember standing there not sure whether to drop to one knee or not, you know, like a knight or something, when *he* says to *me*, 'Don't forget us when you're famous.' Christ. Thinking about it now gives me goose bumps.

The other was Luciano Pavarotti, July 14, 2001, standing next to Charlotte in his dressing room. I'd just performed to close on 70,000 people, sung a duet with Midge Ure. But even so, that meeting was the highlight.

He lifted an arm, welcoming us, pointing first at me, and saying, 'You. You sit here,' indicating a place next to him. 'And you, pretty girl,' he said to Charlotte, 'you sit here,' pointing to a spot on the bench on the other side.

We took our places either side of the great man. I looked across his chest at Charlotte, wanting to share the moment. She looked back at me, obviously feeling the same urge.

'Rehearsal,' announced Pavarotti.

I straightened.

'When I point to you,' said Pavarotti, to me, 'you sing.'

Then he looked at Charlotte. 'And when I point to you, you sing.'

There was a moment of silence. Then Pavarotti said, 'End of rehearsal.'

For a second or so I wasn't quite sure if he was being serious. But he was. He was ushering us from the room, graciously, a giant hand indicating the door, which Charlotte and I took, walking out into the grand Pavarotti waiting room and then back down the corridor to our dressing rooms.

As we walked Charlotte said, 'Now, what the bloody hell was all that about?'

We didn't do the song in the end, funnily enough. Don't ask me why. Things change. Luciano changed his mind, perhaps. Like I say, with some of those big, big names, you wouldn't have it any other way. Imagine meeting Pavarotti and not having a tale to tell, what a let-down. In that way, as in all others, he didn't disappoint. I remember where I was when I heard about his death in September 2007. I was in Japan, on my way from Tokyo to Osaka to do a concert, and I got a telephone call from the label.

Pavarotti's passed away. *GMTV* want to speak to you and *BBC Breakfast News* want to speak to you and…

I remember looking out of the train window, thinking of the man swathed in bath towels. 'You. You sit here.' Thinking, Pavarotti's no longer in the world, what a darker place it is without him.

CHAPTER THIRTY-SIX

'Showtime.'

It's what Gary says when I'm about to go on stage. Or my producer Nick. Or whoever I've got with me for the gig.

I hear 'showtime', and I know I'm on.

As you know, I have my ritual. An anti-ritual, I suppose. I don't get ready. I don't put on my stage gear until the very last minute. Sometimes the band or orchestra are already out on stage, already playing, and I'm still pulling on my pants backstage. That's the way I've always played it, going right back to the club days, to the Lily Savage show, Cliff Richard, Pavarotti at Hyde Park.

Even at Wembley Arena.

Wembley, 2001. I think that was the first gig where I really thought, *Yes*.

Because as a solo artist I'd done mainly theatres up to that point. My first UK tour I was playing 1,500–2,000-seater venues. By the next one I was doing 15,000–20,000 arenas. Wembley was one of them. Funny, only a few years before I'd been in this club called the Phoenix in Ellesmere Port. Why was it called the Phoenix? Guess. Exactly. Because it burnt down three years previously and they rebuilt it. Better than calling it the Old Firetrap, I suppose.

Anyway, I was playing the Phoenix, and there were four or five people in, looking bored, regarding me through the bottom of their empty pint glasses. And you know how I said that I rarely had a bad night after that night in Wigan? Well, this was one of those rare bad nights, hardly able to see a sprinkling of punters through the fag smoke, the silence at the end of each song near deafening. When I'd walked on I'd said, with a touch of sarcasm, 'Good evening, Wembley.'

In reply, somebody coughed.

And now here I was, in Wembley. And it felt as though I'd stepped into a machine that had shot me through space and time, transporting me from the Phoenix in Ellesmere Port to here, to Wembley, where, when I stepped up to the mic and said, 'Good evening, Wembley,' it wasn't a joke. Instead of five people sitting there, bored, waiting for the flyer to come on, there were 12,000 – all to see me. I wasn't a support act for the bingo.

'Showtime.' And I get dressed, ready to play Wembley, not letting a single scrap of nervous energy escape because I need it all for when I'm up there, on stage.

It's not like I'm in a band. It's not The Russell Watsons, five of us up there so the singer can take a break and play his tambourine while the lead guitarist does something flashy. Just me up there, and I'm kind of winging it really, because I don't believe in too much rehearsal. I don't believe in over-thinking things, because when you do that you sacrifice spontaneity and freshness. It gets tired and contrived and the audience can feel it; they know you're just going through your paces. I don't do dancing, either. Even the legendary Kim Gavin couldn't knock me into shape, so, no, dancing's not part of the show, no choreography to fall back on, no practised routine. I'm not like Madonna where I can catwalk to the back of the stage and let some oily blokes prance around for a few minutes. It's all about my interaction with the audience, all about my delivery.

I remember walking out, that first Wembley gig. Striding up to the mic and saying, 'Good evening, Wembley,' and flashing back to the Phoenix – these ironies, they're never lost on me – and it was amazing. Like an hallucination. The dry ice shimmering, coloured by the lights, the music announcing me on to the stage; through it all, the crowd. But up there, you can only hear the crowd. You can't see it. The lights create the impression of a black curtain in front of you, so you lose all but the first few rows of the audience. I knew that, of course, I was accustomed to that effect. Which is why I said then, as I always do, 'Lights,' and the lighting guys know to bring the house lights up so I can see the crowd. A lot of performers wouldn't do that; they don't want reminding of how many people are in the arena, and that's fair enough. I can under- stand that. But as Trevor Barry used to say, I fackin' larve the big occasion, and I want to see them, I want to see their faces, their reactions. I want to see how many are out there because that energy is what I'm feeding off.

So: 'Lights.' This was after my first number, my old favourite, what else but ''O Sole Mio', and the spotlight went down and for the first time I could see the outline of the arena. Looking up, all I could see were people, and they were standing – a standing ovation on my first number. The feeling's a rush. It's exhilaration, a sort of pride. It's an intense, ego-shagging experience. Afterwards you can't sleep. Your mind won't let you because it's still bathing in that moment. It doesn't want to step out of that feeling for a bit. And your body won't let you because it's still drunk with adrenalin, arms and legs twitchy and wired. No wonder so many performers have problems with booze and drugs and whatever. I can see that, I can understand it: they're trying to recapture that moment. Or replace it. Or come down off it.

A standing ovation. First song. Holy crap. Bring out the Branston. Behind me I've got the Royal Philharmonic, in front of me thousands of people applauding. All this from little clubs in the North West.

Not that I've changed. I mean, *I've* changed, of course I have. But the act? What I do? I still use the audience. As the applause lulled, somebody screamed, 'Aagh!'

'Tell me where it hurts,' I replied, and Wembley Arena laughed.

'I love you, Russell,' was another comment, later.

'I love you too, Mum.'

If someone screams something the rest of the audience can hear I'll come back on it, the same at Wembley as at Wigan. It's just the numbers that have changed. In my club days I had a roaming mic. At Wembley I came down off the stage and had a wander through the audience, shaking hands, making friends. 'Hello, love, you all right?'

You won't hear many other performers say this, because we like to maintain the illusion that we're there for our art and the audience is incidental to all that magic. But I don't care who you are, when you're up on stage your job is twofold: to entertain your audience and to get them to come back next time. You do that by knowing that the audience aren't there just for you – they could watch a DVD if they simply wanted to see you sing – they're there for the event, and the audience *is* the event. I sometimes think football's forgotten that. In this era of player power, the game's lost sight of the fact that fans are part of the attraction and fans get treated like a dirty secret, an embarrassing relative: good to borrow a few quid off, but not that good for the image.

Me, I don't forget that. I never forget it. The audience *are* the show, and I make sure they know that. It's the same reason I stay behind after shows for pictures and autographs, for as long as I can, until Gary is pulling me away. The same reason that I don't refuse autographs unless I'm with the kids – and even then I've been known not to refuse. There was a time I was in the Trafford Centre, in Lewis's, and a bloke approached me wanting an autograph. 'It's not for me,' he said, 'it's for me mum and she's a massive fan, she's in a wheelchair.' Giving me the face. 'Go on.'

I looked at the girls and they looked back at me, and all three of us knew I was going to say yes.

'Yeah, course, mate,' I said, 'lead the way.'

Turned out she was in the shoe section. The four of us trooped across the shop until we got to the shoes, and an old dear in a wheelchair.

'Look, Mum,' bellowed the bloke, 'look who I've brought to see you.'

She stared up at me.

'You know who it is,' yelled the bloke, loud enough for the entire Trafford Centre to hear.

'Of course I know who it is,' snapped the old dear, 'it's Nigel.'

'Russell, Mum. It's Russell Watson.'

'It's Nigel. I've got all his CDs at home. I know Nigel when I see him. Hello, Nigel,' she said.

'It's *Russell*, Mum.'

'Nigel, would you sign this for me?'

I took whatever it was, signed it 'all my love, Nigel Watson', gave it back and left, me, Rebecca and Hannah cracking up as we made our escape across Lewis's.

I've had requests even more bizarre than that. I woke up after my first tumour operation. At St George's Hospital in London, this was, and one of the medical staff was there, a bloke saying, 'I'm not supposed to do this, but could you sign this for my missus?'

I swear, I'd only just come round. I was groggy, could barely see. 'I would,' I told him, 'but I can't see it.'

I couldn't. I'd just had a tumour taken out of my head (well, *some* of a tumour, as it turned out).

'It's all right,' he said, 'just scribble on it, anything.'

So I did, I literally did, and he thanked me and went, and as he went I croaked, 'Cheers, mate.'

The thing is, I'm enjoying a great career in the music industry, and I wouldn't be doing that without the people who ask for my autograph. Forget that and you might as well pack up and go home.

CHAPTER THIRTY-SEVEN

And the treadmill didn't stop. Or was it a rollercoaster? Up one minute, when I was singing for President Bush and winning Brit awards. Down the next when I was being branded a love rat and Chelsea fan David Mellor's trying to score points off me, the twat. Up and down, but never stopping.

That year they broadcast a *South Bank Show* about me. Clips from my first major concert. Bridgwater Hall in 2000 it was. My dad interviewed, remembering how he and my mum were in the audience, looking at each other, tears streaming down their faces. Me and Melvyn Bragg, wandering around a Lowry exhibition, Melvyn saying (Melvyn Bragg impression coming up), 'Mums see him as an ideal son; dads as a mate,' which is fair enough, I suppose, a pretty accurate assessment of my appeal; and Sir Alex Ferguson – me and Fergie standing on the touchline at Old Trafford, Sir Alex Ferguson paying me all kinds of compliments. Fortunately we were being filmed from the waist up, so you can't see that I'm weak at the knees.

Then, in May, I was being shipped off to something else, the Laureus World Sports Awards, a lavish annual knees-up held in Monte Carlo. It was one of those where I'd turned up in a white tracksuit and baseball cap and everybody thought I was a rapper until I started singing. 'Hey, man, I thought you were going to be Eminem or something,' yelled one guy across the auditorium, and I added him to my mental list.

During the show itself I sang two songs. I did 'Va, Pensiero' as well as a song from the first record called 'Non Ti Scordar Di Me', and get this, I was introduced on to the stage by Sean Connery.

'Ladiesh and gentleman, we're now going to bring onto shtage the fabuloush voice, the behst-shelling classhical artist in the United Kingdom: Rushell Watshon.'

And who was there to take me off stage, leading the audience in a round of applause? Morgan Freeman. Morgan Freeman, movie star, an elder statesman of dignity and wisdom, leading a round of applause for me, gobby bloke from Salford.

It was as though every time I thought it can't get any better than this, it went and got better. These awards, there were more famous faces than I'd ever seen in one place before. There were players I'd booed on the football field (step forward, Vinnie Jones), singers I'd spent years impersonating in the clubs (step forward, Natalie Cole). There were racing drivers, tennis stars, boxers, models, comedians, actors. I found myself chit-chatting away to Michael Douglas and Catherine Zeta-Jones, who were nice. A pleasant couple.

Stop. You wanted to know that, didn't you? I know, because when you mention to people that you've met Michael Douglas and Catherine Zeta-Jones *together*, the next question is always, 'What are they like?' Always. Much more so than with the likes of Morgan Freeman or Sean Connery. Nobody expects you to say, 'Sean Connery, no, didn't like him, bit full of himself.' Even if that's what you thought, people don't want to hear it. They don't want their mental image of Sean Connery tarnished. Mention Michael and Catherine, though, and out come the shovels. People want to hear the dirt. They want you to go into one about Catherine and how stuck up she was so they can say, 'Hm, thought as much,' and make some catty remark about her accent. And I think celebrities such as Michael Douglas and

Catherine Zeta-Jones are aware of that effect, so they cultivate a kind of detachment. It's like their persona, their celebrity aura, takes over what they're actually about as people. I'm sure that when they're at home they fart and wave the sheets around just like any other couple. But out, when they're meeting people, they're always careful to meet that criterion. So they're nice. Distant, but nice. Pleasant.

Same with Posh and Beckham of course – you see it a lot in celebrity couples, actually. The following year, 2002, I sang at David Beckham's pre-World Cup party, and it's one of those things that always crops up in any interview in the same sentence as singing for the Pope and President Bush. And once again everybody wants to know, 'What are they like?' And the answer is: They're nice, they're pleasant. But they've got that same aura as Michael Douglas and Catherine Zeta-Jones. That same feeling you get that they never quite switch off. Wherever they are, they're always on the red carpet.

David, he's a United player, he helped win the treble. He's above criticism as far as I'm concerned. Victoria, she gets a bad press if you ask me. I've never seen any indication that she's this big bad bitch the media sometimes paint her to be. Sorry if you were hoping for juicy goss, but that's the way it is, tell you what, though, I wouldn't swap with them, hell no. I just couldn't deal with the publicity. Because one of the things I've struggled with about fame – and sorry but it's most prevalent in the UK – is that we like to build people up to knock them down. They don't do that in America. They embrace their talent and they champion it. But here, you can read a magazine, say, I don't know, *Yo! Magazine*, which says Victoria's the spokesperson of a generation. A lovely, great, fantastic, super-duper bird who does loads for charity. Great, you think. Victoria's ace.

Then you pick up *Scumbag Magazine* and you open that and it says Victoria Beckham, what a miserable po-faced cow she is. Not only is she too skinny but she split up the Spice Girls.

Okay, two magazines, two different viewpoints, but really, how can she be both? Could it be because *Yo! Magazine* has the exclusive with Victoria that *Scumbag Magazine* missed out on? And now *Scumbag Magazine* wants to run what they call a spoiler? Could be...

Hm, elementary, my dear Watson.

The way I am, and I'm probably the same as most people in the entertainment industry, is that I can perform a sell-out gig to 15,000 people all screaming my name, but if one person was to shout, 'You're rubbish,' that's the one I remember. There'd be 14,999 people disagreeing, sure, but it's that one critic you hear. The one critic you take to heart. So, bearing that in mind, I can't imagine what it must be like for Victoria and David, constantly reading crappy, contradictory things about yourself in *Yo! Magazine* and *Scumbag Magazine*. Or for David, on the field, hearing fans chanting things about his wife. I couldn't do it myself. I've weathered my fair share of bad press and I don't like it.

Anyway, see what happened there? I felt power of thought. Psychically, you asked me what I thought of Posh and Becks and I replied.

Meanwhile, back at the Laureus World Sports Awards, I met John Salley, a basketball player. He's not that well known in the UK. But in America he's massive, and not just in terms of his profile, either. He's about seven foot six, this guy, one of the most successful players in the country, had his own chat show. His girlfriend was Heidi Klum. I met him after I'd finished my rehearsal, just after the Eminem comment, and I was walking down the corridor with my assistant at the time, a guy named Wes, a Scouser, when we heard this booming voice from behind us.

Chapter Thirty-seven

'Hey, are you The Voice?!'

We turned.

Never mind me, John Salley's got a voice that would rattle the tea cups. A deep, deep Brooklyn bass. 'Yo,' he bellowed, off the Richter scale, 'are you The Voice?'

'Er, yeah,' I said. I was hoping I hadn't accidentally looked down the front of Heidi Klum's dress.

He said, 'Let me tell you something! That's one hell of a mother-fuckin' voice you got on you, son, and that's a *compliment* where I come from.'

I said, 'Thank you very much.'

'Can I get my picture?' he said.

'Yeah, great, of course,' standing next to him.

'You know who this is?'

Yes. This was Heidi Klum, five foot nine of Victoria's Secret model.

'Yeah,' I said, 'I think so.'

'It's Heidi Klum,' bawled John Salley. 'You should get a picture with Heidi. You two look good together. Hey, it might do your career some good as well.'

So I said, 'Okay,' and stood next to Heidi Klum, had my picture taken with the pair of them.

Off they went, with, 'Son, you have got one motherfuckin' voice on you,' as a parting shot.

And still the treadmill didn't stop. Still the rollercoaster kept on rolling. I've got Manchester and Salford in my veins. I'm a home-body. I get homesick. I was missing my kids. I was missing my mum and dad and Crnab and my mates. I saw them for brief snatches when I'd touch down, arriving at the Boathouse in Worsley, which was the house I bought and lived in immediately after I split up with Helen. I'd let myself in, hardly recognising the place, its smell unfamiliar to me, my possessions alien.

And there would be post. Lots of letters. Huge, thick envelopes would be sitting on the mat waiting for me to arrive home.

Sometimes I didn't even open them. I put them on the side, and after a couple of days when it was time to leave again, I'd almost feel relieved to be free of them. It was like they sat there taunting me...

CHAPTER THIRTY-EIGHT

Encore was a mad time. We recorded it in New York so I could keep my head down after the bad press I'd had surrounding my break-up with Helen. And I guess if I had my one period of letting the whole fame business go to my head, my only flirtation with the 'rock and roll lifestyle', it was then. We'd finish recording for the day then spend the evening boozing. We literally drank the nearby liquor stores dry of champagnes we were drinking that much. I developed a taste for cigars. Probably not a good idea for an opera singer, but there you go. I was having my moment of being a big-time Charlie, and anyway, it wasn't a long moment; I think I got a handle on myself pretty quickly. Luckily I'm able to do that, step outside myself, take a look and decide whether or not I like what I see, and I'm single-minded enough to stick with it, too. I remember a time, for instance, I was interviewed by this woman. Most people are nice, just the odd one who wants to pour icy water into your bath. And she was one of them.

It was around the time of *Captain Corelli's Mandolin*, the movie with Nicolas Cage. On the soundtrack I'd sung 'Senza Di Te' and 'Ricordo Ancor'.

'Oh my God, you did that?' gushed this woman, when the subject came up.

'Yeah,' I said.

'Did you get to meet Nicolas? Oh my God, he's absolutely fantastic, I love what he does. He sings as well, you know.'

It was the way she said it. As though to put me in my place and remind me just where I stood on her personal celeb-o-meter. Not exactly the most polite way to treat someone you've come to interview. Not the wisest way to approach someone having their big-time-Charlie moment.

'Oh, right,' I said, cold enough to frost glass.

'Did you get to meet him?' she pressed.

'No,' I replied, 'and he didn't get to meet me either.'

She looked taken aback, a get-him expression on her face. 'Well, he's a massive movie star,' she said, still putting me in my place.

'Well, I'll tell you what,' I hissed. 'I'll be doing movies before he's singing opera.'

Oh, Russell, no.

I cringe writing it now. And almost immediately after saying it then, I thought, Come on, mate, grow up.

Definitely one of those take-a-step-back moments.

Still, during the making of *Encore*, I guess I thought I owed it to myself to let go a bit. I was talking about it with my producer, Nick, the other day, and we were saying that *Encore* is the one record I've made where I didn't have some major turmoil in my life. Yes, in the background was the fall-out from my divorce, my ongoing management problems, but nothing like what I was facing on the other records. *The Voice* coincided with my marriage falling to bits. Making *Reprise* I discovered a polyp on my throat that threatened to end my career. *Amore Musica* coincided with more management problems that left me facing bankruptcy. Then you've got *That's Life* and *Outside In*, both of which I made knowing I had a brain tumour. So by comparison, *Encore* was a happy, uncomplicated period, and it's definitely one of those times that, when I look back on it, feels bright. There was me, producer Nick, another guy, Rory, my engineer, Josh, plus my assistant and manager and we'd sit on a balcony after hours, just caning the champagne until three or four in the morning most days. The next day, into the studio recording. My mate Alistair turned up and he couldn't believe it, the booze we were getting through.

A special mention here for Nick Patrick, who was partner in crime and a great mate. I remember grabbing a holiday in Spain and I was out there with my dad and Nick and there was a particular restaurant we used to frequent, where one night we got through nine bottles of champagne. Now, my dad doesn't drink a lot, so I'm ashamed to say it was mainly Nick and me who put it all away. At one point, the restaurant owner came over to offer us another bottle of Dom Perignon and we told him no, thanks. We'd had enough. But he insisted. This one was on the house. So out came *another* bottle of Dom Perignon.

Later, we got back to the villa where Nick and I decided to sit around the pool smoking cigars. I remember very clearly that Nick was suited and booted, wearing an Armani suit. I remember it very clearly because (being a trifle squiffy) I decided to push him in the pool. And this is Nick all over, but having been dumped in the pool he bobbed to the surface, drenched, his Armani suit probably ruined, and he started puffing on the cigar.

'Look at this, mate,' he said (Nick always said 'mate'), 'bloody thing's still lit.'

He held it above his head in triumph, like the Statue of Liberty with her torch, and started making his way to the side. He's been a great mate – and we've had some good times together. Many of them drink-related.

But if you think for a second this is going to descend into a how-I-lost-it-on-booze story, then sorry to disappoint you. I'll leave that for Amy Winehouse, Pete Doherty and the rest of the rehab crowd. Mine was just a moment in time. A brief period of my life when I needed to let off a little steam.

It was in New York that I met Roxanna Valerio. I met her in a bar and pretty soon we'd fallen in love; immediately, we wanted to be together.

It was her I thought of on September 11, 2001, the day of the terrorist attack on the Twin Towers. She was in New York, but I was in the UK, at a mixing studio in London, a converted steamboat owned by Dave Gilmour from Pink Floyd. We were having lunch, taking a break from mixing *Encore* and half watching TV on a big plasma screen. They're pretty common now, but I distinctly recall this being one of the first I'd ever seen, and all of us admiring it, watching some music channel, 1960s stuff. Then flicking through the channels, seeing the first plane strike the World Trade Center.

And, like everybody else watching, I saw the plane hit, the camcorder footage, the flames, the thick pillar of smoke, and I felt like reality was bending somehow. As though what I was seeing simply couldn't be happening. It was a scene from a film. Special effects.

I spent the rest of the day trying to reach Roxanna. Couldn't get through. It was only a matter of days that we'd all been in New York, too. We'd spent four or five months there making *Encore*, boozing the nights away on our studio balcony, looking out over the New York skyline.

We flew back a couple of days after the attack. We had to get back to master the record. I remember, we were the only people on the plane. At the other end, we took a taxi, and Josh, the New Yorker of the group, looked out of the window, at the place where the Twin Towers should have been. His face told its own story.

CHAPTER THIRTY-NINE

February 4, 2008

Mood swing. Here it comes. Salford bloke in full effect. Gary and Victoria ducking for cover because something's got me started. What? Could be anything. A phone call, something I've seen on the telly or something that reminds me about the classical music mafia, the snobs and critics.

Rant number 157 in a series of God-knows-how-many.

And when I'm like this I get a playground mentality. I want to go back in time and offer them out. Proper Salford, like, 'Hey you, Mr Critic, think you can sing? Come round and let's see who can do it better. I can't project my voice, you say? Not got any power? Fancy it down your ear, then, five inches away? You know what I could do if I wanted to sound like the most powerful voice in the world? I could ask Grant to turn the volume on the orchestra down and the volume on the singer up, and it would sound like, wow, he's got such a powerful voice. But it would be bollocks. A sleight-of-hand on the slider during the mixing process. So if you're serious and you really want to tell if I've got a big voice or not, then you need to come round and stand in my hall, and I'll sing down your ear – and then you tell me I haven't got a powerful voice.

You know what? I used to sing at the international rugby, and afterwards there would be these social gatherings. Canapés and wine, that kind of thing. An upmarket crowd. Anyway, I was at one of these and I must have been hurting over some criticism or some comment because I thought I'd try something out. Chatting with one group, we got onto the subject of voice coaching.

'Oh, where did you train?' I was asked.

I told them I'd been trained by David Dubery of the Northern Ballet, as well as by Sir William Hayward, former pupil of Sir Adrian Boult.

'Ah yes,' nodded Rugby Experiment Group One sagely, 'you can tell. You can hear in the voice how hard you've worked on it.'

Moving on to Rugby Experiment Group Two, and the same question cropped up. Where did you train?

'I didn't,' I said, playing up the part of the untutored oik. 'Never had any training.'

'Well, yes, you know, you can tell. You can hear that you're untrained, it's in the voice. Have you ever considered some coaching?'

Same performance. Same bloody performance. I'm telling you, you can't win with these people.

Where does it all come from, all that stuff? I wonder. Am I ranting because that's how I really feel? Or am I just sounding off?

The morning after that night at the Trump International, Sir Bill told me that a drunken man tells the truth. What about a man whose hormones are in a state of disarray? A man who sticks his head in a microwave every day?

I find myself making little resolutions. All based on 'when I get well, when I've got this bloody thing out of my head'.

I'm going to continue my Italian lessons; do some more song-writing – I co-wrote 'Someone Like You', the song I did with (the delectable) Faye Tozer, and I've long wanted to do some more; I'm going to play some tennis, have some lessons on the piano, pick up where I left off all those years ago...

▲ Laura Bush and I at the First Lady Luncheon
I sang at in 2003, in my capacity as a United
Nations Goodwill Ambassador.

The Prince and I discussing
the British weather. ▼

© PA Photos

◀ My second two Brits.
Someone had mentioned that
they make good dumbbells.

See, I told you I was
nervous with the birds! ▼

© PA Photos

▲ A day at the races.

I had to go all the way to
New Zealand to find this! ▼

▲ I had such great fun working with Sian on *Just the Two of Us*.

My first real acting role, Jeff Wayne's *War of the Worlds.* ▼

© Reuters/Corbis

Where did I leave those fucking keys! ▶

Another very proud moment as I was invited by George Best's family to sing at his testimonial! ▼

© Getty Images

▲ A massively emotional day
as I'm allowed out of hospital
after my second operation.

By Charles Yates

Russell just said to me 'Hiya pop' as if nothing ned

THE father of stricken singer Russell Watson has spoken of his joy at hearing his son's famous voice again following an emergency operation to remove a brain tumour.

Tim Watson revealed that prior to the three-hour surgery on Thursday, the Salford-born tenor, dubbed The Voice, was left unable to speak and was losing his vision.

EXCLUSIVE

Singer Russell fights for life

Opera star has an emergency op for 'aggressive' brain tumour

BY DON FRAME

His manager, Richard Thompson said: "This is a _____ and a far more

RUSS WATS

SET TO D
HIS MA
VO
DUBAI
ST

Brain op Russell gets a boost from his gran

THE recovery of singer Russell Watson got a big boost yesterday—when he was visited by his gran.

The opera star—known as The Voice—has been recuperating after emergency surgery on Thursday to remove a brain tumour. He had a similar operation last year.

Russell, 40, is now off the critical list but still in intensive care at the private Alexandra Hospital in Cheadle, Greater Manchester, where gran Phyllis Aldred, 87, went to see him yesterday.

His manager Richard Thompson said: "Russell's condition remains serious but stable.

BY KEITH GLADDIS

We hoped he may have been able to leave intensive care this weekend but it's become clear we are in for the long haul for him to get better."

BETTER: Star Russell

era singer Russell W
tumour after being r

orror of the

istie Hospital
HS Foundation

ospital

partme

Smoki

OICE'S
OUGH
FIGHT

ke up

M.E.N. TUESDAY
OCTOBER 30, 2007

RUSSELL Watson looks tired and tense as he prepares for a gruelling radiotherapy course yesterday.
The tenor, nicknamed the Voice, will be treated for five weeks to destroy a brain tumour that left him fighting for life in October. But Manchester's Christie Hospital fear the course may also damage his eyesight.
The dad-of-two, 41, said: "It's been a strange new year. It takes a while to get your energy up again."

Russell gets a special visitor fter brain op

par
I th

■ Kirsty drops in on
singer in hospital

■ 'I just wanted to
say get well soon'

DEAN KIRBY

SINGER Russell Watson has received a pep talk from Kirsty Howard during a short hospital visit.

The 12-year-old took some flowers to his bedside at the Alexandra Hospital, in Cheadle, where he is recovering from a life-saving brain operation.

It was the first time Kirsty, who was born with her heart

years and has raised £40,000 for her campaign to save Francis House Children's Hospice, in Didsbury.

A card attached to her flowers said: "To Russell, get well, love Kirsty. X."

Kirsty said: "I just wanted to see him to say get well soon, and to bring him some flowers. He's a very special person."

Russell, known as The Voice, underwent a three-hour operation to remove a brain tumour. He has now been moved out of intensive care and hospital officials said he is 'progressing well'.

Fears have been raised about his

Kirsty reached the £5m target of her campaign to save Francis House children's hospice in October.

Russell has been friends with her since he paid her a special visit during her seventh birthday party.

He performed his song Nothing Sacred.

Suzie Mathis, a spokesman for Kirsty's appeal, said: "Kirsty wanted to see Russell as soon as he was well enough. She wanted to give him some flowers and a big hug.

"He looked well considering what he's been through. He was so pleased to see her. They held hands for a long time. She asked her how he was ___

© Uli Weber

© Uli Weber

◀ Clowning around at a photo shoot for my album *Outside In*.

Loads of stuff I'd like to do.

Sometimes I think about finding someone – someone for sharing new beginnings. I've been single for two and a half years now. During that time I've nearly died twice, so I probably wasn't exactly ideal boyfriend material: 'Not tonight, love, I've got a headache.'

But I'm coming out of it now and there are times I do find myself yearning for a partner. Sometimes, despite all the great help I have around me – the Colonel, Lynne, Gary, Red Steve, all my family and mates – I still feel lonely. Bed sometimes feels a little on the large side.

I don't know, sometimes I think I'm just destined to be single and maybe I'm happier that way anyway, because with what I do, well, it's difficult to expect any female to accept it without being threatened by it. I love what I do, I live it, but if there's anybody out there who understands just what it takes to make what I do work, then I haven't met her yet. And I won't be holding my breath while I wait. With Roxanna, I really did focus my energy on that relationship – to the extent that my career suffered – but it still didn't work out so I've got to the point now where I think it's just not meant to happen; I'll stick with the single life for now – focus my affection on my children and my singing.

Tomorrow is Tuesday, February 5. My last day of radiotherapy. My last day of living with a brain tumour.

In 2002 I was made Goodwill Ambassador for a branch of the United Nations, the World Association of Former United Nations Interns and Fellows. A representative of WAFUNIF, Remy Maradona (cousin of *the* Maradona), got in touch with my manager. He'd just seen me on *Good Morning America* and, firstly, there was something about me that reminded him of Mario Lanza, which was cool with me, Mario Lanza's always been a hero. Secondly, he thought I'd be ideal to help promote his branch of the United Nations. How did I fancy coming in and talking it over?

Sure thing. So we went to the United Nations building in Manhattan, 760 United Nations Plaza, an incredible place, one of those famous New York landmarks. There, Remy took me through what the job would entail and I accepted, taking on a ten-year directive to spread goodwill and the word of the United Nations, a role that included raising money, helping educate young people about safe sex and contraception, getting involved with the land-mine fund, as well as helping to provide learning facilities for under-privileged children in war-torn or third world countries – one of which was Nicaragua. Just over a year later I was collecting my UN credentials in Geneva for a UN assignment, film crew in tow: I was going to Nicaragua.

There, in the capital Managua, I started to get an idea of the place – of its near-ruinous state, still in a process of recovery after a civil war in the 1980s caused huge damage and massive blood-shed. A democratic government is in place these days, but the economy has never fully recovered from the conflict and now there's massive, widespread poverty, a situation hardly helped by Nicaragua's position at the junction of three tectonic plates. A devastating earthquake in 1972 destroyed many buildings essential to the infrastructure of the country – their empty ripped-open shells litter the capital. This, where the standard of living is relatively high.

I was there to open what they call a multi-learning centre, provided by the UN for one of the most poverty-stricken areas of the country, Jinotega. Bumping along a crater-filled road, I became aware of what were the worst scenes of poverty I've ever seen. Everywhere I looked there were shacks, some of them criss-crossed with planks of wood holding them together, some of them with plastic hanging and roasting in the sun, harsh sunlight reflecting from the makeshift coverings. People sitting outside shacks regarded us as we drove past, for my part I suddenly became conscious of my clothes, my hair, my sunglasses. Ashamed of it all, somehow. As though I was flaunting my affluence.

The day before I was due to open the centre, we went to an infant school, handing out sweets and pencils to the kids. Drawn by the lure of candy and the excitement of having a camera crew in the place, they gathered around, tussling and scrapping over sweets and pencils. I couldn't help but think of my two, spoilt rotten with Western comfort. And not just mine, obviously, but kids in general. Heads in Nintendos, widescreen TV blasting away in front of them, mithering for the latest doll or a new mobile phone. I'm not the first celebrity to take the cameras into a poverty-stricken area, so I won't be the first to express this sentiment, but until you go out to somewhere like that, you just don't know how lucky you are. You simply don't realise how much we take for granted in the West. We put a few smiles on faces that day in the infant school, and bumping away on the crater-filled road it felt good to have achieved something – perhaps something a bit more profound than usual.

We opened the multi-learning centre the following day. The locals put on a show and I gave a speech, sang ''O Sole Mio' (which seemed to tickle the kids no end) and then, the best bit – watched them get to grips with the computers we'd provided at the centre. I left Nicaragua hoping I'd be able to return – and that the country would be in better shape when I did. I still hope that one day I'll get the chance.

This was in 2003 – the trip to Nicaragua. Rewind to 2001 and shortly after meeting Remy Maradona in New York, I was formally named a UN ambassador at a reception in Beverly Hills. While in LA I made history by being the first artist to perform at the new home of the Oscars, the Kodak Theater, which had just been reopened. I also gave a performance at a Dreamworks studio event, with guests including Steven Spielberg. Back in the UK I switched on the Christmas lights in Regent Street, then did a Royal Variety Show, where I appeared on a bill that also included Elton John, Jennifer Lopez, Charlotte Church and Paul O'Grady – funny the way things go, back on the same stage as Paul O'Grady.

Shortly after that I flew to Oslo for a Nobel Peace Prize concert held to celebrate the centenary of the award. It was hosted by Meryl Streep and Liam Neeson, and present would be stars such as Wyclef Jean, Natalia Imbruglia, Anastacia, and the big one – the one that really stopped me in my tracks: Paul McCartney. Not only that, but we were going to sing with him. For a finale, the assembled artists would sing 'Let It Be'. My favourite songwriter ever, a bona fide genius, and I was going to sing with him. Bit of a shame about his missus at the time, of course. But then you can't have everything...

Oslo was freezing. Not just that but it was damp, too. As garlic is to a vampire, so the cold and damp are to a singer, especially a classical singer.

The venue was small. A 7,000-seater, although the concert itself was going out in a hundred countries, so had an estimated audience in the tens of millions. The stage was decorated with an incredible aluminium globe.

During rehearsals I got to meet some of the other performers. I fell instantly in love with Natalie Imbruglia, who is even lovelier in real life than she is on TV. I got on fine with Wyclef Jean and I decided that Anastacia was so far up her own arse she was wearing herself for a hat. Okay, let's give her the benefit of the doubt. Maybe she was just having a bad day.

Paul McCartney was there, too, of course, and he watched me rehearse 'Nessun Dorma'. I think I've already told you that I don't give it full pelt during rehearsals, but come on: Paul McCartney was watching. So I turned up the volume a notch.

'That's a bloody big noise you make there,' he said. 'I'm impressed.'

'Well thank you very much,' I replied. 'You know, I've been a big fan of yours since I was this high. I'm really looking forward to the song tonight.'

'Great, mate, that's great.'

Just like two blokes down the pub we were.

For the performance, the members of a hundred-piece orchestra took their places. A choir came on for 'Let It Be', and during his set McCartney dedicated two numbers to the victims of 9/11, plus another to George Harrison, who had died a fortnight or so before.

The 'Let It Be' finale was quite something. McCartney led the song, obviously, and performers paired off to share individual lines. I was with the American soprano, Barbara Hendricks. Lovely lady, Barbara, but I couldn't help be jealous of Morten Harket out of a-ha – he was paired off with Natalie Imbruglia.

Then, following the gig, we were all invited to Sir Paul's dressing room, which was a small, cramped, airless cubicle, hardly room to swing a cat, with just some old sausage rolls and bits of sweaty cheese on sticks for guests to eat.

I'm pulling your leg. Sir Paul McCartney's dressing room was palatial, only Pavarotti's dressing room comes anywhere close. There, we were greeted at the door by Sir Paul and Heather Mills, and...

You want to know what she was like, don't you? Just like Posh and Catherine Zeta-Jones, Heather Mills is one of those 'women of notoriety' who people are just dying to judge. Well, she wasn't my cup of tea, let's put it that way. On the one hand I do think she's had what amounts to years of bad – possibly unfair – press. When you see somebody getting such a hard time in the papers, and the letters pages are full of people queuing up to slag her off, it's hard not to feel slightly sorry for the victim, and I always did for Heather Mills. But then I met her, and I could see why she was getting the press she did. Then, at least, it was all down to the way she behaved, like she was royalty or something. Not exactly the most down-to-earth person I've met, to put it kindly. And I've spoken before about how I like my legends to appear larger-than-life. If you meet Aretha Franklin or Luciano Pavarotti or Elton John, you want them to be a bit eccentric. Normal would be letting the side down. It's a bit different if you're a celebrity wife, though, which is what she was.

Sir Paul, though. Different story. What a bloke.

Every time I thought my life couldn't improve, suddenly it did. Because the treadmill kept on going, the rollercoaster rolling and I was about to hit a massive peak. I'd been invited to perform for the Pope.

CHAPTER FORTY-ONE

'Now, would you look at the sweaties on that.'

The lads from Westlife had introduced me to a word I'd never heard before: 'sweaties'. Noun. Term of affection for the female bosom, frequently employed by members of an Irish boyband.

The fact that we were in the Vatican at the time? About to perform for Pope John Paul II? Didn't seem to faze them much.

It was for his annual Christmas concert, where he used to invite pop and classical acts for a special televised concert at the Vatican before an audience of cardinals and dignitaries. Pope John Paul II died in 2005, of course, and his successor Pope Benedict XVI turned out not to be such a fan of pop music, so he's stopped them. But during Pope John Paul II's tenure they were a yearly fixture for well over a decade. They've stopped them now, so it was just a select few of us who got to perform for the pontiff.

Funny thing is, I can't even remember the call coming in. I mean, it was during a period when calls were coming in a lot: *The Voice* was still selling by the bucketload, *Encore* was poised to come out, we were thinking about recording the next record, which would be *Reprise*; I'd just done the Nobel Peace Prize concert; and I had a sell-out gig at the *Manchester Evening News* Arena to look forward to at the end of the year. It's not like I was 'Pope shmope' about it. Just that if I have something big on, a huge gig, or an important bit of telly, I tend not to believe it until I'm on a plane, or in the car on my way there. Why? The Parkinson effect, probably. He's retired now, of course, but when Parky was on the box, everybody wanted to be on it, me included. I can't count the times I was told that I'd got the show, only for plans to change at the last minute: 'Sorry, they've gone with John Travolta instead.' Later, I would be doing my own version of 'Staying Alive', but not Parky.

I'd met him as well, in Australia of all places. I was doing a signing and who should turn up, but Michael bloody Parkinson.

'Russell Watson,' he said, exactly the way you'd expect Michael Parkinson to say the words 'Russell Watson'.

'All right, Parky,' I said, and after a bit of chit-chat, guess what I was asking him: 'When are you going to have me on the show?' Not until 2007 was the answer, in the end. I was on with David Dimbleby and Dara O'Briain. I sang 'Summer Wind' from *That's Life*, told Parky about my first brain tumour, the story of getting up on the table at Decca, and I gave him a blast of ''O Sole Mio'.

The point is, I've learnt over the years not to get too excited about anything ahead of the event, and it was the same with the Pope. I was going to sing for Pope John Paul II, one of the world's most powerful men, the head of the Catholic Church, a future saint. But I wasn't going to get excited about it until we touched down in Rome.

And then we did – we touched down in Rome. And we were wandering past the Trevi Fountain and I started to get excited. Tourists were milling about on St Peter's Square in Vatican City, gazing up at the jaw-dropping architecture. Huge columns that seem to go upwards for ever. We crossed the square to the Papal Palace. Guards wearing colourful, striped uniforms demanded to see passes. Tourists stopped gawping at the columns to watch us as we passed through.

Inside was breathtaking. Everywhere, eye-popping art. Raphael, Bernini and, of course, Michelangelo, painter of the famous Sistine Chapel, where we were due to meet the Pope. He had this tradition of meeting invited guests and artists due to perform at the concert the day before the performance. He would receive them in the Sistine Chapel.

To get to it we took several flights of marble stairs, all of us gawping at the frescoes on the walls: majestic, detailed, awe-inspiring. A huge archway led into the Sistine Chapel, this incredibly holy place, and we sat down to await the arrival of the Pope.

I have a picture of it on my wall. A couple of them, actually. In the first we're all sitting in the Sistine Chapel and the Pope has taken his seat. I'm sat next to Brian McFadden out of Westlife. We didn't speak much, though. We were waiting for the Pope in the Sistine Chapel; it's not like you're going to chat about *EastEnders* or chart placings. After 'Wow', what else is left to say?

At the side, there were doors. Huge things, solid oak. They must have been 40 feet high. From them came a loud, imperious knocking. Then, as they swung open, we heard music. Difficult to describe, like a bagpipe sound. Next the Pope entered, flanked by cardinals, flag-bearers holding the papal coat of arms bringing up the rear. Bent almost double, he walked with the aid of a walking stick to his seat.

Then, guests were invited up to where the Pope sat. A cardinal bent to the Pope's ear, introducing each guest as they approached, bending and kissing the Pope's proffered ring. I decided to take my cue from those ahead of me, and I, too, leaned forward, took his hand and kissed the papal ring; was given his blessing.

I sometimes wonder about that blessing, in the dark moments. I wonder if that blessing carried me through. Gave me the strength I needed to overcome the throat operation, the tumours.

After we met the Pope, it was time to rehearse for the gig, hours and hours of waiting around in one of the Vatican music halls – waiting for the organisers to get their collective arses in gear, which is where I learnt about sweaties, one of the main things I remember about the Westlife lads. The other being that they were made up having seen the Pope, being good, Catholic lads; a couple of them had brought their mums. And if you're thinking that it sounds disrespectful of them, talking about sweaties in the Vatican, to be fair this was an altogether less sanctified surrounding than the Sistine Chapel. It was, to all intents and purposes, a concert hall.

Rehearsals lasted for the rest of that day and then well into the next, the day of the concert. If I wanted to be diplomatic, I'd say that rehearsals were intense because it was for the Pope's annual Christmas concert, and it would be broadcast to an audience of tens of millions of people on Christmas Eve. If I wanted to tell the truth I'd say that they were intense because the organisation was a shambles.

Eventually, though, we'd all done our bit, including a run-through of a 'Silent Night' finale, by which time it was time for the show, opened by yours truly.

It was packed, the hall full of Catholic dignitaries, and the front rows were taken up by about forty cardinals, red-robed, very smart, hands in their laps, watching the stage inscrutably. On the stage, a 120-piece orchestra. And me.

I did three sacred arias, 'Adeste Fideles', the Schubert 'Ave Maria' and Cesare Frank's 'Panis Angelicus', and it was probably one of the best performances I've ever given. Whenever I'm singing, without wanting to sound cheesy, I always feel the songs. When that stops happening, you might as well forget it, in my opinion. But that concert at the Vatican was something else again. That was emotion layered on top of emotion. There's no getting away from it, it was a spiritual experience.

How could it not be? I'm not a particularly religious person, but I believe in God. I have a faith, shaky as it may occasionally be. And being inside the Papal Palace in the Vatican, surrounded by some of the world's most holy men; everywhere you look, great art made in God's name; singing songs of devotion to Him; that whole experience, beauty and worship so closely inter-twined, I think anybody but the most hardened atheist would be moved. Even my manager. Completely anti-religious. Even he felt something there. A feeling that's very hard to describe without resorting to the usual religious words, so I'm going to use them. It's a feeling of spirituality, devotion, virtue. All of it within me as I sang.

I wonder, too, how I would feel now if I gave the same perform-ance. Then, I was on the upswing of my life and career. I had relatively little in life to worry me. Since, of course, I've had more testing times. I realise now that your preoccupations change. When you're busy doing your thing – whatever your thing is – it's easy to get sidetracked by all the consumer stuff: you're doing your house up, you want to drive a cool car, you're working, you're keeping an eye on the bills, and your kids want the right clothes and all the new toys. It's easy to lose sight of what you're about as a human being. It's natural to forget to stop and ask yourself whether you're behaving correctly; whether you're treating people fairly or not. I've come to believe that you need to consider that kind of stuff. There's no point in paying lip service to spirituality, just answering, 'Yes, I'm a Christian,' simply because that's the way you've been brought up, or, in my case, you've had a moving experience in a holy place. You have to consider those beliefs. And consider them often, not just when it suits you, or when you need something – when you're sick and you want to be healthy again.

I'm as guilty of it as anyone. The state of mind I'm in now, I think about my beliefs a lot. But is that because I've become a more spiritual person? Or because I'm recovering from two brain tumours and I've finished a course of radiotherapy; because I've been put in a position where I've been forced to think about my faith?

When I'm better, and I'm on the road, preoccupied with plane trips, hotel rooms, the tour, the band, the show, will I think about it then? I'd like to think so, but I'm not sure.

I don't know – somewhere along the line we've lost something, I think. Not just me. All of us. TVs, cars, houses, money and fashion have all got in the way. That whole keeping-up-with-the-Joneses ideal. Those things have stopped us from making the connection between the people we are and who we ought to be. Instead we concentrate too much on what we want. So, yes, I do have a faith, though if I'm honest I often wonder if I'm truly good enough – if I'm worthy of that faith.

After the show, I was approached by Archbishop John Foley. Red-robed, he'd been sitting in the front row.

'Russell,' he said, 'that was absolutely magnificent, absolutely wonderful. Um... I feel like I'm intruding, but could I perhaps trouble you for one of your CDs?'

'Yes, of course,' I said. All performers carry CDs around with them, and my manager handed me one from our luggage. 'Who's it for?'

'Well,' he said, 'it's for the man himself. He'd like one of your CDs.'

'Uh, yeah, sure,' I managed. 'Would he like me to sign it?' Immediately thinking, How the bloody hell do you sign a CD for the Pope?

'Oh no.' Archbishop Foley looked taken aback. 'No, you won't need to sign it for the Pope.'

'Right.' I handed him the CD.

'I'm terribly sorry,' he said, 'but I don't suppose I could trouble you for one more?'

'Of course.' I passed him another CD, thinking, Better not offer to sign this one. God only knows who it's for – pun intended.

'Oh,' he said, as I handed him the CD. 'I'd like this one signing, please. This one's for me.'

'Right,' I said, and signed, grinning.

A couple of weeks later, a letter popped through the door at the Boathouse in Worsley. Letters were arriving a lot, of course. Those big, thick envelopes that sometimes stayed unopened.

This one had a little red wax seal, the Vatican emblem. It was a letter from the Pope, thanking me for my CD. It arrived on January 14, 2002, and not long after, I had a second letter from him, this time saying how much he'd enjoyed it. Cool. A review from the Pope. That and the thank-you letter hang on my wall at home.

At the end of 2001, I ended what had been the most incredible year of my life with a sell-out gig at the *Manchester Evening News* Arena.

'Good Lord,' I told the crowd. 'It's only four years ago that I was singing in a pub in Wigan.'

CHAPTER FORTY-TWO

February 2008

Oh my God.

I can't believe it.

Gary's driving me away from the Christie after my last-ever session of radiotherapy and I thought I'd feel happy about it, but this – this is complete and utter elation. I'm babbling at a million miles an hour. *It's over, it's over, it's over.* No more touching soup, no more medieval torture device, no more felt-tip pen on the tip of my nose every day I go (even though the nurses were nice enough to say that that they were going to miss me going 'Beep' when they dotted the felt-tip pen on my nose), no more taking ages to set up, no more clutching the little panic button…

No more radiotherapy at all.

As we drive away from the hospital, I can't help myself. I'm singing and laughing, I'm doing football chants ('Cheerio, cheerio, cheerio!'), beeping the car horn and waving at random passers-by.

It's over. It feels like the first day of the rest of my life.

Two days later

Doctor's got me on steroids – there was some inflammation of the optic nerve. Here's a hot tip: never take steroids. You know you hear those stories about bodybuilders who go crazy having necked too many steroids? I can see why. They turn you into a psycho.

'All that rehab crowd. Amy Winehouse, Pete Doherty and all that lot,' I'm telling Gary, 'they've turned being a drug addict into a lifestyle choice. And you know what really hacks me off?'

'No, Russ, can't say I do,' says Gary.

'They're role models. My kids'll be looking at these people thinking that's a cool way to behave.'

'Yes, Russ,' says Gary.

I get letters from people who tell me I'm brave, and it's nice to hear, of course it is; the one thing that's been great in all this – the one bit of silver lining – is just how fantastic everyone has been. Family, friends, fans, the public. A week or so ago I was at the Christie, in for one of my radiotherapy sessions, and a guy came over to me: 'Just wanted to say, Russell, good luck with your treatment, pal.'

'Thanks, mate,' I said, 'and good luck with yours.'

Some guys on a building site: 'All right, Russell, how's it going? Stick with it, mate.'

'Cheers, lads.'

But I don't feel brave. I don't feel as though what I'm doing is exceptional. It's not through choice I've been sharing my head with a brain tumour. I haven't run into a burning house and saved a baby. All I can do is try and put a positive spin on something negative. That's all I can do. That's the courage I have to offer my situation. Most of the time what I feel is hacked off. I mean, I've got big plans for the future. The radiotherapy's over and you know the Italian lessons I was talking about? I've been taking them. I'm training hard. My sound engineer Grant's in the house, working on a live CD of a gig I did last year at the Royal Albert Hall and it sounds fantastic.

But I'm pissed off, too. Maybe it's the steroids. Maybe I'll read this back and think, Yeah, definitely the steroids. But when you're in the Christie and a guy waiting for his radiotherapy session wishes you luck with yours, then you're looking at the day's papers and it's Amy Winehouse or Britney, the poster girls for self-inflicted misery. Then you get mad. You get seething with the injustice of it. All that real, proper bravery and courage that goes on in hospitals and hospices up and down the country, all day, every day. Quiet, unassuming courage. And those two are in the papers every day because they're screwing themselves up. Messing up their own lives then whingeing about it. And they're front-page news, their records are selling shedloads, people talk about how sad it is, the situation they're in, how they need help. Tell you what, they should get down to the Christie. Go and sit in reception for an hour. That'd put them right; that'd stop them feeling sorry for themselves. Either that or pay Kirsty Howard a visit. A trip to Francis House would sort them out.

CHAPTER FORTY-THREE

July 2002

Francis House is a hospice in Didsbury where terminally ill children live out the rest of their lives. It was opened by Princess Diana in 1991 and since then it's filled the final years of thousands of youngsters in the North West with as much care, laughter and joy as possible, while also offering support to their parents – parents who have to come to terms with the inevitable.

I visit it, when I can, take gifts for the children. I went last week and took my two with me, watching them as we walked around chatting to the children in the hospice. Afterwards, outside, they were quiet.

'You see how lucky you are, don't you?' I said. 'It makes you realise how lucky you are to be happy and healthy.'

'Yeah, daddy, it does.'

Francis House receives less than 4 per cent government funding, so in order to stay open it needs to raise funds. Up until 2006 it needed £5m just to stay open. And what a bloody disgrace that is. *Just to stay open.*

The target was reached in October 2006, and it was mainly down to the work of Kirsty Howard. She was born with her heart back to front, which means her internal organs are misplaced. It's a condition so rare it doesn't even have a name; she's the only person in the UK to suffer from it and only the second in the world. In February 1999, aged three and a half, she was given six weeks to live. She's now twelve. To date, she's had nine operations on her heart. Talk about brave.

I first met her at the Commonwealth Games, the opening ceremony. I was there to sing 'Where My Heart Will Take Me', which was the opening theme for *Star Trek: Enterprise* and had been written for me by my friend, Diane Warren. Not that I'm name-dropping or anything, but this is *the* Diane Warren we're talking about, one of the most successful songwriters in the history of the music industry. One of the most prolific, too. She's been nominated for six Oscars, four Golden Globes and won a Grammy. I'd recorded songs by her on *Encore* ('Catch The Tears) and *Reprise* ('I Don't Know How I Got By'), and we'd formed a friendship. One day the call came in: Diane's written the theme tune to the new *Star Trek* series, did I want to sing it? Thinks for a second. Remembers watching Captain Kirk and co as a young lad. *Yes.* Where do I sign?

Turned out to be a great one too. If you ask me, 'Where My Heart Will Take Me' is one of her best songs – which is saying something. It's become a favourite with me and with the fans. It even ended up being played as a wake-up call to astronauts on a space shuttle mission in 2007.

Funny thing is, I'd been in the frame to perform at the Olympics in 2000, the ones held in Australia, but it hadn't come off, which was a disappointment at the time. So when the call came in about the Commonwealth Games there was a bit of the old Parky effect about it, with me thinking, Yeah, well, we'll see. I'll get excited about it when I'm there.

And then, just as it was in Rome, I got excited about it. A car picked me up in the morning for rehearsals and I got my first look at the venue, the City of Manchester Stadium, which is Manchester City's new ground. It had just been built then, so it was a huge deal to be one of the first to see it. Empty, it was mammoth, magnificent. When it started to fill up it was something else entirely. It filled, and it filled, the spectators taking their seats. Then a Red Arrow fly-past announced the Queen's arrival. Then the show began, commencing with what seemed like thousands and thousands of drummers, the noise of them like nothing I'd experienced before – a noise you feel, rather than hear.

S Club 7 were playing. Each nation was introduced and took to the pitch with flag-bearers and supporters, the pitch thronged with people. There were lights going. Spots, lasers, floodlights. Camera flashlights blinking all over the stadium, making the stands twinkle like a carpet of diamonds. It's people in the audience taking pictures, but the flashlights become part of the show. It's like I say, the audience *are* the show.

There was so much sound and colour in that arena, and in the middle of it all was a little box. A podium, a tiny stage on the centre circle. Which was where I was due to stand.

Waiting to go on, I remember looking up, out through the roof of the stadium, where the sky was a perfect, uninterrupted black; that same black curtain the performer sees at concerts. Framing it were the floodlights, spearing the black mass with light. Into it rose a mist, heat generated by the capacity stadium. I thought back to that first-ever childhood visit to Old Trafford, where I was like a sponge, soaking up the buzz and atmosphere of the expectant crowd. They say you never quite recapture the magic of that first time, the thrill of that kind of event. That opening ceremony, it felt like I did.

There was a steward nearby, guy in a fluorescent yellow tabard. Proper Manc. I was standing there, hypnotised by the light, colour and sound. Buffeted by it. Adrenalin going.

'All right, Russell, how you doing, lad?' said Tabard.

'Yeah, mate, thanks, fine,' I said.

'Yer nervous, then?' he said, indicating the stadium.

'I don't really feel the nerves,' I said, truthfully.

He sniffed as though not entirely satisfied with my answer. 'You do know there's going to be over a billion people watching you tonight?' he said.

I grinned, looked at him. 'I'd better be good then, hadn't I?'

'You better had, son.'

'Ladies and gentleman,' came the announcement, 'to sing a salute to the athletes… Russell Watson.'

The stadium fell as quiet as it was going to get, and I sang, backed by a huge gospel choir.

It's been a long road, getting from there to here.
It's been a long time, but my time is finally near.
And I can feel the change in the wind right now. Nothing's in
    my way.
And they're not gonna hold me down no more,
No, they're not gonna hold me down.

There aren't words to describe that moment. I mean, simply attending an event like that is an incredible experience. To perform. To take centre stage. For a huge stadium to hush and for billions of people to hear you sing. I don't know, there aren't words to describe it. And it spoils you in a way. If you're in a band, you get to share the experience with your bandmates. S Club 7 were probably talking about it for weeks, and Westlife could swap notes about their meeting with the Pope. If you're a solo performer, you don't get that. You have to deal with it alone. You could list your achievements and people will nod, impressed. And they might try to imagine what it's like. But they don't *know*. They can't know. And that can be quite lonely at times.

And then. Bump. Back down to earth. You know what I was saying, how you can get carried away with your preoccupations?

Bump. You meet someone like Kirsty Howard. Lonely? Try being the only person in the country with a condition so rare nobody's even bothered to give it a name. For whom every single day is a day on borrowed time.

'Ladies and gentlemen,' said the announcer. 'To present the Jubilee baton to Her Majesty the Queen, someone who's overcome more challenges than even the greatest sportsman or woman here tonight... Kirsty Howard.'

A little girl. Six she was then. Hand in hand with David Beckham, she approached the Queen. Billions of people watched her do it, her mum, Lynn, a short distance behind with Kirsty's oxygen tank.

I met her later. When you first see her what strikes you, of course, is the oxygen tank, and then the tubes that run from that into her nose. Maybe the first thing you think is, 'Poor little girl.' Then you get talking to her and you swiftly realise you've met your match. We are talking one hell of a driven little girl here. Very bright. An incredibly positive outlook on life and very, very charismatic. To meet her is to fall under her spell, and those who have done so include Becks, Mohamed Al-Fayed, who gave a lot of money to the appeal, and, of course, me. I knew Susie Mathis, who is Kirsty's PA, for want of a better word. I knew her because she used to organise some of my gigs at the Italian restaurants. So the day after meeting Kirsty, I gave her a call.

When you get involved with a charity the first thing you ask is, What can I do? Are there any events I can do, for example. In this case there was a ball that Kirsty had organised, the Angel Ball, and I went along, took a little orchestra and sang, and the ball did really well, raised about £70,000. I did a couple more, then Susie suggested we do a song for Kirsty. I agreed. Great idea. Now to find a song, which isn't as easy as it sounds. But as it happened, there was a song floating around that was written by Jim Steinman, Meatloaf's songwriter. Luckily for us, Jim and Meatloaf had fallen out (probably, as I was later to find out, because Meatloaf is absolutely, categorically, nuts). I was in New York when I heard about the song, saw the lyrics, knew at once it would be a great song for the Kirsty appeal and got in touch with Susie; ended up recording a version of the song and sending it to her.

Two nights later she rang me up from the UK, almost in tears down the phone – thankfully, happy tears. She loved the song.

It was called 'Nothing Sacred (A Song For Kirsty)' and it got to number 10 in the charts. At the time I was annoyed about that, to be honest. Said a few things in the media about how it wasn't getting the backing it deserved. Maybe I should have got myself a drug habit and wandered around Soho in my underpants. Perhaps then we would have had a few more column inches.

On the other hand, it did raise a few thousand quid, and I'm well aware that there are legions of charities that never get that kind of exposure. I get a lot of letters from charities and good causes. You read them and it makes you painfully aware of how much hurt there is out there. You want to help, of course, but you can't because you simply wouldn't have time for anything else. But when I met Kirsty there was an instant connection. Perhaps because Rebecca is around her age – you can't help but think of your own children; how lucky you are that they were favoured by the accident of birth. Or maybe because Kirsty worked her mojo on me.

That end of year I performed at Old Trafford and Kirsty came on to thunderous applause. A week or so later I played another sell-out gig at the *Manchester Evening News* Arena, and we did 'Nothing Sacred'. Kirsty came out to sing some of it with me. She got the biggest cheer of the night.

She came to see me when I was in hospital last October, after my emergency operation. She had good news; her appeal had reached its £5m target and the long-term future of the hospice was assured.

The day-to-day fundraising would continue, though, of course. It wasn't like she was going to put her feet up. You know, if there's a hero in this story, it's her.

CHAPTER FORTY-FOUR

Glad to escape the tyranny of the big, thick envelopes still piling up at home, I'd gone to New Zealand early in 2002. I did lots of stuff there, but a massive gig in Auckland capped it all. We later released it as a DVD; Faye Tozer appeared with me, as did Hayley Westenra. Just before the show, we had a minor panic when my favourite shirt came back from the dry cleaners two sizes too small and we had to comb Auckland for a replacement. We had no luck and I ended up just pulling the shrunken shirt on anyway. I can laugh about it now, but at the time I wasn't a happy bunny.

Despite any wardrobe malfunctions, the show was great. I got into hot water because about halfway through the gig I told 100,000 people that I was staying at the Auckland Hilton.

'Want to come to a party?' I said. 'We're having one at the Auckland Hilton at about half eleven, see you down there.'

Hello? Joke? Didn't stop thousands of audience members turning up at the Auckland hotel. The manager spoke to me. 'Er, Mr Watson, there are a lot of people here who say you've invited them to a party.'

'Really? That was a joke.'

'Well, they're all waiting outside, Mr Watson, they want to come in.'

Uh-oh...

Shortly after my New Zealand trip, I was invited to play

Carnegie Hall, and who should I phone to conduct me at Carnegie Hall but Sir Bill? There was no way I was going to let him miss out on that one.

He flew over, joined us in New York. As well as the Carnegie show I had a bunch of other stuff to do, TV interviews mostly.

'How was the trip over, Bill?' I asked him when he arrived. He was looking slightly more relaxed than I would have expected after the long transatlantic flight

'Well, Russell, it was wonderful, thank you. I was actually quite surprised because they booked me in first class.'

'Did they?' I said.

'Yes, yes. Normally it's either coach or business – business at best. But they put me in first class. Couldn't bloody believe it.'

'Well that's fantastic, what about your room?'

He said, 'Well, that's another thing, it's like a bloody double penthouse suite.'

'Great stuff.'

That evening I met up with Kevin Gore. Remember him? The guy I ended up abusing the night I serenaded Bill Clinton's guests at the Trump. He'd long forgiven me for that incident, thankfully.

'How is Sir Bill?' he asked when we were at our table. 'Is he okay? Is he happy with everything?'

'Sir Bill? Yeah, he's delighted,' I said. 'First class, penthouse suite, the whole shebang. He's over the moon.'

'Great,' said Kevin Gore. 'Listen, Russell, we were wondering, you know, with him being a knight, whether he'd be interested in maybe doing something on one of the TV shows. You could incorporate him somehow on one of the TV shows and he could talk about when he got his knighthood. You know, over here we're really interested in that sort of stuff. So I think it would be great if he could do something like that.'

'Oh, he's not a real knight,' I said. I can't remember exactly what Kevin Gore was doing at the time, pouring a glass of wine, arranging his napkin. Whatever it was, he froze.

'I'm sorry?' he said. His smile never faltered. Only it no longer reached his eyes.

'Sir Bill. He's not really Sir Bill. It's just a term of endearment.'

The colour was now draining from his face. 'Really?' he pressed.

'Yeah, sorry, it's just a joke. You know, it's funny because he speaks in this posh way and because of his demeanour.'

'Right,' said Kevin Gore. And fair play to him, he had the good grace not to make the call there and then.

But Sir Bill was downgraded from his penthouse suite pretty soon afterwards. And when he travelled back, he flew coach.

He was there to conduct me at Carnegie Hall, though, that was the main thing. And that night was a special one for me. The gig came at a time when I was doing really well in the States. I was answering questions from UK reporters about how I'd 'broken' America. How did it feel to achieve what Robbie Williams had failed to do? I'd left the UK with an album at number one in the classical charts, and I had a number one album in America's classical charts, too. Not many can say that. Actually, nobody can say that. Getting number ones in both UK and the US classical charts made history.

So the concert at Carnegie Hall was the icing on the cake. My New York debut. I'd been warned that the audience could be a bit on the cold side, a little restrained. 'Expect a bit of polite applause when you go on, Russell.' But when I walked out there I was met by a wall of sound, all the more powerful for being so unexpected. They were up for it, the audience, and I responded; I was on fire. Backed by the New York Pops and the Juilliard Choral Union, my guest artists Hayley again, and Lea Salonga, I sang 'Va Pensiero', 'Volare', 'Funiculì, Funiculà', 'Where My Heart Will Take Me',

'Vesti La Giubba' – the whole bit. Plus, of course, 'Nessun Dorma'. And the reception was amazing, breathtaking. There are moments, doing those really big gigs, that I'm transported. I mean, I love being on stage at the best of times. That and my kids, that's what I live for. But some of those major, turning-point performances, I've felt something else, like an out-of-body experience. I'm somewhere different. On Planet Russell. I felt that way during the performance for the Pope. The Royal Albert Hall's another venue that does it for me. And, of course, that night at Carnegie.

Not that I ever had much chance to sit around daydreaming about the experience. We did the Carnegie performance, some TV, then we were flying back to the UK for the Commonwealth Games, another intense experience. The following month, back to the States, continuing my love affair with the Americans, this time for a PBS Special at the Trump Taj Mahal in Atlantic City.

A PBS Special is a big deal. PBS stands for Public Broadcasting Service, which is a huge non-profit channel in America with 354 member stations. The specials they host are a great vehicle for artists, because PBS set up the gig, record it, then show it on the station, non-stop, so if you do a PBS Special it'll be broadcast not a few times, but hundreds of times, across scores of member stations. The potential size of the audience you reach is immense. PBS broke Bocelli in America, that's how powerful it is.

Not that we were taking it all that seriously. This was at a time when I'd be up to all sorts just to break up the monotony of the treadmill. A favourite gag in those days was to check into hotels under ridiculous names, or baffle room service at the New York Trump by calling up and using my (legendary, by now) Sean Connery impression.

'Yesh, I'd like to order shome chicken shandwishes, please. My name? Yesh, it's Bond…'

Out in Atlantic City we were still making merry with employees of

Donald Trump. Beforehand, Rory, who was the Alcohol & Restaurants man for the record company, had asked me, as he always did, 'Russell, they want to know what you'd like on your rider?'

The rider is what the venue provides for you in your dressing room. You hear about bands with weird rider requests: Barry Manilow insists on a certain temperature, Van Halen say backstage celery must be trimmed and not peeled; Mariah Carey that all straws must be bendy – although from what I've heard that's one of her more sane requests.

Anyway, time for me to have a bit of fun with the rider, I thought. Nick Patrick was with me. We opened a bottle of champagne and went into conference, coming up with a list of ridiculous stuff to put on the rider.

'What about coloured assorted flavoured condoms?' I said. 'You know, a hundred assorted condoms, spread around the carpet in the dressing room.'

'Okay.' We put that down, making sure that it was clear we wanted them spread around the floor of the dressing room.

Next we added a desire for two blow-up sex dolls, one blonde, one brunette, both wearing suspenders and stockings and with strap-on dildos attached. We also wanted assorted helium-filled party balloons. Then, to top it all off we decided to ask for a non-existent English delicacy, a 'Cheesy Daniel'. Oh, and one last thing, a 'gusset typewriter'.

Off went the list of requests. Not long after, Rory had a call that he told us about, some guy, very camp, saying, 'Rory, hi. Look, it's about this rider. We've managed to get most of what Russell wants, but, you know, I'm struggling with the Cheesy Daniel here, Rory. And to tell the truth I don't know what the hell a gusset typewriter is.'

So we never got our Cheesy Daniel. Or our gusset typewriter. Shame, I'd have liked to see them try and improvise. We did get everything else, though, to the letter, so that when Nick, Rory and I arrived at our dressing room in the Trump, sure enough there were coloured condoms spread all over the floor, helium balloons were everywhere and in one corner stood a blonde blow-up sex doll dressed in suspenders and stocking, proudly sporting a strap-on dildo. In the other corner, a brunette version. All just as we'd asked for.

Nick, Rory and I were still laughing about it when there was a knock at the door, a member of staff saying, 'Mr Trump would like to come in and see you, Mr Watson.'

And in walked Donald Trump.

And he didn't even flinch. He took it all in: the condoms, the balloons, the two blow-up sex dolls. And he said nothing, no response whatsoever, not even a raised eyebrow.

With him, though, was his girlfriend. An absolutely stunning blonde who was clinging on to him for dear life. She was a different story. Her mouth dropped open as she gazed around the room.

'Hi,' said Donald Trump. 'I just wanted to stop by and say what a pleasure it will be to introduce you on stage tonight.'

He stepped forward, his feet crunching on condom wrappers, and held out his hand to shake. His girlfriend followed, staring in horror at the condoms around her feet, stepping gingerly over them. She batted a helium balloon away from her hair. All the time, her eyes wide, her mouth on the floor. I don't think it closed the entire time she was in the room.

At her side, Donald was still carrying on as though every dressing room he visited was done up like a porn star's birthday party. 'What a great pleasure it is to meet you, Mr Watson. I've got your record and I'm a big fan of yours and I'm really looking forward to the concert tonight – can't wait to see it. Now is there anything you'd like me to say when I introduce you?'

Completely oblivious to his horrified girlfriend, who still gazed around the room, every now and then looking down at her feet and shifting her shoes as though fearing the condoms might bite. With a last handshake, Donald turned to leave and she followed, glancing back as they reached the door, her mouth still a wide O of shock.

We were in bits as the door closed behind them.

As promised, he introduced me that night, which went well, just one minor hitch that had become apparent during rehearsals. Natalie Cole. Now, if you think I'm going to say anything rude about Natalie Cole, you're wrong. She's virtually a legend, and her father certainly was. But I've met her a few times and each time she's been a bit... what's a nice way of putting it? A bit out there, I suppose you could say. You know my policy – who wants legends to be down-to-earth? The problem I had on that occasion, though, was that I was due to sing 'The Prayer' with Natalie, a song I'd originally done with Lulu on the first album, and Natalie hadn't bothered to learn it. I was going through the song with her on the day and it quickly became apparent that she had no idea how it went. Maybe she'd been expecting to rely on the autocue. Maybe nobody bothered to tell her it was in Italian. Perhaps she thought that she was so great that she could turn up, sing a song that she hadn't sung before and that wasn't even in her own language, and completely nail it.

If she did, she was wrong on that score. Not exactly a complete disaster, but let's just say it was interesting. Like your divas eccentric, do you? I thought. Be careful what you wish for.

Later that year, I was touring Australia, and the tour brought me to the Sydney Opera House – another of those truly legendary venues, a pivotal moment in my career. The thing with that gig was, I'd sold it out – twice on the trot. The Sydney Opera House, one of the most famous landmarks in the world, and it was packed with people coming to see me. There was a time I'd barely even been abroad. Just going to see the Sydney Opera House would have been a once-in-a-lifetime experience. To play it. To sell it out. Words can't describe.

I loved Sydney. When I'm old and grey and the kids are settled down, maybe I'll go and live there. Who knows? I definitely fell in love with the place. It's beautiful, not quite as crowded as in the UK, the roads less busy. For the gig at the Sydney Opera House, I was staying at the Grand Quay Hotel on the harbour. It's so near you can walk from the hotel to the venue. I just stuck my suit on, strolled a few hundred yards along the quay then into the Sydney Opera House.

'Hey, Russ, mate, you going to put on a good show for us tonight?'

'Absolutely.'

Incredible. I loved it there. If it wasn't for the kids I probably would have stayed. The Boathouse back home was less inviting by the day.

When I used to do the clubs, they'd put posters up to advertise the performance: 'Russell Watson. From Meatloaf to Pavarotti.'

I'd met Pavarotti. I'd had the world's weirdest rehearsal with him. Now it was time to meet the Loaf.

And I think I've already mentioned it, but he's nuts. Absolutely 100 per cent mental, on stage and off.

I met him as part of a programme I was making in 2003, called *Can Russell Watson Cut It?* Cut what? Being a rock and roll singer. The idea was to take me, the classical singing guy, and pit him against one of the most legendary rockers ever, Meatloaf, me picking up tips from other hairy blokes along the way. I'll be honest, it wasn't like it was a huge challenge. I mean, it took me out of my regular singing comfort zone, but only by a small margin; it wasn't anything I hadn't done before. Still, it was fun. I flew to LA and made the rounds. When it came to interviewing Gene Simmons out of Kiss, I was picked up by a Hummer – a stretch limo Hummer, about 40 feet long, fitted with plasma TV screens, a bar, the works. Opening the door and looking down this vast expanse of car, I saw Gene Simmons reclining in leather seats.

'Hey, man,' he grinned, 'just thought I'd bring something small for us to sit and spend the afternoon chatting in.' He was mad. Not Meatloaf-mad, but mad all the same.

Chapter Forty-five

In New York I spoke to Slash out of Guns 'n' Roses, too, and we ended up going out for a drink at the Rainbow Room. Slash is what you'd call a cool cat. That stage presence he has? The hair, the hat. That's Slash off-stage, too.

At the time he was auditioning musicians for his new band – Velvet Revolver. He held court at the Rainbow Room, a Guinness not far from reach, cigarette permanently on the go – just before the smoking ban, this was. Goodness only knows how he copes with that.

'Hey, man,' he drawled. 'You know, you're a great singer. I think you'd work really well in this band I'm putting together. It'd be great, man. You should come down.'

'You know what,' I replied, 'I'd love to, but I'm just crazy, crazy busy on my own stuff right now.'

Slash nodded wisely. A long, slow shaggy nod like he knew the deal. 'Yeah, man,' he said, 'yeah, I know that, man.'

Next for the performance with the man himself. The loaf they call Meat. I'd grown up listening to him, I'd sung his songs in the clubs, I knew what he was all about and he didn't disappoint. There's something epic about Meatloaf: if he was a film he'd be in widescreen. Yet on the other hand there's also this manic, genuinely bonkers edge to him, and those two sides work off each other. So what you're left with is this huge ball of energy, bounding from one place to the next, never shutting up, wiping the hair from his eyes, bawling at people, bursting into song, always out of breath.

'With rock, you can't do anything wrong,' he yelled at me, demonstrating how to thump your chest in time with the drum beat, then running breathlessly around the stage during rehearsals, doing some more shouting. I stood, holding my microphone, just watching this super-caffeinated guy do his stuff. There's extrovert; then there's Meatloaf.

I was asked if I felt nervous about the performance and said no (because I fackin' larve, etc). His drummer piped up, 'Anyone who isn't nervous on stage with Meatloaf is plain old crazy – you just never know what's going to happen.'

Still, it went off well. We sang 'Bat Out of Hell', a real blast from the past for me, and there was a moment when I sang a part, then he sang a part, and it was like the battle of the voices. After that we did 'Couldn't Have Said It Better', and all told it was a cool experience. Not up there – face it, I'm not a rocker – but cool.

That May I performed at a huge memorial concert in Washington, singing 'God Bless America' during a moving ceremony to honour America's war dead. I was still working hard, there was a new album to record; something wasn't right, though. It was my voice. There was something up with my voice.

Plus, of course, those letters.

CHAPTER FORTY-SIX

They kept arriving, the letters, and suddenly I was broke. Really, really broke. Looking back on that time now, it's dark. Very dark.

It dates back to when I first started to get noticed as an artist. I'd got involved with a management company and it seemed like an amazing deal for someone in my position. And for someone in my position *then*, it had its advantages. Financial security, being the main one. The problem would come (as it turned out) if I was ever successful. If that happened, I stood to be giving away a large amount of my income.

Round about that time was the Old Trafford performance, the Cliff Richard meeting. Things started to move for me. This management deal just seemed like a leg-iron.

So I consulted a firm of lawyers in Manchester, told them I didn't want to work with this company any more. By this time I had a new manager and there was a meeting set up with the old company, the idea being to hammer out some kind of settlement. Pay them off, in other words.

Unfortunately, no settlement was ever reached. After a year with this firm of lawyers – a year that cost me almost £125,000 in legal bills, with little to show for it, still tied into the deal, I fired that bunch of lawyers, went and found a second set, this lot supposedly more music-orientated than the last lot.

I was with them for three years and ended up paying them almost three-quarters of a million pounds. Still the case remained unresolved. All it seemed I got for my money were letters. They were posh-looking letters but they didn't seem to be worth the money.

So, I went to another set of lawyers. This lot were the Real McCoy, I was told, and they wouldn't be charging silly fees without getting a resolution. The bills kept arriving, still posh-looking, only now they had a different letterhead. I was with that firm of lawyers for twelve months, I paid them a six-figure sum and the case fell apart.

It gets better. Me and my manager had a company together that went to the wall owing thousands. I can't go into details and they'd be too long and boring anyway, but it was me who ended up paying every penny of that catastrophe. I had no choice. The bank had their claws into my house – they wanted it if I didn't meet the company debts.

I'd return from Canada, Australia, America, Miami, *South America*, and there would be piles and piles of letters and papers – envelopes two inches thick: Special Report. Witness Report. Barrister Report. Then a bill because somebody needs to pay for all these reports and that someone was me. There would be bills for lawyers' services in the issue of the management dispute; bills for lawyers' services in the small matter of my divorce; bills from my accountants and letters from the bank reminding me they had their eye on my house.

At first, I was pretty happy-go-lucky about it, believe it or not. I just had this belief that things were going to turn out fine. My manager was looking after my affairs, I had good accountants, my lawyers were doing their job. All this legal and money stuff I thought came with the territory. I can see now that I was hopelessly unbusiness savvy and have no one to blame but myself for the financial mess. All I was really concerned with was performing and singing.

And still those letters kept dropping to the mat. And it started to get me down. I'd go away for three months. I was the biggest-selling UK artist in the history of classical music. I'd be performing for royalty, for the Pope, at the Commonwealth Games. I had sell-out gigs. Yet, I might go away for a couple of months, earn £150,000, then come home to find lawyer's bills for £200,000 on the mat.

Even so – even with all that – I kept positive. Don't think I'm trying to spin you a sob story here because I'm not. Throughout the whole business I kept going, thinking that if I worked hard enough I could pay everything off. My career was doing well. I had the earning power to get through.

I thought that right up until the point I almost lost my voice.

'I've got some pictures for you. We can have a look at what I've just seen. That all right with you?'

Dr Phil Jones had just shoved a probe up my nose. You know that trick magicians do where they pretend to push a pencil up their nostril then pull it out of their mouth? It was a bit like that, except for real.

'Right,' he said, 'do you see this?' He pointed at something on the picture that looked like the mouth of a cave, indicating a dark area. 'These are your vocal cords, and I don't know whether you can see – if we just zoom in here... Right, you see that lump there?'

'Yes,' I said, my voice sounding small in the consulting room.

He looked at me sharply, at the expression on my face. God knows how I must have appeared to him. Like a man walking the plank. A convict on his way to the gallows. 'Well,' he continued, 'that lump is a vocal polyp. Firstly, it's not a nodule, which is... well, it's a shame, actually. It's a shame because nodules often go away of their own accord, or they can go away with therapy. Polyps don't go away, I'm afraid, and therapy's not much use. You have to have them surgically removed, and if you don't it'll get bigger. And if it gets bigger it'll cause an indentation on the opposite fold. And if that happens, it'll cause your vocal folds to bow, like this...'

He held up his hands in an O shape, as though he was holding a large invisible Easter egg. I'd heard about this effect before. It's what happens to singers with age. Their voices sound strained as they get older because the vocal cords, or vocal folds, which is what doctors call them, start to bend. And the effect of that in the voice is to give it a shake, which is the vibrato going out of control. Like I say, you hear it in older singers. Frank Sinatra, towards the end, his vibrato started to get out of control.

And the same thing was going to happen to my vibrato. Only not in the twilight of my career, but now. Still in my thirties. I was still in my thirties and my vocal cords were going to look like the large invisible Easter egg Dr Phil Jones held out in front of him.

'And you could lose some of your register,' he stated, flatly.

I looked at him. You've got to remember, this happened before all the tumour stuff. Apart from the births of my daughters, I was virtually a hospital virgin. Up until that moment, I'd been invincible, hardly ever ill. I was Thai kick-boxing then, so as fit as a fiddle. To me, this news was like Achilles being told, 'Right, Mr Achilles, let's take a look at this picture of your foot...' Samson learning his haircut was a *really* bad idea.

Suddenly I was no longer invulnerable.

'The operation, then,' I managed, 'is this a relatively easy procedure?'

'Oh yes,' said Phil Jones, 'it's a piece of cake...'

I let out a deep breath I didn't even know I'd been holding.

'...unless you sing opera for a living.'

At first it was a throat infection. There was a run of arena concerts that I should have cancelled, but of course I couldn't afford to cancel them because I had hundreds of thousands of pounds' worth of lawyers' bills to pay. So I went ahead and did the concerts. I shouldn't have done. These days I think that having sung with a throat infection caused the problems. Plus, of course, my singing wasn't what it should have been.

To be honest, we all do it, perform with a sore throat. Any singer will say the same. You shouldn't. It's stupid. It's like playing football with a broken ankle. But all singers do it, probably because you can't see it. With a broken ankle, you can see if it's swollen, it hurts to walk on it. If there's something going on in your throat, it's just a sensation. 'Oh, it's fine, I'll have a little gargle with TCP and it'll be right as rain.' The show must go on. Especially if you need the show to keep your house.

So the shows went on. Immediately after was my next project, the recording of *Reprise*. But in the studio it was clear my voice was suffering. I was struggling to achieve my full range, plus my throat was still sore. It stayed sore for longer than it ever had before. Normally I'd get a sore throat and after two or three weeks I'd be fine. This went on for five, six, seven weeks.

One of the songs needed a lot of falsetto, which is a register of the voice that emanates not from the chest, the way you should sing, but from the back of the throat, hence the name 'falsetto', false.

When I came to do the falsetto parts, instead of the sweet choirboy-like noise I was expecting, I got a sound like a brickie clearing his sinuses. A strangulated, gravelly croak that I knew at once wasn't right.

I now know it was the polyp, of course. What had happened was that the lump on my right vocal fold was preventing the two vocal cords from pressing together and it caused a crack in my voice. My chest-voice was fine, because that sound bypasses that area of the vocal folds. The falsetto had gone.

'That falsetto's not working, is it?' said Alistair Gordon, one of my great friends. He co-wrote 'Someone Like You', the song on my first album I later released as a duet with Faye.

Chapter Forty-seven

'No,' I said.

'You might want to get that checked out then.'

'Sure,' I agreed. But guess what? I didn't. I'd lost my falsetto for a while before, but it always came back and I assumed it would return this time. Like a cat or something. Here, kitty, kitty. Here, falsetto.

So I decided I'd be fine; that I'd probably just done a bit too much singing, been working my voice too hard.

I kept thinking that for another four or five weeks until eventually the penny dropped that I was going to have to go and get it looked at, and I booked an appointment at the Wythenshawe in Manchester, the Department of Speech and Language Therapy, with Dr Phil Jones.

Right up to the appointment I still felt armour-plated. Me? Ill? Couldn't be. Trying to ignore the little voice. The one telling me that something might be wrong. The one making my guts churn with nerves.

He stuck the probe up my nose. A huge thing, it has a camera on the end, the idea being that it can take an up-close picture of your vocal cords. It's supposed to go up through the nose, all the way down through the back of the nasal passage and then down the back of the throat to the voice box; only, because of my nerves, my voice box had closed off. Getting it in turned out to be a harrowing, painful experience. They needed to ram some kind of bar down my throat to open the voice box.

(Funny, by the time the operation was over I'd had so many of these things rammed up my nose that I used to do it myself. No injections or gel, just 'hand it here' and up it went.)

That first time though, we got there in the end. Phil Jones took his pictures, identified my polyp, told me it was a simple operation – unless you sing opera for a living. Which, of course, I do.

'So if you were a plumber,' he said, 'I'd do the operation, you'd probably have a sore throat for a couple of weeks and then go back to normal. But you're not. Your voice is your instrument, so any scarring, any deviation on that piece of equipment, can be catastrophic. We've got to get it right.'

There was a pause. I felt conscious of the room around me, as though the atmosphere had changed, the air become more dense. I felt it pressing in on me.

What came to mind was a story I'd read about Julie Andrews. She'd had surgery to remove nodules from her throat but the operation had left her unable to sing for two years. *Unable to sing for two years.* My mind flashed on the piles of bills at home.

'I believe I can get it right for you,' said Phil Jones. 'I've worked on singers before, and I think I can do it for you, and that you'll be singing again within six months.'

But I was hardly listening. I was thinking about Julie Andrews, about surgeons with scalpels and lasers scraping things off my vocal cords. *Unable to sing*, I kept thinking. Julie Andrews couldn't sing for two years.

I was with Roxanna and we left the hospital, me explaining to her what Dr Phil had told me, that if the operation went well, I would be singing just as I always had within a few months. If something went wrong…

He hadn't given me the worst-case Julie Andrews scenario. There was that at least. What he'd said was that if something went wrong I could lose part of my register. Which meant I couldn't sing what I sing. I wouldn't lose my voice exactly – I'd lose The Voice.

Roxanna and I walked from the hospital to the car. Tears were streaming down my face.

CHAPTER FORTY-EIGHT

Home was no comfort. Fat envelopes sat mocking me and I wasn't getting on with Roxanna. We were arguing because she wanted us to move to America. She wouldn't understand that even if I wanted to, I *couldn't* move to America. I couldn't leave Rebecca and Hannah. End of story. She just didn't get it.

We'd been together for four years at that point. We were engaged and she'd moved from New York to Manchester and the Boathouse in Worsley. The problem was, Roxanna missed her family, and there was always this suggestion that we both go and live in America.

I loved America, and I loved Roxanna, but my kids live in Manchester. They lived with their mother in Irlam, and still do, and I see them whenever I can.

You can't do that if you live in America.

And the money stress was still mounting. I was plagued by dark thoughts. Like vampires they came out at night: I'd lose the house. The operation was going to go wrong. I'd be left with nothing – no money, no career. Just a sideshow. A footnote.

I've often wondered if it was that period that either awoke the tumour in my head or somehow caused one to grow. It's not congenital, I know that much, and whenever I've asked if it could be stress-related, I'm told, 'Well, it could be. We're really not sure.' But come on, all that stress has got to go somewhere...

That time was a period of my life when the years spent slogging round the clubs paid dividends. In the end I was able to cope with the situation because I'd become used to it during the early part of my singing career. I was accustomed to being broke and being in debt. I'd got used to people chasing me; to being hassled for money.

God, it rankled though. It's one thing not having two pennies to rub together when you're performing at the Old Firetrap for £60 on a Tuesday night. Quite another when it's a packed Wembley you're playing. This was a time when I should have been financially secure, yet here I was again, broke. I was making a hundred times the amount of money I made during my club days and I still didn't have two pennies to rub together; still couldn't afford to go out and buy a new sofa without asking my manager. I remember going to him and telling him I needed a new sofa for the lounge and he said, 'We've not got enough at the moment, Russell, you might have to wait until next month...'

I'd just come back from a sell-out UK tour and I couldn't buy a sofa for my house.

In the end, despite the fact that it felt like the end of the world at the time, it was that little polyp on my vocal cords that put the brakes on the whole show. Unable to sing, my career went on hold. And at last I stepped off the rollercoaster. The treadmill finally, after three hard years, came to a standstill. I had a week's grace between the consultation with Phil Jones and the operation, and for the first time since I signed to Decca in 1999 I was able to take stock.

I started asking questions. Why wasn't I getting bank statements? That was one of the first. I'd hardly noticed before, and if I had noticed I probably wouldn't have given it a second thought.

But I wasn't getting statements. I didn't have credit card statements, either. Nor company statements. The company that had gone belly-up, for which I was meeting six-figure costs.

I'd never bothered to ask about stuff like bank statements before because I was on the treadmill. I was performing, doing the job I love. Isn't that the way it's supposed to be? I was a famous person. I had 'people' to deal with all that boring money stuff. People who ultimately couldn't protect me from financial problems and who I suddenly realised were costing me more money attempting to.

I rang the accountant, spoke to the bank and to the lawyers. Started asking a few questions. And what a shock to the system that was. Me asking: What's going on? How much is such-and-such costing me? Why is it costing me that? Why am I paying for that? And the main one: Why is this case still dragging on?

My third set of lawyers ended up costing me a six-figure sum and the case fell apart. Up to that point I'd paid over a million quid in lawyer's fees, and I didn't have a thing to show for it. The other lot, my opponents in all this, they were on a no-win-no-fee agreement, so it could drag on for ever as far as they were concerned.

I can't palm off all the blame. I was an idiot: I didn't take any notice of my financial position and I was stupid enough to leave my affairs to other people. I went into it with the same happy-go-lucky attitude I had when I was at school. It thought it would all be fine. But it wasn't.

CHAPTER FORTY-NINE

'Are you ready, Russ?'

My mate, Gerry – Gerry Clifford – picked me up in his van, gave me a lift to the Wythenshawe hospital.

'Yeah,' I said, 'I guess.'

I lied. I wasn't ready. Don't laugh, but I thought I was going to die. What I'd done, I'd gone onto the Internet looking up the details of my procedure, reading up on the general anaesthetic. Of course, I now know that the Internet's the worse place to look for advice or information on medical matters. You can have an itchy toe, you look it up online and the next thing you know you've got gangrene. But that's a lesson I learnt the hard way. I was admitted to the hospital the night before my operation and I spent that night convincing myself the procedure would kill me. I'd have some fatal allergic reaction, the laser would slip: Opera Star's Operation Tragedy. Or if not that – if not an operating theatre fatality – then I'd lose my singing voice, or even lose my voice altogether. I don't mind admitting, I was scared. This was my first operation, the first time I was going to be hooked up to breathing apparatus, out cold, have surgeons delving around in my body. Scared pretty much covers it.

I didn't sleep much that night, if at all. They came to me early to take me into the theatre. And as they wheeled me in, I made a deal with myself. I decided that when it was over, things were going to change. I was going to take control, make some changes in my life. Change management for a start. Take the reins of my financial dealings.

It felt like I was in a bad way going into that operating theatre. In a dark place. It felt like everything I'd worked towards had fallen to the floor and shattered. But things were going to be different. Let me get through this, I thought, and I'll get my act together. I won't ever take anything for granted again. Just let me get through this.

'Are you ready, Russell?' said Phil Jones.

'Yeah,' I said. 'I'm ready.'

And this time, I was.

Three days later I was knocking around the house – the one the bank were so eager to take – and I was mulling over the instructions I'd been given by the hospital, the post-operation advice I was supposed to heed: no talking for ten days. No singing for six weeks.

For most people, that wouldn't be a problem. Ten days of monastic silence might be a treat. For me, it was hell. I'm a voice person. I'm the one who's always talking, who never shuts up. I felt like I was muzzled and it got me down. It was hell for another reason, too. If I couldn't talk for ten days – and not sing for six weeks – how on earth would I know if the operation had been a success? It's one thing to be told. They'd pronounced it a success, of course, another pipe up the nose. But there was only one way to find out for sure. I had to hear it for myself.

I had a huge downstairs gym at the Boathouse. It would go, of course, along with the rest of the house, a victim of the money problems I was hoping to bring to an end, but then, it was my sanctuary, and I crept down there.

I stood in it, in among all the stuff, feeling down, a bit sorry for myself; the future stretching out ahead of me looked bleak and uncertain. I'd promised myself I'd pull myself up by the bootstraps, but I wasn't sure if I could do it without my voice. Roxanna had suggested that if I did lose any of my register I could try sticking to pop, drop the classical stuff from my repertoire. I'd looked at her and shook my head no. Telling me not to sing the high stuff – the stuff that I'd made my name singing; that I loved singing. It was like asking a footballer to hobble around the pitch on one leg. That voice is what I am.

I looked around the gym. Swallowed. I opened my mouth and... sang a note.

A high note. A note that I hadn't been able to produce for close on nine months. For a second it felt as though I'd had a brick wall in my throat and someone had just smashed it down and now there was a 90mph wind whooshing through it. It felt so open and clean and unbelievably smooth.

I dropped to my knees on the gym mat, put my head in my hands and said, 'Thank you. Thank you, God.'

It was back. *I* was back.

Okay, the voice was all right. It would need months of work, of course, to bring it back to full power, but it was going to be all right. Now I had to untangle all the legal mess, and if only it was as simple as making a pledge on a hospital trolley. This stuff that needed sorting out wasn't going to float away on a cloud of my good intentions.

I fired my manager. I had my reasons for firing him, but what I do want to say is that in the early days he did well by me. He was very enthusiastic, he had lots of energy and drive. But largely, as a result of agreeing to this management deal in my early years, going into 2004 I was broke, on the verge of bankruptcy. It went to the wire. I was *that* close to being declared bankrupt.

The upshot was I had to undertake a voluntary financial arrangement. I reached a settlement with the management company – that figure was added to the voluntary arrangement, a cumulative ball of minus figures that included all my accrued debt plus everybody's costs. You name it. If someone drank a cup of coffee that day, it went on my bill.

In the end, it was only because I was able to prove I had the capacity to earn more that I was able to escape bankruptcy. Now all I needed to do was get out and earn it.

CHAPTER FIFTY

I don't usually feel the cold, but it was bloody freezing the night of the Prince's Trust event. It was February, an icy night. My breath fogging in front of me as I entered Windsor Castle.

The event was a charity do hosted by Prince Charles and Camilla in the Grand Ballroom of Windsor Castle. And what a beautiful hall that is: the walls lined with coats of arms, flags, swords, spears and shields. Its acoustics are great, too, and I did my five or six songs then was approached by a rather serious-looking chap, clearly attached to the Palace.

'Mr Watson,' he said, bowing slightly, 'the Prince would very much like to meet you. He's requested you at his table. Is that all right?' He extended an arm, gesturing at the Prince's table on the other side of the hall.

'Yes, yes, of course, that would be fine.' Following my serious pal, I weaved my way through the tables, returning the odd smile from other guests, everybody suited and booted.

At Prince Charles's table I was ushered to a seat next to him and he stood slightly to greet me. We shook hands as I sat. 'Wonderful performance,' he said, 'absolutely wonderful.' He has that way of speaking where he looks as if he's thinking very hard about what he's saying. And then he listens the same way. As if he's thinking very hard about what you're saying.

I thanked him. We got chit-chatting. I was telling him how the performance was one of my first since the throat operation. Talked about the operation, then the vocal coaching I'd needed afterwards. He listened, nodding intently, eyebrows knitted together, concerned when I told him about the discovery of the polyp on my vocal folds. 'Goodness. Goodness,' he said. 'That must have come as quite a shock. Quite a shock.'

'And everything's all right now, is it?' he asked when I'd finished, his eyebrows arcing up and away.

'Yes, yes, everything seems to be working perfectly.'

'Well that's wonderful. Wonderful. Everything certainly sounded as though it was working perfectly.' Then, 'I wonder, Russell, would you mind having a word with Camilla? She's a great supporter of yours.'

Supporter? Right, she turns up at all the matches, home and away, I thought, making myself grin as I walked over to the other side of the table; they sat opposite one another in those days.

'Oh, Russell,' she said, as I took a seat next to her. A spare chair had magically appeared in time for my arrival. 'That was absolutely wonderful. I was hoping that you'd sing all night. Would you sing us another song, Russell?'

I said, 'I'm really sorry, I can't now, the band have left. I'd love to have done, but...'

'Oh,' she said, 'such a shame. I do love your music, it's absolutely wonderful,' and she sat there raving about how great I was, while I sat there smiling, nodding my head, thanking her, deciding that she was lovely, a really lovely woman. And she was a big fan, too. Which always helps.

After hearing how great I was from Camilla, I went back across the table to speak to the Prince, who said he thought I'd made a good evening something special, that I'd been the icing on the cake, and would I be an ambassador for the Prince's Trust?

I said yes, of course, because it's not the kind of offer you're supposed to ask for time to think over, and I got the official letter a couple of weeks later, plus a handwritten letter from Clarence House, from the Prince.

So there I was, a newly minted ambassador for the Prince's Trust. I did a couple of events for them, going along to sing and talk to the kids about music, and there was a big charity event for them I was due to do, but had to cancel when I got ill. So in the end I haven't done as much for the Trust as I would have liked. I think I've got a fairly reasonable excuse, mind; it's not exactly dog-ate-my-homework, nearly dying of two brain tumours. But even so, it's one of those things, like the UN ambassador role, that sadly fell by the wayside during the time I was ill. I'm hoping, when I'm fully better, to put some more time in there. I'd like to.

Certainly Charlie hasn't forgotten me. He sent me a letter after the most recent operation, wishing me well and saying how concerned he and Camilla were. I get a Christmas card off them, too. Can't be bad.

One last thing to say about that Windsor Castle visit. The strangest thing happened. I collected my coat and it was only when I got to the car that I realised a Windsor Castle coat hanger had become tangled up inside it (cough). It was a solid oak hanger with the royal crest emblazoned on it, but by the time I discovered the mistake it was too late to turn round and give it back. Windsor Castle had shut. So, I thought, Well, I pay my taxes, technically it sort of belongs to me anyway, so I kept it. For a while it hung in pride of place at the Peacock Farmhouse, which was where I moved after selling the Boathouse to help clear my debts. But I had a spate of thefts at the farmhouse – never found out who the culprits were – and one of the items that went missing was the coat hanger. I'd also lost a watch that had been given to me as a gift, but, to be honest, I think I was more gutted about losing that coat hanger. I could probably have replaced the watch; it would be more difficult to get another coat hanger. There was no way another one was going to accidentally get tangled up in my coat.

Next stop, Tokyo Imperial Place, residence of the emperor. I was invited there as part of another charity event, this one for Save the Children. Once again I did my set, about half an hour's worth, and afterwards up came a palace official – the Imperial Palace version of the serious-looking chap from Windsor Castle.

'Emperor wants you to sit at table with him now for dinner,' he said without punctuation, bowing slightly as he spoke. 'You want dinner?'

I hadn't officially been invited for dinner, so this was a great honour. I was escorted to the head table and the next thing I knew I was sitting at the table with the emperor on one side, the empress on the other, just chewing the fat. As you do. They spoke excellent English, which was lucky. It would have been a short conversation otherwise; my Japanese is restricted to a series of impressions that sound suspiciously like Cato out of the *Pink Panther* movies. One day I'll learn it, perhaps. Let's get the Italian out of the way first.

And again this was one of those surreal situations where I thought, What am I doing here? How the bloody hell did *I* get *here*? I'm a Salford lad. Fifteen years ago I was on the lathes and now I'm having dinner with the Emperor of Japan and his wife – *drinking vintage Dom Perignon with the emp, for God's sake* – thousands of miles away from home, not a single connection with Japan. The reason I'm here, the only reason, is the voice. Insane.

The emperor and his wife always leave first. The rule is that everybody else must be seated when they first enter the room, then again when they leave. They are always the last to enter a room, always the first to leave it. Their departure was announced over a microphone. The emperor and his wife stood to leave, and as they did so, the emperor turned to me, saying, 'Very nice to meet you,

Mr Watson,' and he shook my hand. Like everybody else I remained seated as they left, then, after they'd gone, my serious-looking mate came darting over.

'You know what happened?' he said, very excited. 'You know what happened?'

Uh-oh, I thought, breach of protocol: Opera Star's Emperor Blunder Sparks International Incident.

I said, 'No, what happened?'

He said, 'Emperor never shake hand. You know what happened? Never shake hand. Great honour. You lucky man.'

And that was it, apparently. The emperor liked me so much he'd shaken my hand.

My run of making friends with members of royalty burped to a halt towards the end of that year, 2004. It wasn't like I hadn't met the Queen before. I had, on many previous occasions. Just that she didn't remember me.

'When's the fucking Queen going to come out, then?'

This is our old friend Chris Torrent. We were at Buckingham Palace for an event called Celebration of 100 Years of British Music. Me, every single musical icon you can possibly think of and, for some reason, the surprisingly sweary host of *Who Wants to be a Millionaire?*.

'Where the fuck is she, then?'

We'd been given the chance to look around Buckingham Palace; we'd had canapés and glasses of champagne and now – Chris was right – the Queen was keeping us waiting. The real royalty was letting the rock royalty know their place in the food chain. And we are talking some serious big names here: Eric Clapton, Paul McCartney, Robin Gibb, Elton John... just anybody who'd ever graced an arena stage in the last twenty years was standing in that room in Buckingham Palace, having a chinwag.

Chapter Fifty

Eventually, the time came and we were arranged into a row to meet Her Majesty, who entered the room, smiling, Prince Philip and assorted aides in tow. She began at one end of the line, asking, 'And who are you?' to whoever it was who was standing there – somebody very famous anyway. Moving along the line she came to Robin Gibb.

'And who are you?'

'My name's Robin Gibb, ma'am.'

'And what do you do?'

'I'm one of the Bee Gees, ma'am.'

'Oh yes, yes,' she said. 'Yes, yes, I know those.'

Come on, I thought, she must have met Robin Gibb before now. Even if she hadn't, doesn't Her Majesty ever switch on the telly?

Eric Clapton was beside me in the line. Maybe she'll know Eric Clapton, I thought. Then again, perhaps not. Bet popular music's not something the Queen pays much attention to. Maybe it's a case of seen-one-stadium-rocker-seen-them-all.

But after Eric, it was me. She should know me, I thought. Not that I'm more famous than Eric Clapton or Robin Gibb; or even that Her Madge is a big fan of classical music. But I'd sung for her just the other day, at the Remembrance Festival. We'd shaken hands afterwards and she told me how much she liked my perform-ance. I was an ambassador for her son's charity. Her memory can't be that bad.

The Queen reached Eric Clapton. 'And who are you?' she asked.

'I'm Eric Clapton, ma'am.'

'And what do you do?'

Eric cast a sly sideways glance along the line of music legends. 'It is said in *some* circles, ma'am, that I'm a reasonably good guitarist.'

A little tremor went along the line as everybody fought to contain themselves.

The Queen gave Clapton a slightly thin smile, then moved on to me and said, 'Ah, Russell, how nice it is to see you again.'

Only joking. She didn't. What she *actually* said was exactly what she'd said to everybody else on the line. 'And who are you?'

'Russell Watson, ma'am,' I replied.

'And what do you do?'

'I'm a singer, ma'am,' I said.

'Oh yes, yes,' she said. 'Of course,' and moved on. Priceless.

CHAPTER FIFTY-ONE

The tumour would take its time to make its presence felt, though. In the end, what it did was wait until my career was on an upswing to strike. Shortly after I'd won *Just the Two of Us*, and when *The Ultimate Collection* was flying off the shelves and I was about to record a new album, riding the crest of that wave.

Rewind to before all of that, though, and things had been going badly. Why? That would be the Curse of the Manager Problems again.

After releasing my manager, I joined up with a big management company, a very well-known outfit at the time, and was given one of their guys to look after me. We don't mention his name either. Nor do we mention his secretary who I had the pleasure of speaking to many, many times over the barren year I was with him. Me and the secretary were able to form our priceless relationship because the manager was never, ever there. Literally months would go by without the two of us speaking.

And what happens in a situation like that is that the air starts to go out of your career. There had been... 'problems', let's just say, caused by previous management, a slightly 'forthright' style that had put a lot of noses out of joint, both at my record company and with sections of the media. As a result, the phone had stopped ringing. Or, rather, it wasn't ringing as often as it should have been. What my career needed at that time was a bit of bridge-building, which should have been my new manager's job. But there was no construction work going on. There was just a building site, empty, a crusty old cement mixer and a bit of plastic sheeting fluttering in the wind.

I've got to give the company their due. Joining them, they did help me to create some important business relationships: they found me a new accountant, for a start, one who had experience of dealing with these voluntary financial arrangements; plus they put me in touch with a lawyer, and as a result my legal costs started to decrease.

Other than that, though, any work that came in would have come in anyway. What I needed was for someone to get out there and push me, build those bridges. But that building site stayed deserted, the plastic fluttering in the breeze, and instead of a manager I got the secretary. No, she couldn't tell me where he was. No, she didn't know when he'd be back. Yes, she would pass on my message. Yes, she had passed on the message I left yesterday. Etc. Etc.

Her whole attitude was, just get back in your box. What had happened, this guy spent half the year in the south of France, and he'd handed a lot of his work over to the secretary. She and I didn't see eye to eye, so nothing got done. It seemed that she'd have sooner eaten the contents of an ashtray than done anything to help my career.

What do you do? I'd get frustrated, end up having a go at her. Next thing you know, the phone would be ringing and it was him, the first I'd hear from him in weeks: 'Don't you upset my secretary.' What a mess.

Coupled with that, the Roxanna situation had deteriorated. We'd got engaged and I put my all into that relationship – so much so that my career was taking a back seat. My career was hurting and I was seeing less of my kids, all to try and meet expectations she had of me, which, as it turned out, were just way too high. We split. We were actually in New York when we split. She wanted me to stay; I told her I had to go.

And I left.

It was like the final scene from *Brief Encounter*. It caused me so much heartache at the time. We had a couple of dogs together – a beagle, Chula, and a Shitzu, Muttley – We'd gone over there with them, but I came home alone. No girlfriend, no dogs. I arrived back, jet-lagged from New York, into a house that was suddenly no longer a home; that just seemed cold and empty. All the familiar sounds and feelings were absent. No Roxanna, no dogs running around my feet. And I thought, What do I do now? What on earth do I do now?

The Colonel and Lynne were there for me. They mopped up, as usual. Looking back, it's funny, because one of Roxanna's parting shots was that I'd find someone else – someone in the music business. 'You'll have forgotten me in no time,' she said.

Well, I haven't, and I haven't. And what that relationship showed me was that relationships are not for me – not any more. I'm able to take an analytical look at things. At the time, though, God, it was so traumatic.

Have a look at the cover of *Amore Musica*. Do I look a bit glum to you? Well, now you know the reason why. It ended up being my lowest-selling album. Sold 110,000 copies in the same space of time that previous albums had sold six or seven times that amount. The accompanying tour was also a disappointment. It was great to be performing and I loved the material, but the receipts were down.

I jumped ship from that management company. Just in time as it turned out, because the ship sank.

At least I got out in time. Not exactly unscathed, but still. Now I needed to get my career back on track. And perhaps I was owed a lucky break by then, because I got one. Rick Astley pulled out of *Just the Two of Us*.

CHAPTER FIFTY-TWO

February 2008

Walking around the house, I go into the bathroom the girls use when they stay at the weekend. A towel on the rail is wonky. Not hung right.

I tut, straighten it, then walk into Rebecca's room. Like the rest of the house it's tidy.

I'm not going to say I'm obsessive compulsive about stuff like that but, well, I'll let you draw your own conclusions. I just like the place to look nice, that's all. I spend enough time here these days...

On the floor above, Grant is mixing the live album. Every now and then I go up there to see how he's getting on. It's sounding good: crisp and powerful. Listening to it reminds me of the old me, in my element at the Royal Albert Hall. Listening to it buoys me up, makes me yearn to get back on the stage, back into action. Soon, mate, soon.

I leave Grant to it for the time being. Instead I pad down the stairs, pausing a moment to look at the bust I have on the landing windowsill.

It's of Kirsty Howard. A brass bust her mum and dad had made. I think they had five of them done as commemorative gifts for people who had worked for the charity, and they gave one to me. Sometimes, if I'm feeling sorry for myself (like now, perhaps?), I'll catch sight of it. Just seeing it there makes me pull myself together. I take a look at that and think, come on, get on with it, Nobby. You think you've got it hard, every day alive is a bonus for Kirsty. Every day she defies medical probability.

I glance into the lounge. Silent. Empty. Tidy. From the kitchen I can hear Gary talking to the man who's come to the fix the boiler. They're discussing the relative merits of some fixing or other.

I decide I'll give that a miss, the great boiler-fixing debate. Instead, I stick my head through the doorway of the office. Victoria's in there, sitting at the computer. On the walls hang my framed discs. The platinum and gold discs you get for selling lots of records.

'Victoriah,' I say.

'Yes, Russ.' She looks around from the computer.

'When you've got a moment later, can we go through some stuff?'

'Stuff?'

'Bills and stuff.'

She smiles, bless her. But we both know I drive her mad with it – my insistence on going through stuff.

Still, that's the way I am these days. I paid off my voluntary financial arrangement two years ago and I am never going through anything like that again. So these days I run my business from the top. I can't just concentrate on singing any more, I've got to be shrewder about things, I have to lean on people: on Gary and Victoria. On my management. Because if I don't, then things don't happen. And that goes right down the line. I don't blindly trust people to look after my affairs any more, I do it myself. This is why I drive Victoria mad. If we get a letter from the lawyer and they want money I need to know what it's for. If a bill isn't correctly itemised, I'll be on to Victoria.

'What's this for?'

'It's for such-and-such.'

'Yeah, but that doesn't tell me what it is. Find out, would you?'

I *have* to do all that now. The bit of me that wants to not worry and be happy-go-lucky and have a laugh has to pipe down, and business bloke has to take charge. It's not necessarily the way I saw myself in my forties; I've had to force myself to be this way.

I feel so *changed* these days, that's the thing. Such a different person from the bloke I was. Don't get me wrong, I know that everybody changes. But sometimes I feel as if I've been denied the luxury of changing gradually. My life-changing events have been sudden. Some of them sudden in a good way. Some sudden bad. And when you're living as fast as I was they come at you quickly, they hit you, turn your world upside down. Smash and grab. And afterwards you look at yourself in the mirror and you're a different person.

I was living life at a hundred miles an hour. When you hit a wall at that speed, it stings a little.

And I look at the albums in the office and they're like markers, of my music, and of my whole life. I look at *The Voice* and it brings back not just the thrill of being signed, but the pain of my marriage failing. *Reprise*, when the polyp that might have ended my career was discovered. A whole skip-load of management problems during *Amore Musica*. *That's Life* and *Outside In* – my two brain-tumour albums. *Encore*'s the only record of mine unshaped by traumatic events. The others I look at and think, After that album, I was different. I'd changed.

For the better, I hope. Because if there's one thing the events of my life so far have taught me it's that (cliché alert) you have to look on the positive side of things. For instance, looking at *Amore Musica*, me all glum on the cover, maybe it should bring me down, remind me of the 2003 that I once told an interviewer was my worst year ever. The worst year of my life.

But was it? Really, looking back, was it? The throat operation was a harrowing experience but developing that polyp made me step off the rollercoaster to carry out some essential maintenance. And it's lucky I did, because that rollercoaster was a death trap. What was waiting for me if I'd stayed on it was burnout, and financial ruin.

But I got the polyp, stepped off and turned my life around. Took a while, but I did it. So I gained something positive out of that experience. From the tumour? What have I taken from that? I'm still having tests. And how it's changed me I'm still mulling over. I'll have to get back to you on that.

Later, when the boiler man's gone, and I've finished torturing Victoria with questions about invoices, I decide to have a laugh, cheer the place up a bit. I get dressed up in pyjamas, a hat and a false moustache, then take a walking stick and go down to the bus stop to wait for a bus.

Yes, I may have changed a lot. But sometimes, I think, sitting in the shelter waiting for a bus in my pyjamas – maybe not *that* much.

CHAPTER FIFTY-THREE

February 2006

It may have escaped your notice, but I have reservations about talent shows. Yes, I know, my own career was launched off the back of one, but come on, that was slightly different. It wasn't like I won the Piccadilly Radio Search For A Star competition on Saturday and by the following Thursday you could buy my CD in Tesco. There was a long period in between where I learnt my trade and found my musical feet. What these TV shows tend to do is remove that process and, in doing so, they destroy the romanticism of the music industry.

It's true, there have always been Svengalis, but back in the old days the Svengalis had to graft, too. They didn't have that quick route into the charts that seems to exist now. They didn't have the country's best marketing tool, TV, at their disposal.

And even the rock bands these days all seem to come out fully formed. Bands like Keane who come from rich backgrounds so they get their guitars bought for them. I had to do a paper round to pay for my instruments. All that graft, all that blood, sweat and tears, seems to have gone out of the industry.

I feel for them, really, all these oven-ready chart acts. They bypass the climb and most of the time it's the climb that's the making of you. It was for me, plus I really enjoyed the experience.

Okay, so *Just the Two of Us* wasn't exactly a talent show. Nobody's trying out to be a singer and pinning all their dreams on making it as a career. It's not about building up the hopes of kids and then making them look stupid on TV. It's a reality show. But still, I guess I couldn't help but consider it part of the whole talent-show culture, and I wrestled with that for a bit.

Plus, of course, I was the stand-in. I was the guy they parachuted in to pick up the pieces after Rick left. Again, that's not a situation to inspire you. So I went into it feeling a bit negative about it.

On the other hand, I knew that it could be just the platform I needed to get my career back on the rails. I'd joined a new management company, Merlin Elite (and just to put your mind at rest, I'm still with this management company. Richard and Giles, my managers there, have been brilliant for me, totally turned my fortunes around, which is more than any other managers have achieved), so this looked like being the ideal time to do a bit of that bridge-building I was talking about.

I met my singing partner, Sian Reeves, at a hotel in Manchester. We didn't hit it off.

Before I came on the scene, she had been partnered with Rick and the two had met in the same studios. They'd seemed to get on well. They'd done a bit of rehearsing together, each done pieces to camera saying how much they were looking forward to the experience, then left at the end of the day. Only, Rick never came back. At the time there were mixed reports as to why he'd left, with some saying that he'd been out of the limelight for too long and nerves got the better of him; others that he'd simply decided it wasn't for him. Later it came to light that he'd pulled out of the show because it would conflict with the Oscars, where his partner was nominated for an animation-film award. Whatever, he unceremoniously bowed out.

So Sian was in bits when I trundled along, me wearing a base-ball cap and a lot of apprehension. Her confidence was gone. She felt betrayed, abandoned, rejected. She'd convinced herself that Rick had left because she was a useless partner.

'I need a knight in shining armour,' she'd wailed. And she needed him fast, too; there were only a few days to go before the first live show.

I wasn't her knight. Not at first anyway. In the studios the day of that first meeting, we had a laugh about Rick leaving. We sang his song 'Never Gonna Give You Up', changing the words to 'never gonna let you down'. I knew that it was tough for Sian having to adapt to another person, and I did a piece to camera saying how I felt it was my job to pick her up and give her the confidence she needed.

Privately though, I was thinking, *Oh, bugger*.

What I knew of Sian beforehand was what I'd seen of her on TV in *Cutting It* where she played a bit of a mad, nervy character. Turns out there was some typecasting going on there. In real life she's a bit of a mad, nervy character. She was non-stop and that, plus the blow of Rick leaving, had left her behaving like a tomcat on Red Bull – needing comfort one second, claws out the next.

'I'm freaking out,' she kept saying, at volume.

Great, I thought. This was going to be tough.

We had three days to work on our first performance, time that we mainly spent coaching Sian on her voice. Still we didn't click. Her nerves were shot and I was grumpy because I wasn't even sure I wanted to do the show. We niggled at one another.

On the first day of the series, we got to meet our competition. I'd been overjoyed to find out that Alexander O'Neal was in the line-up; it was probably the main reason I did the show. I'd thought, If a legend like him can do it, then I can.

Alex was partnered with Fiona Bruce, the newsreader. Penny Smith from *GMTV* was with Curtis Stigers, another great singer; Natasha Hamilton of Atomic Kitten was with Mark Moraghan out of *Holby City*; Jo O'Meara from S Club 7 with Chris Fountain from *Hollyoaks*; TV presenter Gaby Roslin with Martin Fry, out of ABC; soul singer Jocelyn Brown with TV presenter Matt Allwright;

and another great soul singer, Beverley Knight, with TV presenter Nicky Campbell.

There was some serious singing talent in that line-up.

The judges started as they meant to go on, hacking into us for our first number, 'Can't Help Falling In Love With You'.

Stewart Copeland, the Police drummer, accused me of not supporting Sian, starting a Copeland vs Watson theme that would continue throughout. All of them were fairly dismissive: 'Well, you tried hard,' seemed to be the overall verdict.

Backstage, presenter Vernon Kaye said he thought we'd done well to perform the song with so little time to get it together. We looked as though we'd bonded in a short space of time, he said.

'Yeah, yeah,' we agreed, lying through our teeth.

Bonded? We couldn't stand the sight of each other. When the cameras weren't pointing at us, Sian and I were more than happy to go our separate ways. I was hanging out with Alexander O'Neal, who turned out to have a personality as big as Heathrow. I nicknamed him 'the Motherfucker' on account of his language.

'*Motherfucker*,' he used to exclaim, often for no apparent reason. Chris Tarrant's got nothing on Alexander O'Neal; you really need the brass bands when he's around. He'd be in full flow and even the presence of the cameras didn't stop him.

'Alex,' I told him, 'you can't say that.'

'Why the fuck not?' he roared.

Alexander O'Neal doesn't talk, it's more like a public-service address.

'Why can't I swear? *You* swear.'

'Yeah,' I said, 'but not when the cameras are rolling.'

'Listen, man,' he boomed, 'I was listening to your shit today and when you've got a voice like you've got, you can say what the fuck you want. Don't you fucking forget that.'

'Right, Alex.'

The next day things hadn't improved between Sian and I. She was apparently intimidated by my voice. It was too loud, she said.

'Does it matter?' I came back, thinking, Get a grip. 'They can just turn my microphone down.'

Her nerves were the other thing. She kept going on about them and I tried to explain to her that all that nervous energy is what performers feed off. But I'm not sure any of it was getting through.

Nerves. She was getting on mine. I was getting on hers.

We did 'It Takes Two' that night, and Sian did a great job. I'm sure she'd be the first to admit that she doesn't have a show-stopping voice, but she can act. Which makes her a great performer. All of that went into her performance on 'It Takes Two'. 'If you can sing loud, I can dance loud,' she'd said to me during rehearsals, and she was as good as her word.

Judges were harsh, of course. Actually, Cece Sammy said that Sian's voice had improved, which it had. But elsewhere they were less kind. Trevor Nelson told us we were as subtle as a heart attack. Stewart Copeland said he didn't believe it – and it wasn't meant in a good way. Lulu told us she thought we were too fast, a bit over-eager, and Sian wailed that she'd sung too fast because of her nerves.

'I thought she was brilliant,' I said, putting an arm around her shoulder.

And I did. I really did. Doing that programme Sian was so far out of her comfort zone she may as well have been on a different planet. Trouble is, it was me who had to try and reel her back to earth.

The next day, things deteriorated between us and we were bickering in the studio; only, we were doing it in that excruciating forced-smile way when you've got no choice but to get on with someone you don't like.

Still, there was no hiding the animosity and much of it was caught on camera. The way the production span the story at the time was that Stewart Copeland's comments had needled me and ignited some kind of primal competitive urge. Like I was going to show that Police drummer a thing or two and the casualty of my chest-beating competitive nature would be Sian, drowned out by the sheer volume of my Battle Voice.

'This competition's supposed to be about two personalities coming together,' cried Sian, who was really down that day, 'but Russell doesn't care what I sound like. It'll just be him standing on that stage tonight.'

It's true, Stewart's comments had needled me. But not much; it's not like they extended into genuine rivalry. If we saw each other in the green room afterwards we'd greet each other as normal. All that on-stage banter was part of the storyline of the show and, in fact, when it was over, he gave me a call saying that he'd written a song he thought would be great for my voice, me being such a diverse singer.

Having said that, he did initially get my back up with his comments directed at my performance. The way I saw it, Sian was there to have her performance criticised – that was the programme – but I wasn't. I was there to help coach and accompany her, not to get reviewed, thank you very much. And in any case, if I was going to take criticism for my performance, I wasn't going to take it from a bloody drummer.

Funnily enough, they changed the format of the show for the second series, tweaking the rules slightly so that the judges would only comment on the performance of the guest celebrity – presumably because other professional singers felt the same way.

So, yes, there was an element of competition to my attitude that day. Maybe I did want to prove something. Not that I actually *had* anything to prove to Stewart, of course. Just that I do have a competitive streak. And Sian and I were still winding each other up, doing our smiley-bickering bit, and it all came to a bit of a head, Sian in tears, me wishing I could call the whole thing off. I was having headaches, too. Bad ones. And they hadn't been helping my mood at all. I didn't know it then, of course, but it was my tumour growing. Pushing down into the nasal cavity.

Sian and I had a head-to-head, cleared the air.

'Russell realised he needed to be a bit more supportive,' Vernon later said on the VT. And that was certainly part of it; I think in the end we both just calmed down a bit. We'd each come into the partnership with a chip on our shoulder and instead of pulling together we were pulling apart. Once we realised that, things started to improve.

And they really did improve.

That night we did 'All Right Now' and ended the song hugging. Stewart Copeland went into one about my performance. Not my vocal performance. He was talking about the fact that I'd let Sian do most of the dancing. This from a guy who spent his career sitting behind a drum kit.

'Come on,' he said. He had this way of holding his hand when he spoke, like he was chopping with it. 'You can't just stand there.'

'Just a second,' I countered. 'Weren't we saying a few moments ago that this was a *singing* competition?'

'Touché.'

Afterwards, I did a duet with Alexander O'Neal to end the show, 'To All The Girls I've Loved Before'. During rehearsal he'd been in full brass bands mode.

'*Motherfucker.*'

One of the assistants approached him to attach a small lapel-microphone for sound-checking.

'Can I just put this on you?' she asked.

'You can put what the fuck you want on me, honey, you can put whatever you want on me.'

Completely larger than life. An 18-certificate force of nature.

'You want to know something?' he roared across the studio at me later, 'you want to fuckin' *know* something?'

'Yes, what is it, Alex.'

'There are going to be ten-motherfucking-million, mother-fucking cocksuckers watching us singing this shit tonight.'

'Right,' I said. Frankly bemused.

'What do you think about that?' he barked.

What did I think? I thought I'd rather stick with the advice I'd been given all those years ago, about imagining Mum shouting at the kids not to get felt-tip pen on the carpet. I preferred that image to the motherfucking cocksuckers.

CHAPTER FIFTY-FIVE

Our next performance was our rock and roll number, 'Great Balls of Fire'. It involved dancing: a Reeves speciality but a Watson weakness.

Sian rose to the challenge of being the one to boss me around for once, and during rehearsals I watched her confidence flourish. Go, Sian. The atmosphere in the studio had changed, too; in fact, if there was one day where we finally put all the niggles behind us, then that was it.

'You're right, Russell, I do have it in for you,' said Copeland, hand-chopping when we'd finished our performance that night, 'but I'm gonna have to bury the hatchet because you supported, you grizzled and you move pretty good for an opera singer.' Lulu told Sian she made a good rock chick. Backstage, Vernon observed that we seemed to be gelling together well. And this time, he was right.

Meanwhile the off-stage atmosphere was friendly and congenial, but competitive. The public had now voted off Gaby and Martin, and Fiona and Alex, so everybody had stopped worrying about an early exit and secretly we were all eyeing the final prize. Sure, it's all laughs and smiles and didn't so-and-so do well for the cameras. But behind the smiles, we all wanted to win. After all, we were a competitive bunch. We're in music and showbiz, and people in that industry like to win. They're there because they've strived and worked hard to get where they are. So everybody in the vicinity was a competitive human being – otherwise they wouldn't have been in the room in the first place.

Plus, it was very hard and very intense. I was lucky in that respect. Once again, my background in the clubs stood me in good stead; I was able to hop between the different genres of music because that was how I'd earned my stripes. Some of them struggled, though. Jo from S Club, for example, was used to doing pop, so the bigger numbers, the West End stuff, were hard for her. It was tough enough just for the professionals. For the celebrity guests...

Put it this way, I could understand why Sian was like a bag of nerves.

Jo didn't speak to me much. Nor her partner. I got on well with Beverley Knight, though, she was lovely; plus Jocelyn was exactly as you'd expect her to be: 'Hey, baby, how ya doing? Come over here and give me a big hug, baby.'

She'd crush me. 'Whoah, you are so good. I could just eat you all up, baby, I could just eat you all up. He's so fine.' All woman, she was.

Like I say, Alex had been voted off by then. No doubt to the relief of some of the contestants and crew; put it this way, he didn't mind living up to his reputation. I'd had the vote of confidence off him, though. One day I was suffering from a sore throat and Alex brought some throat tablets to my dressing room. Later his manager said, 'You know Alex really respects you, man. He never does that, he's never gone to somebody else's dressing room and handed them stuff, he must really like you, man.' We ended up recording 'To All The Girls I Loved Before' and it went on my next album, *That's Life*. The Stewart Copeland collaboration I was unable to do because of my illness.

By now I was really enjoying Sian's company. It had got me thinking, and I did a piece to camera, saying, 'You know, at heart

I'm a boy's boy. I like my football and my boxing. But a bit of female company has been very, very nice.'

Sian told the crew she thought I was shy – a bit scared of girls, 'but I've broken through his barriers and we've made a connection'.

We had. By now we'd relaxed and we were having a laugh. That night's number was 'Annie's Song' by John Denver, and the whole day we amused ourselves by singing it in hillbilly accents. The actual performance was probably the only time we sang it together without cracking up laughing. Then, of course, at the end came the kiss. 'Annie's Song' almost became her Snog. The audience loved it and Lulu was doing a bit of stirring about it during the judges' sum-up. Copeland, meanwhile, was still trying to use us as target practice: 'Russell.' Doing the hand chop. 'This kind of schlock is what your voice is for. Sian, you were... adequate.'

All good TV, I'm sure, but that 'adequate' knocked Sian for six and during rehearsals for the next show she was in bits. We were due to perform 'All I Ask of You' from *The Phantom of the Opera* and she was so anxious about it during rehearsal she couldn't even sing it to my face; she stood facing the wall.

'I can't do this, Russell,' she kept saying, hiding beneath the peak of her baseball cap.

'You can,' I insisted. But nothing I said seemed to keep the confidence gremlins at bay.

In the end I took her to the Wyndham Theatre, hoping the change of scene might do her good. It seemed to do the trick, and at least she was able to look me in the eye after that. Even so, the night didn't go well.

We did a rousing version of 'Nothing's Gonna Stop Us Now', but Sian's voice was showing signs of wear and tear and even though we put everything we had into it, it wasn't her best vocal performance. Trevor Nelson probably hit the nail on the head when he said, 'We've been encouraging this couple to get it together – and they have. But they've had so much fun they've lost a little vocal control.'

Then came 'All I Ask of You' and the song didn't start well. The key was out of her range and she struggled. When it finished she burst into tears and I gave her a hug; not for the first time I felt protective of her, only just resisting the urge to pick her up and whisk her out of there. She was in pieces.

But it brought us together. As the competition wore on, and we were continually slated by judges and regularly placed in the bottom three for the public vote, we developed a kind of siege mentality. It was me and Sian against the world. We thought every show was our last and that backs-to-the-wall atmosphere brought us closer together. I don't know – I sometimes wonder if that's when I'm at my best.

The next day was tough.

'Russell, I really don't think I'm in a good space right now,' was the first thing Sian said to me. The previous night had really knocked her confidence.

But she's a trier, Sian. She's a real fighter and I think that somewhere inside she was beginning to relish the challenge.

I know I was. Bloody hell. For the first time in years I was waking up in the morning with a spring in my step. Merlin, my new management team, were sorting things out; there were people on the building site at last. I wasn't having to deal with the secretary any more. I was performing on the big stage. And more importantly, for the first time in what felt like years, I was having a laugh. Working with Sian we had a giggle. Sure, there was lots of tears and wailing, too, but that's actors for you. Next second we'd be riffing off each other, cracking each other up.

The headaches, though. I still had these blinding headaches.

CHAPTER FIFTY-SIX

We were the underdogs, Sian and I. But we've both got bottle. After the *Phantom of the Opera* song, probably our worst performance, I did a piece to camera saying I wasn't sure Sian could come back from it, the dent in her confidence was too great. I was just laying it on for the show, though. Of course she could do it. And the next night she rebounded full of fire.

Our first performance, 'You Don't Know Me' was well received by the judges. Sian's voice was strained. All the singing, not to mention the crying and wailing, had put a massive load on it, but it had acquired a smoky, husky overtone that suited the song. Our next performance was 'Barcelona' – my signature number – and she gave it her all. No, it wasn't the most technically perfect rendition of the song, but it had gusto. To me it sounded great.

The judges hated it. 'You looked like you enjoyed yourself,' said Trevor Nelson, 'and that it was your last performance on the show. Not adequate.'

'He's talking bollocks,' I whispered in Sian's ear, just for her and a few hundred thousand lip-readers to pick up on.

Copeland did his hand thing. 'That was nauseating but huge.'

'Hey,' I came back, 'so are you.'

That night, Jo O'Meara and Chris Fountain were voted off, even though they were well ahead of us on judges' points. Once again, we'd escaped the boot. Sure, the judges may have hated us, but the public loved us. Story of my life, really.

We were still the underdogs going into the final. Our fellow finalists Natasha Hamilton and Mark Moraghan had had an uneven run to the final, but they had nailed their version of 'Kids' and the judges clearly loved them. Even during the final the panel behaved like Sian and I were just there to make up the numbers. They made the right noises, of course. Our 'Great Balls of Fire' went down well. Even Copeland had to admit it.

'You absolutely slammed it,' he said, doing the hand-chop.

'You guys have had a tough time during the competition,' added Cece, 'but you were on the money for that song.'

We did all right on points for that one. Natasha and Mark came on next, though, and the judges were all over them, awarding mostly nines. Our turn next and we did 'Annie's Song' again. Once more, it almost became 'Annie's Snog' at the end, and by now Sian's voice was sounding very husky.

'Patchy,' said the judges, before handing out high marks to Natasha and Mark for their next number.

It felt like we were the walking wounded. Sian was fast losing her voice; the judges thought we were second best; we'd had this incredible journey to the final, full of heartache and tears and laughter; and during it all we'd formed a wonderful relationship. Now here we were, battered and bruised, feeling like no bugger thought we had a cat in hell's chance. It brought out the best in us. Okay, maybe we were the future runners-up, certainly the experts seemed to think so. But we weren't going out without a fight.

So we did the Meatloaf song, 'I'd Do Anything For Love (But I Won't Do That)'. 'This song says so much about how Russell and I came together,' Sian told Vernon, 'and I think it could be our best yet.'

It was, but, true to form, the judges didn't think so. Stewart Copeland said Sian was shouty. He was wrong, we nailed it. Now we were way behind on points. It was up to the public.

As the votes were totted up, all four contestants sang 'Your Song', the Elton John number. Then we were lined up at the back of the stage, and after a long, long pause, they announced the winners.

It was us.

I punched the air. I don't think Sian could believe it. As the other contestants hurried on, we moved to shake the hands of our co-finalists. There was a lot of celebrating that night and let's just say I did my fair share – even with a headache.

And I think in the end we won it because of our story. Sian and I had gone on a journey through the series. We'd changed over the course of that journey and ultimately the public were supporting us not because we outshone the other two – on the whole their performances were probably better – but because we'd rolled up our sleeves and got down to the business at hand – and we'd had a laugh doing it; because we'd started with a barely concealed dislike for each other and ended the series with a close friendship.

That friendship, of course, became the subject of some newspaper rumours. Specifically, that Sian and I had become an item. Later I went to the wedding of the producer, Charlotte Oats, and Sian was there with her other half. It was a bit uncomfortable; there had been all this stuff in the papers, after all. I'm not sure how happy I'd have been in her partner's situation.

The truth, of course, is that we never were an item. Nothing went on. Did I like her? Yes. The two women I've met during my career about whom I really did wonder, What if... were her and Faye. But both were in relationships and I would never have tried anything on.

So for the answer to the question: 'Did anything happen between you and Sian?' I'd have to refer you to the title of the Meatloaf song we sang for our last performance. It ended up having a special significance.

Anyway, after all my hang-ups about reality shows, it turned out to be a great experience. From it came not only being mates with Sian, but a much-needed career boost. The record company were friends with me again, thanks to the bridge-building now going on, and *The Ultimate Collection* was released, flying to the top of the charts. People were reminded I was still around. I met the producer, Charlotte Oats, who's become a great friend, and we were making plans for a new album to be recorded in LA.

Next, I was due to star as Nathaniel Parsons in a tour of Jeff Wayne's *War of the Worlds*. Things were taking a huge upward turn. I felt like I was finally waving a not-so-fond farewell to the bad times.

Still, though, I was eating painkillers daily. Hand constantly at my forehead as if to knead away the hurt that now seemed to have made a permanent home behind my eyes. *War of the Worlds* should have been a major thing for me, a chance to try and gain some acting chops. When I joined the cast, though, I wasn't a well man.

When had they started, the headaches? When did the tumour first begin to make its presence felt?

I can date it back to 2003, I think. A year that I was having all sorts of problems, little knowing that the biggest one was growing in my head. I'd gone on holiday with Roxanna, my first holiday in a long, long time. We went to Scotland for four or five days and while there I started getting this pain round about the bridge of my nose. A harsher, harder headache than anything I'd ever had before, which up till then was just the usual, I guess: hangovers, a touch of man-flu.

This one was in the headache Premier league, though. It was like a sharp dagger twisting that started off unpleasant, very unpleasant, then got worse.

The more I thought about it, the more tablets I took, the worse it seemed to become. It was particularly bad in the evening, and if I had a glass of wine it was agony. We came home and still I had this piercing headache each day. It was worse if I tried to concentrate. Watching television was painful, and as for trying to command stealth missions on the PlayStation, forget it.

I put it down to a migraine. I gobbled pain-relief tablets, wore sunglasses a lot, avoided alcohol and TV, and rode it out.

It was suggested that the problem might be my vision so I went to a place in London for an eye test. They gave me the all-clear.

There was a little problem with the periphery vision on my left side, they said, but it was probably something I was born with. So it wasn't my vision.

After about a fortnight, the headache went. The bad guys rode out of town, and for a few days at least, the dust seemed to settle.

I now think that during that fortnight in 2003, something was happening in my head. A tumour developing in my brain. It was getting bigger. It was working its way down the front of my brain and into the space behind my eyes, where it was growing fat. It was expanding and pushing into the nasal cavity. It was eating through the bone.

And then they appeared to stop, the headaches. Not completely, but at least this particular batch of agony seemed over. My left eye, which had swollen, healed. I was able to move among normal people without wincing.

From that time on, though, I was at home to Mr Headache on a regular basis. On average once a week I'd have a monster behind the eyes. By then I had the throat problem, so any symptoms I was experiencing elsewhere I put down as side effects of that. Plus, it wasn't as though the headaches were always located in the same place. One week I'd get it down the side of my face. Next week's might be behind the nose. The week after a stabbing pain behind the eye that I now know was the tumour putting pressure on the optic nerve – that almost cost me my sight.

Funny, really. It means the tumour was in there when I had the operation on my polyp. If only I'd known. I could have arranged some kind of two-for-one deal. Remove one polyp get tumour free of charge. But no, I lay on the operating theatre thinking the polyp was the worst of my troubles. As Homer would say, Doh.

I tried not to let the pain affect my work. But even so, I came on to the cast of *The War of the Worlds* suffering from serious, debilitating headaches.

It was to be the first stage production of Wayne's famous concept album, and Jeff himself was personally in charge. I was playing Parson Nathaniel, and when I first became involved I was bang up for it. I thought it would be great and that it was a good opportunity for me. As with a lot of singers, there had been constant talk of me doing some acting: there was a proposed film version of Mario Lanza's life story, starring me as Mario Lanza, that had been green lit but then fell through; I was constantly being asked if I'd ever thought of trying my hand. So this was a good chance to combine singing with acting. Parson Nathaniel, who was played by Phil Lynott on the original album, had dialogue and songs, so if I turned out to be a bit crap at the acting I always had the singing to fall back on – and I knew I could do that. Plus, this production was a big deal. It was the first-ever live version of the album; they had a huge CGI animation of Richard Burton's head, the narrator; there was a mammoth model of one of the alien tripods that would appear on stage; and they'd made a prequel film to add to the story. It was due to start in Brighton in mid-April then tour arenas. We were going to Cardiff International Arena, the Royal Albert Hall, Birmingham NEC, Manchester MEN and the Glasgow Clyde. One of the shows, at Wembley Arena, was to be shot for a DVD.

So, yes, all told it should have been great. It *would* have been great – if I hadn't been in so much pain all the time.

They did a 'Making Of' feature to appear on the DVD and I appear on it, complaining about my headaches. Viewers probably thought that was all I did, but God it was bad. I used to turn up for rehearsals in agony. Pills rattling in my gut. Sunglasses on. Head down trying to ignore the searing pain crouched like a sick dog behind my eyes.

During rehearsals I had to wear the sunglasses on stage, because the lights were making the pain so much worse. I couldn't even watch *EastEnders*, how the bloody hell was I supposed to cope with an alien invasion? There were times I had to cut rehearsals short if the pain became too intense.

One night, there was some kind of do after rehearsals and a woman from the orchestra string section approached me. She felt it was her duty to tell me that she and some of the other girls in the orchestra had been talking, she said. They'd been saying, 'Who does he think he is? Always swanning around with sunglasses on.' I tried to explain to her that it was the headaches – I was still calling them migraines then.

Yeah, she said, right. But she just thought I ought to know that she and some of the other girls in the orchestra thought I was getting a bit too big for my boots.

Thanks for that.

Things didn't improve. The day before the first show I was running in Kensington Gardens, fell and twisted my ankle, tearing ligaments. Jeff and the rest were telling me that I couldn't do the show, that they were going to have to bring in the understudy because I wasn't in a fit state.

'I'm doing it,' I told them. Think I was going to go through all of this, the blinding headaches, the contempt of the string section, just to cry off after the third date? No way. I was given cortisone injections to reduce the swelling, the ankle was strapped up and I threw myself on. Here I was playing Parson Nathaniel, a man wracked with doubt, being driven slowly mad by witnessing the destruction of everything he believes in, and I was dragging myself around the stage like a wounded animal, searing agony in my head. I think they call it method acting.

The tour did well. And rightly so. It was a great show and the reviews were fantastic. Most were nice about me – it was certainly good to hear that I had made my role my own; after all, I had big shoes to fill – but it's always the bad ones you remember. One said

I had an unconvincing limp. An unconvincing limp? My ankle was the size of a melon. That was my *real* limp.

I enjoyed it, mainly. I enjoyed meeting and working with Jeff. I enjoyed the acting, and simply being part of such a large-scale show was incredible. But even so, when I look back it's one of those dark times. All I remember is the headaches. My moods were up and down, too. I now know that it was the tumour affecting my hormones, and it made me irritable. That expression, like a bear with a sore head. That was me. The sore head was real and getting more real by the day.

With the run over, I took myself back to Manchester and went to see a specialist, a neurologist. I told him my symptoms: the headaches like daggers; problems with my peripheral vision; very, very tired and lethargic. By now the pain was so bad that I'd started to convince myself I had a brain tumour. What I wanted was someone to tell me not to be so daft. Of course it's not a brain tumour, it's just...

'Stress,' said the specialist.

He'd looked in my eyes. Shone a tiny torch at me. Done a few checks.

'But I'm not stressed,' I said. 'The only thing stressing me is the fact that I can't see out of my left eye properly and I've got severe headaches.'

No, he said, it was stress. He gave me some extra-strong headache tablets to take and told me I needed to 'de-stress'.

'Don't worry,' he told me, 'you haven't got a brain tumour.'

Thank God for that, I thought, leaving. At least I'm not dying.

CHAPTER FIFTY-EIGHT

'I can't handle this, mate,' I said to Nick.

'Just hang on, Russ. Hang on.'

The worst place to be with a head full of broken glass and road-works is on an aeroplane. But that's where I was. On the plane to LA with Nick on our way to record the new album, feeling as though my skull was trying to tear itself open. Within about an hour of taking off the headache had become unbearable. The cabin pressure, I suppose. I didn't dare have a glass of wine or two to help me sleep, which is what I do normally.

'Are you all right, mate?' said Nick.

'To be honest, mate, I'm just trying to focus on not screaming at the moment.'

At the front of my head was a jackhammer. *Boom, boom, boom.* Needles were being jammed into my temples. My whole head felt like it was throbbing. As though it was pulsating like those grey brain-heads you see suspended in fluid in sci-fi films. I tried to settle, to position my head on the seat, but I couldn't get comfortable. *Boom boom boom.* I closed my eyes. Found that I hardly dared open them. Each time I did, my vision seemed to have deteriorated and it was getting worse and worse. It was like looking through a kaleidoscope – but a kaleidoscope that was gradually narrowing as my field of vision decreased. At the sides, nothing. I couldn't see Nick sitting next to me. Nor could I see anything below. It was as though my sight was slowly being letterboxed.

We landed. I've never been so grateful to get off an aeroplane. A thirteen-hour flight, *boom boom boom*, the whole way. Nick led me past customs and through the terminal, my sight now reduced to barely a slit.

'You'd better get to bed and get some rest,' he told me. 'Maybe tomorrow we can get out, get some fresh air, play a little bit of tennis and see if that helps. Might clear your head a bit.'

That's what we did. The next day the headache had receded and I was well enough for a game of tennis. At least, I thought I was.

We started with a knock-up, then began the game proper. I remember it well; he kept smashing balls at my backhand and I wasn't reaching them. What am I saying? I wasn't even *seeing* them. It was as though the balls came over the net towards me then simply disappeared in mid-air. My sight was closing in even as we played.

'God,' I said, 'I can't even see the ball,' after yet another smash flew past my backhand.

'Yeah, yeah,' he came back, 'any excuse.'

'No, I'm serious.' I passed a hand across my forehead. I was sweating. Not just from the exertion of the tennis either. 'I'm serious, I can't see the ball any more.'

We played on. Still more of his shots came over the net then, *powf*, vanished into some other dimension, just the sound of them plopping to the clay behind me. All on my backhand, all on my left side. The optic nerve it would turn out to be. My growing tumour grinding against it.

I became more anxious, more worried, as the game went on. This isn't stress, I was telling myself.

'It's stress,' I heard the Manchester neurologist in my head say.

But I was playing tennis. In LA. I was about start work on a new album with a group of guys who were my friends. My career was back on track, my personal life stable, I was in the best financial position I'd been in for ages, and I wasn't losing my sight back when I was broke. I wasn't suffering pain like airbursts in my head every five minutes then.

And the balls kept whizzing to my backhand, vanishing, *powf*, and sweat was running freely down my forehead as I became more anxious, more frustrated.

Until I launched my racket at the clay, swearing loudly in frustration and anger. It thudded loudly into the surface, a metallic *chonk*. And on the other side of the net, Nick straightened.

'Are you all right, mate?' he asked, concerned.

'No,' I said, pressing the balls of my thumbs into my eyes. 'No, I'm not all right. I can't see the ball on this side.' I indicated to my left. 'As soon as you hit the ball to this side of me, it disappears. I can't see, Nick. I can't see out of my left eye.'

He came to the net. 'Mate, I think we'd better get you checked out, hadn't we?'

And I knew. I knew that the Manchester neurologist was talking out of his backside. 'Stress', my arse. There was something in my head. It hadn't liked the cabin pressure in the plane. It was awake. It was angry.

The Cedars-Sinai Medical Center in LA is an enormous, imposing metal and glass complex, stretching high up and all around you.

It was inside that building that I was diagnosed with my brain tumour.

I got an appointment soon after the day of the tennis match. In a consulting room full of machines I was tested. And a bit more thoroughly than my Manchester friend had managed. All the kit came out. I found myself wearing goggles, inserting my head into apertures, having things shone in my eyes. X-rays were taken.

Next they came to do what they call a VFT – a Visual Field Test. The aim of it is to check peripheral vision and it involved me putting my head into another aperture, this one cone-shaped. I wore a patch over my right eye, the idea being that I should use my left to look for test lights. I was supposed to click a mouse when a light blinked on.

I put my head in the cone-shaped aperture, waited for a light to flash. I shifted on my seat to get comfortable, conscious of my fingers on the mouse, daft things running through my head like, How sensitive is the mouse? How hard will I have to press? What if I accidentally click it? What if I see the light but don't click quickly enough…?

And I stayed like that for ten minutes, politely waiting for lights to start flashing. Until at last I got fed up and asked a nurse, 'Excuse me,' I said, 'but when does this test start?'

'About ten minutes ago,' she replied.

I hadn't seen a thing. Not a thing. Next they did my right eye and the story wasn't so bad on that side. But the left. With the left I saw nothing.

Shortly after that, I had a consultation with a doctor. He had my tests. He wasn't messing about.

'You have a pituitary tumour,' he told me.

I looked at him. I swear I felt it move in my head. As though it heard its name called out.

Pituitary, I thought. That's a gland. The one they tell you about at school that's responsible for making your balls drop. It controls and regulates the flow of hormones around the body. It was as though I suddenly became aware of those, too. The hormones, whizzing, unregulated, through my body.

'I've got to be frank with you here,' said the doctor, 'from the pictures and results I'm getting, I would say it's a big one. I can't say whether it is cancerous or not – they're usually not – but it could be. You have to go for an MRI scan, and you need to get it removed sooner rather than later. This thing is big; it's putting a massive amount of pressure on your optic nerve. You need to get it out of there, Mr Watson.'

For some moments I just sat, staring out of the window. From the outside I'd been impressed by the building, the size of it, the sun winking off metal and glass. Now I saw it for what it was: a place where people edge ever nearer to death.

And sitting there, God-knows-how-many-storeys-high in the Cedars-Sinai Medical Center in LA, four thousand miles away from my kids, I felt so alone. I was thinking about how I wanted to be back in Salford right now. Thinking I was going to die. Feeling homesick so badly it was like a physical sensation.

The doctor's voice dragged me back into the room.

'We can get you an MRI scan in three days, Mr Watson. Until

then, you have to try not to dwell on it too much. Nothing makes a tumour worse than knowing you've got one.'

Leaving the Cedars-Sinai afterwards, it felt as though my head was heavier than it should have been. I'd suddenly become aware of this parasite, squatting in my head. I wanted to reach in and peel it away from the surface of my brain. To reclaim my head, which no longer belonged to me. As if I was now the host for something dark and malignant.

My thoughts were scattershot: *I knew something was wrong the dreams were right I'm going to die. I'm going to die.*

We were recording at Capitol Studios. It had long been a dream of mine to work there. Every singer is the same. Frank Sinatra recorded there. Ike and Tina Turner. Nat King Cole. Before the trip I could hardly contain my excitement just at the thought of being there, all that history seeping through the walls. When I'd pictured it in my mind, it was preserved in the 1950s: old analogue equipment, Frank's hat on a hat-stand, a cigarette smouldering in an ashtray.

The next day, I went there. It wasn't preserved in the 1950s, of course; it was bang up to date. There were no cigarettes smoking in ashtrays, no half-glasses of bourbon lying around. What there was, was a sense of these legends in the walls – and on the walls.

Walking along a corridor towards our studio I stopped before a photograph on the wall. Frank Sinatra. What would Frank have done if he were me? I wondered. What would Frank have done if he'd been told he had a growth on his brain? Frank looked down at me from the picture. I'd have gone out on the lash with Dean and Sammy, he said.

Thanks for the advice, Frank. Fat lot of good you are. Because what should I do? Four thousand miles away from home. Something dark and slithery attached to my brain.

I decided how I was going to cope. I was going to work.

'Right,' I said, Nick turning as I entered the studio, 'let's get on with it, shall we?'

And I told nobody. Not a soul. Not Nick, not the record company – especially not the record company – none of the team who made that record. I didn't even ring home and tell the Colonel and Lynne. My loved ones I didn't want to worry. Anybody involved in a professional capacity I wanted to keep it from in case they wouldn't let me finish making my record. So for the next three days I kept my tumour to myself. I tried to take the doctor's advice. I tried to keep my thoughts clear of tumours. Instead I put my heart and soul into my voice.

I can hear it there, when I listen to the album these days. I can hear the voice of a man who thinks he's going to die. 'When I Fall In Love', 'A Very Good Year', 'Born Free'. I can hear it all on the record.

I ended up recording Tuesday, Wednesday and Thursday. On Friday I returned alone to the Cedars-Sinai and had my MRI scan. The following day the doctor rang with the results.

'I'm sorry to say, Mr Watson, that I was right, it's a big one.' He cleared his throat. 'If you can imagine two golf balls in a figure-of-eight shape on the front of your brain...'

I don't have to imagine, I wanted to shout. *I don't have to imagine it because it's there.*

I put a hand to my forehead, pressing the tips of my fingers into the flesh, trying to feel for the tumour. Come out, come out, I know you're in there.

'I actually don't think I've seen one that big before,' he added. 'You need an operation pretty quick. I suggest you get it done over here, now, next week if you can. I've got somebody that can do it for you...'

But I'd stopped listening. We ended the conversation and for a moment or so I sat motionless on the bed, the room seeming to settle around me. Then I dragged myself onto the covers, pulled my knees up to my chest, and lay, foetus-like. And I cried. My hands to my head, this vessel for an invading tumour. I lay and cried until there were no more tears left.

When I'd finished, I washed my face and made some calls. It was time to tell people. I told the Colonel and Lynne, I spoke to my management. The doctor had advised going into the Cedars for the operation but that would have meant spending months in America during the recovery period. Worse, having the operation without seeing my children first.

No way. Not that. If I was going to die, I wanted to see my kids before it happened.

It was agreed to book the operation for when I returned. I had two more days recording vocals for the album and I went back into the studio for the next session. Still I told no one.

People knew, of course. Nick knew something was up. I even did a piece with *GMTV* during the process and even they worked out I wasn't myself. But I threw myself into the vocals during the daytime.

Night-time was different. There was no sitting out on the balcony drinking off-licences dry and smoking cigars. That was another guy. He belonged to another life. Instead, I went back to my room at the Four Seasons and counted down the hours, turning things over in my mind, feeling my vision worsen, always aware of that thing in my head. I'd study myself in the mirror, peering at the glass to see if I could make it out. As though I might see a figure of eight raised in the flesh of my forehead.

Nothing makes a tumour worse than knowing you've got one.

The headaches seemed to pound harder. Vision on the blink. I'd sit there mulling over stuff: my marriage, my relationship with Roxanna, the throat operation, selling off my home to pay my debts.

One night, at about ten or eleven o'clock, I went out onto the balcony. I looked down and realised I couldn't see. Not because it was dark – this was LA, it's never dark. But because I couldn't *see*, not even a few feet below me. I could make out my hand in front of my face, but as I pulled it away it seemed to dissolve.

Down below was nothing, blackness. Out in front of me, the same. And I thought, I could climb over, look out into the blackness and take one step. I could just fall into the dark and there would be no more pain.

I shook the thought away.

Come on, Nobby.

I pulled myself together, turned, went back into my room, sliding the balcony door shut with a thud. Let's get it together, eh? Let's just keep it together.

I flew back to the UK. I had time before the operation to tell those who needed to know and see the children. They came over the night before I was due to drive to London for the procedure. The Colonel was there, too; he was coming with me to the hospital.

And I remember, I was playing with the kids. We were jumping on my bed. And for a second, I forgot – I forgot that the next day doctors were going to go inside my head and scrape away the tumour that lay inside.

But a second later it came back. A rush of fear and a longing to get old. The kids jumping up and down on the bed, grabbing onto each for support, hair bouncing, faces split by grins. It came flooding through me, keen and sharp as a scalpel. *I don't want to die. I want to live and see my children grow up.*

I stepped away, let myself into the bathroom. I wrapped my head in a towel so that nobody would hear me, and I sobbed. Huge sobs that shook my whole body. All that emotion punching its way out so suddenly and so violently that I could barely control it.

Coughing. Choking. Trying to catch my breath at the same time. Feeling my face burn.

I was gone about twenty minutes. Then I rinsed my face, opened the bathroom door. Got back on the dancefloor.

I have to be careful what I say here. I mean, it's a matter of public record where I had that first operation done but I don't want to name the hospital, because as later became clear, the operation wasn't a success.

For five hours they worked. They drilled into my skull through the gap between the lip and the gum. A surgeon with a scalpel equipped with a tiny camera scraped at my brain, working from pictures relayed to a screen. And they scraped. And tumour came out. They withdrew, then packed the drill-hole they had made. And most of the tumour probably sat in a silver tray, which was, no doubt, whisked away so that I would never see it.

But not all of it.

I wouldn't find out for a while, but to all intents and purposes the operation had failed. It seemed they may not have removed all of the tumour.

The period afterwards was hell. Coming round, I couldn't see. My vision was at its all-time worst; all I could make out were shadows. Even so, my first thought was, At least I can see. Seeing shadows was better than seeing nothing.

'Your vision shouldn't have been like that,' Mr Leggat told me, over a year later, after a second operation to remove what was labelled in the press as a second tumour; but that was, I'm convinced, the same one.

'In fact, I would have been surprised if you hadn't woken up with an *improvement* in your vision, far less a deterioration.'

It was a busy London hospital. They needed the beds. By day four they were sweeping me out of the door and I returned home. I was there for a day. Unable to move, unable to see, short of breath, struggling even to get to the bathroom, I went to stay with the Colonel and Lynne.

I've introduced you to the Colonel and his missus, Lynne. You know the Colonel looks like a cross between Kenny Rogers and Steven Spielberg. You know I see them both almost as surrogate parents. But even saying that doesn't do justice to the effect they've had on my life.

Simply put, they've been the single most solid fixture in my life for the last twelve years. They've been there for me. When I first met them that night at South Shore Cricket Club, I was an unknown, struggling with the mortgage, still trying to pay off Jonesey every week. They liked what they heard. They liked me. And they got behind me.

The Colonel runs a successful business; he's not short of a few bob. He'd done a bit of DJing in the past, but that was about the extent of his contact with the music business. What I'm saying is, he had nothing to gain by getting behind me. He and Lynne just liked my voice. We got on, and they were happy to put the word around about me. Tell you what, South Shore Cricket Club may have been empty the night I met the Colonel, but it was packed when I went back there. The Colonel helped financially, too. I needed to make tapes to sell in the clubs but couldn't afford the studio time. He paid for sessions in Lollipop Studios, a local studio, so now I had tapes to sell in the clubs. He helped out with the CDs, too. The CD sent to Cliff Richard's management was paid for by the Colonel. When David Bryce pointed at a picture of me on the

CD: 'I receive this CD in the post and it's got a picture of this young chap on the front, so I play the CD and there's this... *voice*,' he was pointing at a picture of me paid for by the Colonel.

They bought me shirts and trousers so I could smarten up my act. When I started doing some of the clubs in Blackpool, I was far from home and they let me stay at their house. The Colonel would accompany me to gigs and he used to help out – almost like a manager. He helped out with bookings, then in the club. The band would come in wanting to know what songs I was doing that night.

'What songs am I doing, Bob?'

'Here,' the Colonel would say, pulling out bits of paper. 'I'll go through the list with you, lads.'

It was during those days that the Colonel nickname first came about. It's not that he looks like Elvis's manager Colonel Tom Parker – he doesn't (he'll probably give me a clip round the ear for saying this, but he looks more like Colonel Sanders), but he took to calling me the King (because he's a huge fan of Elvis; because he said I sounded more like Elvis than Elvis), so in return I called him the Colonel. Nobody calls me the King, of course, but for him the Colonel stuck somehow. Even Lynne calls him the Colonel these days.

He and Lynne are the people I turned to when I needed a hand, and never once did they come up lacking, not once have they asked for anything in return. I remember, I had this gig in the Bahamas. This was before the Decca deal, when I didn't have two pennies to rub together, and I did the gig, but when it came to leaving and coming home, I'd either lost my passport or had it stolen, and I missed my flight. It was the Colonel who made the calls, who gave out his credit card details so I could fly home. I couldn't have afforded the journey. I'd probably still be out there now if it hadn't been for the Colonel. I'd be busking for my fare home.

And bloody hell, we've had some laughs, too. Nights at his

place when we've got completely trashed and jumped in his pool, Lynne going, 'Get to bed, you two, you're drunk.' But neither of us taking any notice, diving right in.

There was another night during the Paul O'Grady run. Oh dear. Paul had this do and I went along with the Colonel. We ended up getting stuck into the Baileys of all things. My advice is if you're ever going to get drunk on Baileys, don't. And if you do, buy yourself a bigger bucket.

By the end of the evening the Colonel and I were both legless. I was supposed to get back to Salford that night, but I was in no fit state to attempt the trip. Instead, I stayed at his, and the effects of the Baileys had really kicked in. Let's just say I had a good long chat to God on the big white telephone that night.

The next day I had to perform again, but I was as sick as a dog. Who's there to help me? Lynne. She ended up driving me to the show so I wouldn't miss it – and I didn't.

You know what the Colonel always says: 'We knew from day one Russell would get to where he has. The first night I saw him play that club was empty but he performed as though it was full. He's no different in front of ten people than he is front of a hundred thousand.'

And I know it sometimes sounds as if my relationship with the Colonel and Lynne has put my mum and dad into the shade, but it's just a different relationship. My mum and dad gave me a wonderful, uncomplicated childhood. From them I learnt manners, respect and how to tell right from wrong – all the things you would want a kid to learn. But their horizons were never as broad. When I told my dad I was packing my job in at the engineering factory to do singing, he thought I was mad to jack in a secure nine-to-five job for this wild, pie-in-the-sky idea. He thought, Oh, it'll never last.

But he's my dad, and I wouldn't expect anything less from him.

Dads want secure, comfortable futures for their kids. They don't want to see their kids' dreams shatter, their hearts break. I don't blame him for that attitude; I'd probably be the same if it was my kids.

The Colonel and Lynne were different, though. They'd give me a kick up the arse every now and again. They made me believe in myself. Both of their kids have gone to university, so maybe they ended up putting a bit of that parental drive my way, pushing me, offering support and advice and urging me on.

I don't have that many friends. I mean, I know lots of people, I have 'friends'. But my real, close friends I can probably count on the fingers of one hand. The Colonel and Lynne are two of them. If somebody like that came along now, I'd be wondering about their motives, but the Colonel and Lynne knew me when I didn't have a pot to piss in. They've seen me through the good times and they've seen me through the bad. I can't thank them enough.

After the operation was one of the bad times. I was wasted. Felt absolutely terrible. Vision was awful. If I got out of bed, I was exhausted. I was short of breath. Could hardly get out of bed to use the bathroom.

I was anti-social, too, didn't want to mix with anyone. I couldn't have a proper conversation. I remember being at the hospital and my managers were there, Giles and Richard. My assistant at the time, Adrian, was also in the room and the Colonel was there, too, My room, full of all these people, me in bed.

And it hit me. All this noise. The Colonel and Adrian were chatting, Giles was tapping a text message into his BlackBerry and it was all too much. I felt the weight of all these people and their lives. I felt as though they had brought all of themselves into the room and the huge presence of them was pushing down on me, pushing me into the bed.

The conversation. Adrian laughing. *Tap, tap tap* on the BlackBerry.

'Get out,' I screamed at them.

They stopped, looked at me. I clutched my hands to my skull, digging my fingers into my temples. 'For God's sake,' I shouted, 'what are you doing in here? What do you want? I just nearly died. Why are you tapping on your phone, why are you having a conversation? Get out of my room.' My head in my hands, saying, 'I can't deal with this,' and hearing the catch in my voice as I began to cry.

And I was like that for weeks. Back at the Colonel's I lay in bed. I was bed-bound for about a fortnight, lying there feeling like an empty shell. It was as though all trace of the old me had gone. Like they'd scraped out my former self along with the tumour. On the outside I was the same; on the inside, I was hurting. It was a dark, dark time. I don't like to go there.

I made it through that time thanks to Lynne, who was really responsible for nursing me back to health. After what felt like years of lying in bed suffering, I was at last able to get out and move around, I could use the bathroom and just about manage the stairs. My vision had improved, just as I'd been told it would. I thought I was starting to get better.

Then one night some of the Colonel and Lynne's family had come round. I'm not sure it was meant as a surprise, but I didn't know they were coming and I walked into the kitchen, which suddenly seemed full of people. Couldn't handle it.

'Hi, Russ, how are you doing?'

'Hello, Russell.'

Immediately couldn't handle all of those people in one place. A room full of people I knew were all there to see me and wish me well. But no. No, it just wasn't happening.

'Oh God,' I said, 'I'm sorry. I'm going to have to go,' and I left the room.

Some ten weeks after the operation and I was still the shell, but I was back at home, walking around a bit more, and Richard came up from London to see me. We went for a stroll down to the local pie shop and when we got back, I took off my coat.

'Bloody hell, Russ,' said Richard.

'What?'

'You're drenched, mate.' And I was saturated. My shirt stuck to my back. I was exhausted and all I'd done was take a stroll down to the pie shop. It took me months to get my strength back. It took even longer than that to overcome the psychological side effects. I didn't want to see anyone. I didn't want to leave the house. I didn't want to *do* anything.

And of course I now know that it shouldn't have been that way. After my second operation I had none of this. I was up and about in days. I was back in the gym after a fortnight, talking to my managers, thinking about my career, working on this book. But back then I had no way of knowing that it shouldn't have been this bad. I'm convinced that it was so painful because the tumour hadn't all been scraped away. They'd left some in there, and it was growing back.

CHAPTER SIXTY-ONE

The first thing I did when I was well enough – my first proper day back at work – was a guest appearance on *Just the Two of Us*, the second series.

I was originally down to do the programme, to defend my title, and I'd been paired with an actress from *Hollyoaks*, Loui Batley. But I'd had to send a sick note: 'Please may Russell be excused from this series of *Just the Two of Us*; he has a very poorly head.' And sadly for Loui they didn't find her a replacement partner, so she wasn't able to do it either.

Anyway, they invited me on to do a guest appearance on the second show and, for the first time ever, I almost bottled it. Being around all those people, all the cameras and lights, and technicians, researchers, make-up, everything. The whole time my body was screaming at me. *Go.* You don't want to be here. *Go.* I spent the day at war with what my battered instincts were telling me.

At first, I was sitting in the audience and Vernon came to interview me. If you see the footage now, I'm clearly in a bad way: I'm speaking slowly, I look uncomfortable and close to tears, I'm unable to look Vernon in the eye and when I smile it seems forced and automatic, like I'm fighting nausea.

Which I was. Inside I was churning, trying to control the mess in my head. My senses were on high alert and I became super-aware of the people sitting around me – again I had that sense of them as a large presence. When Vernon arrived to speak to me it was as though he'd brought an army into my personal space. I was trying to be the old me, who laughed and did impressions throughout interviews. This new me was having to concentrate on the questions, work hard on the answers. What had once been second nature I now felt like I was doing for the first time. The cameras seemed way too close, the silence of the other audience members unbearable.

But then I got up to sing. It was 'You Don't Know Me' from the album we'd recorded in LA that I'd decided to call *That's Life* – a title to honour all the trauma I was going through.

And up on stage, singing, I felt, for a few minutes, better. It was as though getting up there restored a bit of life. A bit of the old me. Before, Vernon had asked me if I had any advice for the contestants and I'd struggled through the answer, which was just to think of pleasant things. Go to your happy place, in other words.

My happy place was up there, on that stage. Returning to it seemed to replace some of my scraped-away soul.

As well as having to cancel *Just the Two of Us*, plus various other bits and pieces, I'd had to postpone my UK tour, and I picked it back up in March 2007. I was itching to get back. The appearance on *Just the Two of Us* had been hard but it had shown me one thing: I belonged on stage.

On the other hand, I wasn't sure if I'd be able to cope. I'd got through *Just the Two of Us*, but what if I suddenly froze on stage? This wasn't just a kitchen full of friends. This was venues full of people. I was still having a hard time walking down to the paper shop. Could I cope with all these people?

It went well, though. I enjoyed it. But something wasn't right. I didn't get the same old spark from what I was doing. I still wasn't feeling well. This was six months after the operation and

I was constantly tired, fighting lethargy the whole time. If I tried going to the gym or doing a workout it would be a grind; I'd do fifteen or twenty minutes then feel tired and listless. Where before endorphins would be racing around my body, keeping me bouncing on my toes, now I needed a sit down, like an old man. And I wasn't old; I'd turned 40 the previous November. Maybe if you're 13 that seems old but trust me, it's not old. It's not so old that a previously fit guy needs a lie down after a few minutes on a Stairmaster.

I also had this weird feeling. It was as though when I shook my head I could feel something in there, waggling around. As though I could somehow sense that it was back, perhaps as a slightly tattered version of its former self – tendrils of damaged tumour waving about on the surface of my brain.

'It really has knocked you for six this, hasn't it?' said Nick, one day.

I looked at him. 'Yeah, mate. Yeah, it bloody has.'

I was beginning to wonder if I'd ever feel well again.

The audience reaction was astonishing. My fans know I'm not just kissing their collective backside when I say that they're an amazing, loyal, supportive bunch, because they are. From them I had cards, letters, flowers, presents, countless messages left on my website. And they turned up to support me, too. Every night on that tour I'd feel a wave of goodwill coming off the crowd. It created some intense, emotional nights. The first two or three I came off the stage in tears. The show at Manchester's MEN Arena, my homecoming show, was incredibly emotionally charged. Birmingham Indoor Arena. The Royal Albert Hall – one of my 'Planet Russell' venues – there were times when it was brilliant. And don't get the impression that I was walking around with a face like a wet weekend the whole time, either, because I wasn't. I stayed positive. I thought that if

I kept doing what I do, then eventually I would get better. If it took a year, so be it. But I still had that nagging feeling. The feeling that something wasn't right. When I shook my head, I was sure I felt it in there.

CHAPTER SIXTY-TWO

'There's been some regrowth. I need to see you.'

My endocrinologist, Peter Trainer. He's a Scot. Very direct. Doesn't mess around. He's a bit strident, you might almost say. There's no, 'Pour yourself a drink, Russell, I've got some bad news, take a seat why don't you,' with him.

Just, *There's been some regrowth.*

Something whooshed through me that seemed to detach my mind from my body, as though my essence wanted to escape its rotted host, and for a second I was thousands and thousands of miles away, up on some other plane, looking down at this bloke on the phone. Looking at this thing who was once more surrendering his body to the parasite. No control over his own life, no say in who or what gets to live in his head.

Regrowth.

It was supposed to be a routine scan, just to check everything was all right. 'Feeling good, are we? Excellent, then this should just be a formality.' I'd had the scan done in a hospital in London but Dr Trainer was based at the Christie in Manchester and it's there I went the following day.

I went with Gary. He drove me. I know that it was a bright, sunny day because I remember gazing out of the car window and seeing summer outside. It was dark, though, to me. I caught sight of my reflection in the rear-view, just my eye, a bit of forehead, baseball cap. I'd done a lot of TV over the last few months, a lot of telling concerned-looking hosts about the tumour I'd supposedly had removed. I'd become an expert at tracing the figure-of-eight on my forehead. 'The size of two golf balls,' I'd told everybody.

There was some regrowth.

Dr Trainer is one of these guys who's unflappable. But he was fazed. I could see from the expression on his face when I walked in how fazed he was. Just seeing his face like that, I was thinking, This isn't just *some* regrowth, is it?

'Russell, I'm afraid I don't know how to tell you this, because you've been through a very difficult time...' He paused for a moment or so, as if trying to select his words carefully. Sitting there, I was willing him to continue, leaning forward, wanting to hear the worst. Get it over with.

'The tumour seems to have grown back very quickly. In actual fact, we don't know whether it's grown back from scratch, or if it's tumour that was left over that has increased in size. We don't know.'

I was getting used to these moments by now. These moments of being told the worst. I felt dizzy and my palms were sweating, and his words had an immediate psychological impact because I felt ill, immediately ill. An instant psychological effect that came on like a light, and I looked at him, hearing myself say, 'Peter, I need to get out of here.'

My voice small in the room. Hot all of a sudden.

'Let me just quickly explain,' he said.

I need to get out of here, I thought.

He drew a diagram of a bean-shaped thing, big.

'But that's the same size as it was before,' I managed, looking at it. 'How can it have grown back that quickly?'

I need to get out of here.

'It's very unusual,' he said. 'But...'

I was pushing my chair back, standing, already turning to take myself away, saying, 'I need to get out, Peter. I'm sorry, I've got to get out of here.'

'It's grown back,' I told Gary outside the room.

'Oh God,' he said.

It hadn't gone. I had to go through it all again.

At home, I clutched my head. I screamed, 'No. *No*. This can't be happening.'

Because, how could…

How could it happen again?

Just as before, it was as though the tumour's symptoms had been magnified by the knowledge that it was in there. I found that I pressed my fingers into my temple, almost wanting to dig the thing out, fighting tears and dizziness and nausea – a wave of something that felt like utter defeat.

That would pass, of course, that feeling of defeat. Because that's the incredible thing about us humans. When you think you're beaten; when you think you can't take any more, you rise to the challenge. And I would. From somewhere I'd find an inner strength.

I needed to take the first steps to find it, though.

I picked up the phone, rang the Colonel. My hands were like jelly. I could hear my voice shaking as I tried to make the horror into words.

'It's come back, mate,' I told him.

There was a pause. A long, long pause.

'What's come back?'

'The tumour.'

'Oh, fucking hell, mate,' he said. 'Oh, mate. Oh, I'm sorry, I can't talk.' I could hear the tears.

Lynne came on. 'What is it, love? What's up, Russ?'

I told her, then asked, 'Can I come over?'

'You get yourself over here right now, Russell,' she said. 'Right now.' And I almost broke down with gratitude, there and then.

I went there, my refuge. All the time thinking, It's grown back. Once again I faced surgery. There was an album to record, too, *Outside In*. For a second time I planned to keep the information from the record company: I needed to make the album.

Meanwhile, I had the scans sent to a specialist in America, a guy called Rafe, who rang me at the Colonel's.

'Russell?' he said.

'Yeah,' I said, 'have you seen the scans?'

'Yes, I have, I've got them here.'

'It's grown back pretty quickly, hasn't it?' I said.

'No.'

'What do you mean?'

'Russell, I don't think this is regrowth. I'm looking at these scans and in my opinion, it's the same tumour.'

'Are you serious?'

'Yeah, looks to me like they didn't get rid of all of it. You're going to have to get it out, man.'

Dr Trainer had recommended surgery. But he also thought that there was a slim chance it could be treated with radiotherapy, and that was a possibility I liked the sound of.

I desperately didn't want surgery. No more scraping tissue from my brain then another six months of hell afterwards. What if it went wrong again? An operation, a long, agonisingly hard road to recovery, think I'm out of the woods, go for a routine MRI scan, sorry, it's grown back, you need another operation, another long, agonisingly hard road to recovery. And so on and so on. Repeat till fade.

So I decided to start investigating both radiotherapy and surgery. If it could be zapped using radiotherapy then that's the treatment I wanted. If it needed surgery, then I wanted the best surgeon I could find.

Meanwhile, I started recording *Outside In*. And something happened. Perhaps because I was back in the recording studio with Nick and Grant and my mates. Or maybe because by investigating the different treatment possibilities I was at last taking some control over what happened to me. But I started to cope.

I remember my GP, Dr Ahmed, rang me one evening: 'Russell, it's Dr Ahmed, how are you?' he said.

'Yeah, I'm good,' I told him.

'Really?' he said. 'Well I'm a bit concerned about that really.'

'Why?'

He said, 'Well, are you in denial?'

I almost made a joke about the river in Egypt, stopping myself. Instead, saying, 'I don't know, what do you mean?'

'Well, you know, you're just carrying on, you're making a record. I'm just concerned that you're in denial. You must take this seriously and get it sorted.'

I came off the phone wondering. Was I in denial? I mean, the nights were tough, sometimes sleepless, but there was nothing as bad as that evening in the Four Seasons. And when I cast my mind back, thinking how dark that time was compared to this, I began to wonder. I was having a laugh with my mates. We made a film one night, the lot of us larking about playing football, except in fancy dress. I was cheerful and laughing. I'm not sure. Perhaps I was in denial. Did the fact that I almost made the Egyptian river joke mean I was in denial? Or maybe I began to wonder if this tumour wasn't all that dangerous; that it was easily beatable. Like this tumour was bad, but not as bad as the last one.

If that's what I was thinking – that the tumour wasn't so bad this time round – well, I was wrong. God, was I wrong about that.

I concentrated on making the record. And once again, I can hear the pain of what I was going through on that album. Singing 'O Holy Night' and 'Adeste Fideles'. It was as if I was singing for my life.

I met with a radiologist who told me the tumour was too advanced for radiotherapy. *Great*. It would have to be surgery. I finished recording *Outside In*. I made an appointment to see a surgeon called Vinko Dolenc, who was reputed to be one of the best in the world at the type of procedure I needed.

'Best'? Did that mean that somewhere there was a worst?

I made another appointment for the following Monday. This time to see Mr James Leggat, who was reputed to be the best in the UK at this kind of procedure.

As it turned out, I'd be seeing Mr Leggat sooner than I planned.

The night before my appointment with Dr Dolenc, Richard came up. We were supposed to eat out, but I said I'd rather eat at home; I hadn't been feeling well during the day, slightly nauseous. We stayed in, got a takeaway, and I opened a bottle of wine but then didn't feel like drinking a glass.

I'm usually a night owl, but this evening I was tired, went to bed about 10.30 p.m., saying goodnight to Richard, who was staying the night. In bed I fell straight to sleep.

At about 2 a.m. I awoke, feeling sick. I wasn't unduly worried; I'd got used to feeling sick, after all. I tried to get comfortable, ride out the waves of nausea in my guts. Not long after I got out of bed and went to fetch a bucket. Along with the nausea I was battling fatigue, and I wasn't sure I'd make it out of bed if I needed to be sick.

Which I was. I leaned over the side of the bed and my dinner splashed to the bucket. Food poisoning, I thought. Must be food poisoning.

And then my head began to hurt. I've had headaches before, believe me, but this one had to be the worst. I was burying my head in the pillow, screaming. Then leaning over the side of the bed, being sick again, desperately trying to take hold of the pain in my body, trying to rationalise it. Food poisoning, I was thinking. Just food poisoning.

By 6 a.m. I was vomiting every quarter of an hour. By now it was just yellow bile, but I felt rank with sickness, it was in my mouth and my nostrils, the smell of it making me dry-heave.

Vaguely, I heard Richard leave. He left about 6.30 a.m., quietly letting himself out. By the time I heard him it was too late to call out. I don't think I had the strength anyway. Much, much later, he said to me, 'Why didn't you come to my room and tell me you were ill, mate?'

Because I couldn't move, that's why. I didn't have the strength.

He left at 6.30 a.m. Between then and when Gary arrived at 11 a.m., I was alone. I lay in bed, heaving, holding my head with the pain of the headache, still telling myself it was food poisoning, thinking, Great, just finished the album. Got an appointment to see a surgeon tomorrow. What a time to get food poisoning.

(Richard wasn't sick, though, said a little nagging voice. Didn't he eat the same?)

Gary arrived, thinking it was strange that I wasn't pottering around, mumbling to myself the way I usually do in the morning, so he came upstairs, knocked on the door, looked in, said, 'Are you all... Russ, what's wrong?'

'I don't know.' I actually didn't care. I just wanted the pain to stop. 'You'd best call a doctor, mate.'

Dr Ahmed was away on a family holiday, so a duty doctor came. He was worried, especially about my temperature, which at the time was 38.2 degrees. And if that sound high, it would go on to rise to 38.9 at its worst – which is just about the highest it can go without it being fatal. Death was really out to get me that day.

The doctor prescribed me antibiotics, told me to call if things got any worse, then left.

331

He then made a call. And thank God he did. He called Dr Ahmed to let him know he'd attended me. He told Dr Ahmed my symptoms.

'Get him to a hospital, right now,' Dr Ahmed told him.

They called an ambulance.

I was getting worse. My vision was deteriorating badly. At first I was seeing colours, neon colours, as though I was squinting up at the lights on Piccadilly Circus. Then it started to fade, like some internal dimmer switch was gradually rotating to the off position.

Christ, it's the tumour. It's not food poisoning, it's the tumour. I made it angry. It's hurting me back. Maybe this isn't the weaker offspring. Perhaps this one's the daddy.

I thought then, I'm going to die.

Oh God, I'm going to die.

And I begin to drift into unconsciousness, unable to move, unable to even speak. This is it. It got me.

The ambulance men arrived.

CHAPTER SIXTY-THREE

Which is where we came in, of course. The ambulance men, the tapping on the back of my hand, the shout that I was haemorrhaging.

I came that close to the tumour imploding, flooding my brain with poison. I came that close to losing my sight thanks to the pressure the tumour was applying to my optic nerve. They calmed the swelling.

When I came round I spoke to Mr Leggat who told me he needed to operate; who told me that he wanted to operate – that he thought he could do it for me. Finally get this thing out of my head.

No. I was shaking my head at Mr Leggat, who sat before me, urging me to have the operation. No, I was thinking. No operations and certainly not *now*.

Because I had convinced myself I would die. If I was a cat I'd used up my nine lives. The operation would kill me – I've never been more certain of anything. As soon as I was well enough I was going to leave because if I only had a couple more days to live, then I was going to bloody well live them. No way was I going straight into surgery. I was a dead man.

He watched me carefully. 'I'm telling you,' he said, 'that you need an operation on this. It's not going to go away and I can get rid of it for you.'

I was still shaking my head. 'Believe me,' he said, 'this is as good as it gets for a man in your position. It's when I come into this room and say I'm sorry, Mr Watson, there's nothing we can do, we can't operate, it's irreversible, the damage is done – that's when you need to worry. That's when you need to consider getting your affairs in order. But I'm telling you that I can. I'm telling you that I can sort this out for you. Think about it.'

I did. I lay in bed for some time, thinking about operations. Thinking about death. Nurses would come into my room. They had this thing they were doing, to check I was still with it. They'd ask me if I knew where I was; then the date.

'Hello, Mr Watson, do you know where you are?'

'Yes, I'm in hospital.'

'And do you know the name of the hospital?

'It's the Alexandra Hospital in Cheadle.'

'Excellent. And do you know the date?'

'Sweetheart, I don't know what date it is when I'm well.'

A little later a different nurse came in and asked me the same question, but by then I'd had a look on my phone, so I was able to give them the date. A nurse would walk in and I'd have a surreptitious check on my phone when she wasn't looking.

A nurse came into the room, asked me her questions, which I passed with flying colours, then I said to her, 'Could I see Mr Leggat, please?'

Not long later he was back in the room.

'I need to see my children first,' I told him. 'No operation until I've seen them.'

He nodded, pleased I'd reached the right decision. 'You'd better get them over here, then,' he said.

I'd convinced myself I would die. When Helen brought the kids to see me before the operation, inside I thought it was the last time I was seeing them. So when I woke up after the procedure, I thought I was in heaven, and the angels were Rebecca- and Hannah-shaped. They seemed to materialise in front of me and I could see them perfectly, vivid and in colour, hair and smiles, because my vision had improved.

My sight had improved. I must be in heaven.

Around me, machines went beep, beep, beep. I was wearing an oxygen mask, tubes attached to the veins in my wrists, breathing apparatus shuttling up and down by my side.

And of course I wasn't in heaven. They don't have beeping machines there, at least I hope not. But I was in the next best place, because the girls were either side of my bed, Hannah on my left, Rebecca on my right. I looked from one to the other. Could they see me smiling beneath the oxygen mask? And I reached for their hands, felt the touch of their hands in mine.

The feeling. It was nothing like anything I'd ever experienced before. It was of life, and love and relief and hope, all rolled into one. It was every other emotion I've ever felt multiplied by a billion, and it seemed to lift my soul from the bed, hurtling me into a euphoric state above and beyond anything I'd ever felt before.

The touch of my girls' hands. It was like God was in the room with us.

I took things one day at a time. I was dreading the same long road to recovery that I'd had before, but the signs were good right from the start: improved vision, a generally improved sense of well-being, plus, after five days, I was able to take my first steps. Sitting back down afterwards it was like I'd run a 100-metre sprint and I said to Gary at the time, 'I've got a long way to go,' but it all started coming back really quickly.

Then I had my radiotherapy. No walk in the park, not exactly a fun time. But you know what? I did it. I stayed fit, I stayed positive, I counted down the days, and I got through it. We won't know for months whether or not the tumour's finally gone. But all the signs are good. I'll be on pills and injections for the rest of my life and I can expect Fun With Hormones every now and then, but otherwise, I feel great.

In fact, I feel better than I have in years. *In years.*

Earlier, I said that I try and take something positive from these really harrowing experiences, even if it does sound like a cliché. I also said each experience has changed me, and I was still mulling over how I'd been changed by this one. I'd get back to you on it, I said.

Well, I've learnt to sit back and enjoy what I've achieved. Before, I'd always been so frightened of losing it, because I'd worked so hard to get it. I'd see singers drift off and the next thing you know they didn't have a record deal and they couldn't get arrested. They'd be standing in the line-up on *Never Mind the Buzzcocks* and the panel wouldn't know who they were. That terrifies you as a singer, especially when you've worked so hard to get there in the first place. It's why you get so scared of losing it.

But what I've learnt is not to let that terror take over. Don't let it rule your life to the exclusion of everything else. Yes, so you might fade out of the public eye. Better that, than to fade out of your children's lives.

Having these tumours – being given a second chance, I suppose you might say – it's strengthened my relationship with Hannah and Rebecca more than I could ever have imagined. It's made me a better dad. Since recovering, I've taken the decision that my career won't keep me away from them any more. It used to. But now, if I want to be with my kids, I will be, simple as that. Doesn't matter if I'm not in the papers, or in the charts or on the right chat shows. Doesn't matter. So what. It used to – all I ever used to talk about was my career – now I just switch off. Switch the phone off. Spend time with Hannah and Rebecca.

And you know why, don't you? You know why I've realised these two little girls are never again going to take a back seat. It's because during everything I went through, all I thought of was them. If you'd asked me before I would have said they were the most important people in my life, because they were. But it would have been an empty soundbite compared to the way I feel now. When you nearly die you get a short, sharp lesson in what matters in this life. You don't nearly die thinking, I wish I'd worked more, I wish I'd spent less time with my kids.

No, you lie there half-cooked thinking the exact opposite. And if you're lucky enough, and you live, you won't make that mistake again.

Because let me tell you, there's nothing like nearly dying to give you an appreciation of life. You think you have it, of course – you mindlessly tell yourself that you're living life to the full. But then Mr Leggat informs you your brain nearly imploded and you start looking at life differently. You start pausing to admire the flavours, realising you'd just been mindlessly slugging it back before.

And then, of course, there's that old saying that whatever doesn't kill you makes you stronger. The tumour tried its best, but I beat it, and I'll notch that up to one of life's experiences. And I'll know that the next time I'm out on stage I can channel that experience into the sound. Singing Schubert's 'Ave Maria' to an audience after an experience like this – believe me, I know – it adds something. It adds something to the performance.

So all told, I feel great. Like I say, better than I have in years. Full of new life. I'm going to make the most of things now: of my relationships, of my time. These days I find myself trying to cram as much into each day as possible. Even going to bed suddenly seems like a waste of life to me. I don't want to waste it sleeping. I want to feel and taste and touch and breathe. I've suddenly got this desire to feed, to learn from life.

And I want to sing.

TV offers have been coming in, of course. Everybody wants to know about the tumour, my 'how I cheated death' story. There's a Trevor McDonald special in the works. I'm also on the panel of a prime-time BBC Saturday night show that's coming up. All very exciting, of course, but what I'm really looking forward to is getting out there and performing. We're going to record a new album. There's talk of a big summer tour coming up and it'll be big, could be quite daunting. The first major performances since nearly dying, surgery and radiotherapy. A different singer will walk out on that stage. A different man. Could be scary. Might feel the nerves a bit.

On the other hand, you know me. I fackin' larve the big occasion.

February 24, 2008

It's Sunday, about 9 p.m. I'm in my bathroom upstairs, washing my hands, listening to the noises I can hear from the floor below. Rebecca, Hannah, the Colonel and Lynne.

Every weekend the Colonel and Lynne drive over from Blackpool. They're bloody saints, they really are. Lynne cooks usually. We mess about with the girls. Sometimes we watch a DVD together, play some games of pool. What with knocking around the house so much lately, I've improved at pool. I'm even beating the Colonel these days...

The sound that rises to me is the people I love, just mucking about down there, and it makes me smile at myself in the mirror.

And then everything goes black.

And I think, Oh no. Christ. Oh no. Please. Not again.

My hands shoot out in front of me and I'm holding onto the bathroom top, suddenly unable to see myself in the mirror.

Next thinking, No – no it's not totally black, I can see. I can still make things out. Shadows, mainly, but I can see.

In my head I hear the words, *Pressure on the optic nerve.*

You were lucky not to lose your sight, Mr Watson.

'Hello?' I call. 'Hello?' And I find the bathroom door, my hands outstretched like some bad Boris Karloff impression, seeing shapes and shadows but nothing more.

'*Rebecca*,' I shout. '*Hannah*.'

'It's all right, Dad. The electricity went off, that's all, Colonel's got it.'

The lights come back on. I stand in the doorway of my bathroom not knowing whether to laugh or cry. Heart pounding. Palms sweaty. Shaking slightly and taking deep breaths to calm down.

'You all right, Dad?' comes the call.

'Yeah, love,' I call back. 'Yeah, I'm fine. I'll tell you about it in a second.' And I leave the bedroom, come running down the stairs, towards the kitchen where I can hear them all.

By the piano in the hall, I stop a second. Look down at the keyboard. I plink a key and try a top C, which I nail. There's a moment of silence and then a round of friendly, not-so-serious applause from inside the kitchen. I grin and go to join them.

Vincerò.

Acknowledgements

To my dear friend Francis Yeoh for all your support in the last few years... Many thanks for the fabulous memories that you gave both myself and my family, from your amazing island, Pangkor Laut resort. Your hospitality is without rival...

Ged Mason, Salford's second biggest star ha ha... one of my few good and long-standing friends, thanks for being a mate and don't forget, I'll soon be beating you at squash again!

Steve Gleave, my best friend growing up, and still to this day, I'm happy to say, one of my best friends. I send you and Rob my deepest sympathy and love for the loss of your father Tom this year.

To all my family, Mum and Dad, Hayley and Dave, Stefan and Josh, my gran and Auntie Lindy, Auntie Sue and Uncle John (congratulations on the announcement of Colin's marriage to Ann this year).

To my precious girls Rebecca and Hannah, the most important people in my life and my heart, for ever...

Merlin Elite for all your fabulous support, drive and commitment during this difficult period.

Gary Johnson and Victoria Davis who have been with me throughout the last few months, seen the highs, the lows, the ups and downs. Many thanks, guys.

Special thanks to all the staff and doctors at the Alexandra in Cheadle for nursing me back to health. The Christie Hospital in Manchester, thanks in particular to all the staff at the Radiotherapy

Unit at Christie's. My surgeon James Leggat. My endocrinologist Tara Kearney, for being patient with my hormones.

To Diane Withers, for all the visits and lovely food you have brought me this last few months, many thanks indeed. Il Pomodoro in Poynton is the best Italian restaurant around!

To my best friends the Colonel and Lynne, I think I pretty much sum up sentiments and regards for them in the book. But thanks a million for all your help and support, you really are true friends in every sense of the word!

Red Steve, my good friend and fellow football fan. Thanks for being around, mate.

Grant Ainsworth, for being more than just a work colleague, you're a friend as well.

My dear friend, and without doubt the most inspiring producer I have worked with, Nick Patrick. Many great times and fond memories remain from all our work together, long may it continue.

Alastair Gordon, one of my longest-standing and most trusted friends... I look forward greatly to the brothers pop and the next tour!

Special thanks to Simon Crane, Simon Moran, Dave Williams, Trevor Barry, Jeff Leach.

RUSSELL WATSON
THE ULTIMATE COLLECTION
— *Special Edition* —

Make *Finding My Voice* an even more enjoyable read by listening to the music behind the story. *The Ultimate Collection – Special Edition*, Russell's musical biography, contains all the hits from *The Ultimate Voice* as well as the brand new album *Russell Watson Live at The Royal Albert Hall*.

Disc One features the songs that made Russell the musical superstar he is, including 'Volare', 'Nella Fantasia', ''O Sole Mio', 'Barcelona', 'You Raise Me Up', 'Nessun Dorma' and many more.

Disc Two is a stunning full-length album recorded live from the Royal Albert Hall and allows you to relive again and again the magical experience of Russell live in concert.

The Ultimate Collection – Special Edition is the perfect partner to *Finding My Voice* and a must for all Russell Watson fans.

AVAILABLE ON CD AND DOWNLOAD